W9-BWG-154

A BOOK

A BOOK OF HOURS

Music, Literature, and Life

A Memoir

M. OWEN LEE

continuum
NEW YORK • LONDON

2004
The Continuum International Publishing Group Inc
15 E. 26th Street, New York, NY 10017

The Continuum International Publishing Group Ltd
The Tower Building, 11 York Road, London SE1 7NX

Printed in the United States of America

Library of Congress Cataloging-in-Publication Data

Lee, M. Owen, 1930-
    A book of hours : music, literature, and life : a memoir / M. Owen
    Lee.
        p. cm.
    ISBN 0-8264-1586-5 (hardcover : alk. paper)
    1. Lee, M. Owen, 1930- 2. Catholic Church—Italy—Clergy—Biography.
    I. Title.
    BX4705.L449A3 2004
    282'.092—dc22

                                                                2003023226

FOR FRANK OVEIS

Much happened during the year I taught in Rome that is not recorded here, and some of what is here has been transferred from other years spent teaching in other places. There is not a character in this book, apart from the narrator, who is not an amalgam of two or more people the narrator once knew. That much said, this is a true story. Of the century now past.

Part 1

1

T HE PAST IS ALWAYS PRESENT TO ME. It becomes more
vivid as it moves onward. Like some long-spanned piece of
music, it shapes itself with repetitions and echoes of its first
beginnings. Like some corridor lit at the far end, it is less mysterious
the more it recedes.

The first years, full of first loves, grow increasingly vivid as I age.
More and more I discover in the past a place where I can meet myself.
There, Theophilus, nothing can be changed, every present action is
anticipated, and the present, so bewildering, begins to form into intelligible patterns.

In memory, everything is made more, not less, real. What once
seemed sorrows are now joys to remember. Today, when I move into
the past, I can see more clearly what it means and why it happened as
it did. I am at peace with it.

I had much to learn, and I still had most of my youthful ideals
about art and faith when, half-way through my life, I spent a year
teaching in Rome.

*How many doors how many floors how many windows are there in
it . . .*

Villa Soratte is six stories on one end, four at the other, spanning a
slope north of the city. It is the largest building I'll ever have lived in.
It houses everything the university has and is. Classrooms, offices, living quarters, chapel, library—all share the same roof. It is bewildering, this first morning, to walk the terrazzo floors and vast, empty
corridors interrupted by unadorned marble stairways. Yet the villa is a
friendly place. It is full of welcoming echoes, which fall lightly on the
ears. And even in the oncoming heat of a summery morning, it is cool.

If to stay to if to stay if having to stay to . . .

It was an August night of only intermittent sleep. I spent it uneasy from jet lag, awake after an hour, battling mosquitoes, pulling the sheets defensively over my head, admitting defeat, rising to unpack, trying again to sleep, rising again to find the chapel, to check the faculty lounge, especially its record collection, returning to my room, unfastening the heavy shutters and staring out into the night, watching the moonlit stillness in the tops of the cypresses and old ash trees.

This morning I discover for myself that from the roof you can see south to Rome and north to Soracte.

"You will see Mount Soracte from the roof!" That's what they promised back in Chicago when I asked about the campus in Rome.

While the city far to my left is sprawling under a summer haze, the mountain stands far to my right, isolated in clear air, saw-shaped from this vantage point, and lordly.

When this you see remember me . . .

The sun rises and, almost paradoxically, the view of the mountain hazes over. In the other direction the city, its hills and domes and monuments, gradually comes clear.

The front of the villa is lined with balconies designed to catch the sun all year, for as much of the day as possible. The villa was once a clinic. The long driveway and most of the façade are lined with lazy palms and Rome's characteristic umbrella pines. Just beyond the gates, the heat and dust and exhaust fumes and billboards begin. Already there is the noise of suburban Roman traffic.

Four saints prepare for saints . . .

I descend to the floors below and turn corners on corners. An occasional voice echoes down a corridor, a tingle in the ears, the English or Italian discernible more by inflection than by any intelligible words.

Prepare for saints . . .

Why, this first morning in Rome, should my head be full of *Four Saints in Three Acts*? That deliriously American piece. I must be giddy from the trip and the sleepless night.

Scene Two. How many saints can sit around. The Italian teaching staff are gathering in their large common room, preparing to instruct in their own language. In the smaller faculty lounge, I interrupt a conversation in English long enough to exchange handshakes with three of the *forestieri:* with Manfred Schöne, from Vienna, who will teach fine art and drama; with Fr. Andrzej Zielinski, Polish-born, who will teach theology; and with the great bear of a man they are talking schedules with—not *Saint Ignatius with it Tuesday,* but Fr. Jack Costello, for two years now the president of this Italian campus of Chicago's Catholic university. He is the only one of the three who extends much of a welcome. He smiles and promises to look me up later that morning, then goes back to scheduling the class hours of the somber man from Vienna and the scholarly little Polish priest.

I'm taken in hand by the registrar, Maria Parenti. A woman larger than life. *Saint Teresa half in and half out of doors.* "You mustn't mind that Fr. Zielinski seems unfriendly at first. He has a reputation for being inscrutable, but everyone who shares his office with him eventually makes him a friend for life. And Herr Schöne—no one is so respected by the students. Very *intelligente.* He doesn't associate much with the rest of the staff, but he's a good man, a good family man. *Simpatico.* You'll see."

She shows me the library—the largest English library in all of Rome—and the classrooms, the bookstore, the accountant's office, where she personally cashes my first check, and the improvised coffee bar where diminutive Pino, with a broad smile, serves us caffe latte and panini.

If to stay to if having to stay to . . .

A few sips of the coffee and the zany American opera, with its windows and saints, has gone out of my head at last. To business. Maria, over her latte, listens carefully to my concerns. There are problems I must solve immediately—a course to be reinstated, a part-time instructor to be hired, last-minute textbooks to be ordered, letters to go off. Maria, a widow long established as factotum at the school, is helpful, but I find that not everything can be done as soon or as easily as I would like.

Pino just shrugs and smiles. What did I expect? This is Italy.

In the office assigned me, I set the little busts of Homer and Virgil in place before lining my Greek and Latin books up alphabetically by author. I'll be teaching classics. I'm happy that the villa's library is so well stocked, as I have with me only a few dozen books and only a vague idea, from student applications, which of the classic authors I'll be teaching. All will depend on individual students' needs. The number of classics majors in a group of two hundred American students, even of two hundred students who come to Rome for a year, might be only nine or ten. If, to continue their programs back in North America, they need Pindar or Plato in Greek, or Plautus or Propertius in Latin, I'm to supply the instruction in those authors. But the groups, in any case, will be small.

I'll also offer, to larger numbers, a course each semester on the classics in English translations. The Greekless and Latinless are often keenly interested in classic drama, myth, and epic and remark that the writings of twenty or even thirty centuries ago seem more accessible than those only two or three centuries old. Every civilization has its classics, but the classics of Greece and Rome are, have been for centuries, and remain still for those who haven't surrendered to more recent trends in education *the* classics, for their lasting influence, their enduring myths, their humanity and wisdom.

To teach a group of thirty students lost in wonder over the *Iliad* in English, students who see themselves in the persons of Andromache and Hector, who find their own secret feelings in words first sung some thirty centuries ago, to hear the silence fall on the room and know that you have had a part in their experience—that is to know what teaching is.

I was nineteen when I first fell silent reading Homer. When I first read, haltingly in Greek, about the Trojan hero Hector, and felt the inexpressible tenderness and toughness in the passage where, though he knows he soon will die, he consoles his wife Andromache as he leaves for battle, and doffs his helmet and kisses his infant son.

Nineteen, and at a turning point in my life. After reading a dozen or so lines of the passage in Greek, touched with the wonder of the scene but impatient with my poor skills, I left my room and hurried to the college library to find and read, in an English translation, the whole of the scene between Hector and his wife. And then I turned to the ending of the *Iliad*—or rather a page close to the end, for Hector dies in book 22 of the twenty-four-book poem.

That library was Troy that day. Reading rapidly in English, for page on page, I felt for the first time what it was to acknowledge one's weakness, to strive nobly, to fail, and yet somehow to triumph. I wept over Hector's death, over Andromache's grief and her anxious fears for what would happen to their infant son. But I felt too the quiet joy and wonder anyone feels in the presence of a great work of art. Something of me was in this very old poem, and one part of my life was from that day fixed. I wanted after that to read and teach the classics, though I suspected, and I was right, that nothing in them would equal the *Iliad* for insight into what I had in my heart.

Sallust, Seneca, Suetonius, Tacitus, Terence, Tibullus, Virgil—that about does it for the Latin shelf . . .

"Enjoy the peace and quiet while you can. It's not going to last." The soft, thickly accented, un-Italian voice startles me.

"Oh, hello, Father."

"You at least can call me Andrzej."

He stands in the office doorway, bespectacled and pretending to be bemused. Diminutive. Dressed in his cassock while I'm busy in shirtsleeves.

"I see Virgil up there on your bookcase. Sentimental stuff, bad propaganda. Now, Homer—that's at least better. But what do you expect the peasants to make of it?" I presume he means the students.

He steps inside. "They will be here this afternoon, you know. And we will be expected to educate them. An impossible task."

"Come on," I laugh as he scans the row of books. He is hardly as inscrutable as Maria said he would be. "I've heard that teaching is all your life."

"You've heard no such thing. And if *I* must hear such things I'm certainly not ready to be told them by you. This year is going to be terrible, terrible."

The more he says in that pessimistic tone the more you know that he means exactly the opposite. He probably likes Virgil as much as Homer, though just now he is frowning at both of them, as if the two little busts were trying, and failing, to impose their authority on him.

"Do I have to share this office with you? Why do I get *you*?" He turns and stares at me.

"Just your luck, I guess. I'll be careful to restrict myself to the hours I post."

"Do you smoke?"

"No."

"Well, I do. Do you keep long office hours?"

"No."

"Well, I do. Do you keep plants?"

"Never."

"Well, I don't either. I suppose you'll want that desk chair for your own."

It's a small chair, and I'm half again his size. "If you like I'll get myself a movie director's chair with my name on it."

"What name?"

"Luke."

"A silly name. Nobody named Luke ever amounted to anything, after the important one. He exhausted the name."

"You may be right."

"Are you going to play that radio in here?"

"Only Wagner." That, of course, is issued as a challenge to this European.

"Wagner! All that screaming. Terrible, terrible. And that detestable German he writes!"

"Don't you like poetry?"

"I write poetry."

"Oh." So much for Wagner. "Have you said Mass yet this morning?"

"Of course. Haven't you? It's after nine."

He's ahead of me, as he always will be. Still, he agrees to concelebrate with me the next day.

I don't think sharing the office with Fr. Zielinski is going to be a problem.

The morning presses on. I take the stairway to the chapel, a remarkably plain retreat with white walls, and I vest for Mass. The sacristy adjoins my room. Never before have I lived so close to the sacramental presence of the God I serve.

A priest prays the Hours and offers Mass daily and preaches God's word as well as he knows it, striving more each day to know it better. He also listens. Students away from home—this far away, and some of them for the first time—often need to talk out their problems. And devout students want more than that. They want the graces God sends through his sacraments. God sends his grace in many ways, but his sacramental graces he gives—a humbling thought—through the priest who performs the sacramental rites.

No one who is chosen to be God's instrument can pride himself on being chosen. He has done nothing to deserve it. Priests are, like all men, like the men they are chosen from among, frail and fallible. Often they are less gifted than those they serve. Many of them seem as unsuited to their calling as the twelve apostles, illiterate fishermen, must have seemed. God has his own notions of who will bear witness to his presence in the world, and he chooses some unlikely subjects to be his instruments and to speak his word.

Any priest would be absurdly presumptuous if he thought he understood that word. But, if he is a good priest, he believes it and tries to understand it, preach it, and live it. That word, by and large, is love. The world makes sense because the God who fills it loves and guides and gives of himself. He sent his son to tell us that.

Alone in the chapel, I speak the words the Son once spoke, "This is my body." I lift the sacramental bread on high, believing that at that moment he speaks through me and that the words mean truly what they meant when he first said them.

On the day I was made a priest, there was a mighty wind roaring outside the church. I remember being told that day that henceforth I would be an *alter Christus*, another Christ, to the people I served. A loving God was breathing his spirit into me and sending me forth, inadequate as I was, charged to serve the people from whom and for whom I was chosen.

I remember too the sweet, inescapable, persistent thought that was the companion of every quiet moment through the ten years before that. The thought that, perhaps, God was calling me. If God spoke to me—how can anyone ever be sure he did? —he spoke in the quietest way, at the quietest times, blessing my ears, filling my sleeping hours, overwhelmingly present when I rose each morning. I thought then that if I gave myself to him, and to no one else, if I consecrated my life, then every act of that life, conscious or unconscious, would be consecrated. Everything I did would be a prayer. My life, stretching out before me then as the greatest of imponderable mysteries, would have meaning. It would share in the goodness that God himself is. I hesitated. There is always hesitation at the moment of being called. But eventually the thought of giving my life away was too beautiful to resist.

"This is my blood." Again, as the text of the Mass prescribes, I speak the words he spoke and lift above my head the cup filled with wine that is more than wine.

I offer the Mass for my Irish father, who died nine years before on this day, and for my German mother who, in a few hours halfway around the world, will be attending early Mass and praying for him and for me.

"I hope I'll see you in here a lot."

I can hear the voice before I see the ruddy face, for I have left the altar and am back in the sacristy, struggling, in an unceremonious moment, to slip the chasuble over my head.

It is my president, looking in on me as he promised. I fold the chasuble and snap to. Maria has told me he was once in the armed forces.

"I'm ready when you need me, Father."

"Good. We'll need you often. Over and above your teaching, you'll say early Mass here every Tuesday and Friday for the students and take your turn, every fourth week, for the high Mass on Sunday. We'll also want you to take groups of students during the year for Mass at some of the basilicas—St. John Lateran, St. Mary Major, St. Paul's Outside the Walls."

"Fine. I'll like that." I lay the stole over the folded chasuble in the traditional cruciform pattern. He is in shirtsleeves, busy about too many things to have dressed formally this morning.

"How did you sleep last night, Luke?"

"Not too well. How do you say mosquitoes in Italian?"

"*Zanzare.* Just think of 'Banzai.' Italian mosquitoes are the dive-bombing variety."

"I found that out."

"You'll also find some mosquito netting in the closet dispensary down the hall. But it's just as well to get used to such inconveniences. Italians don't use mosquito netting. By the way, Fr. Hallagan will be in the room down the hall, past the big window. Johnny Hallagan. From Philadelphia. He teaches history. He's a little late getting in this year, but he'll tell you what you need to know, if I'm not available. A very nice fellow. Likes music, used to play the trumpet. I think he knows the classics pretty well, and much besides."

"Thanks. I'll need some help, at least at first."

"The piano, by the way, is in the big room at the bottom of the main stairway. Maria tells me you play."

"Yes. But not professionally."

"That's just as well. It's not a professional piano. You know that the students will be here by late afternoon?"

"Yes. I'll be ready for them."

"There's a good man! You know, I'm always edgy until after I give them the first talk. If you need me, I'm on the intercom. Till later . . ."

The morning moves toward noon. Still in shirtsleeves, I find, at the bottom of the stairs, the school's only piano, the usual multipurpose upright, set on wheels so it can serve both classroom and social functions, chipped and unhandsome but still proud, and capable at least of resonant E-flat chords.

E-flat is the key you play in when you test a piano. I strike the closing measures of *Tannhäuser*.

This year I hope that, living in Rome and moving north of the Alps on long weekends and holidays, I'll be able to see some opera. I've never lived in a city where I could see it for several months out of a year. And I've never until now had the opportunity to travel easily to other cities where opera is available every day, virtually the year round. In Germany, for a few marks, you can hear not just the standard repertory but new repertory and unusual repertory from the four centuries of opera's history.

Music was my first love. Not Homer, and not Catholicism. Music. I loved the songs that, in my childhood, everyone regardless of age or musical sophistication knew and sang. Month by month they came and went in succession, by George Gershwin, Jerome Kern, Richard Rodgers, Cole Porter—each song more memorable than the last. The best of them had some harmonic change, some subtle modulation that, at the time, the 1930s, seemed wonderfully new and strange.

Then, a radio broadcast from the Metropolitan Opera in New York changed all that for me. One Saturday afternoon I heard *Tannhäuser*. My first opera. Nothing I had heard before touched me as that new music did. Now, three decades later, I can still remember in detail the sound of first hearing Wagner's strange, new, wonderful harmonies.

They are under my fingers now as they were that Saturday when, with only a year or so of lessons, I found them in an old book and sought them out at the keyboard of the ten-dollar piano my father had bought for me. That first afternoon, the thrill of having under my fingers the very sounds that were echoing in my ears was something akin to those later discoveries— first looking into Homer, or first deciding what I was going to do with my life. More than that, discovering what music could be was a self-discovery. In the E-flat chords of *Tannhäuser* I felt, at eleven years of age, that I had touched and sounded something that was part of myself. A part of me deeper than I had known before responded.

Any of the great operas can tell you something of your own self. But *Tannhäuser* of all operas tells you of your self at a time of crisis. It tells of a questing German who, through his music, reaches a state of awareness that makes it impossible to return to the older, simpler, more innocent ways he once knew. Torn between two worlds, he struggles toward some understanding of himself. There is a sign of his healing: the pope's staff, blossoming with fresh leaves. The Father of Christendom had said that Tannhäuser could no more find forgiveness—that is, find and heal himself—than the papal scepter could blossom. But the scepter, long since severed from the wood that once gave it life, does blossom. A miracle is wrought, in nature and in the soul of the music-maker struggling toward self-understanding.

Under my fingers, the music swells to its conclusion.

"So you have found the piano . . ."

It is Manfred Schöne, thickset and scowling. He does not look like your ordinary teacher of fine art. He makes the room his own as he enters it.

"Yes," I laugh as I strike the last chord. "Do you recognize the music?"

"*Tannhäuser.* I've slept through it a few times. *Der Gnade Heil,*" he quotes as he grasps the back of the upright like a pulpit and looks down on me. "The salvation of grace has been granted to the penitent. It touched me when I was young."

"This year I hope, like Tannhäuser, to cross the Alps and hear some singing in the opera houses of Germany."

"And do you hope, like Tannhäuser, to be refused absolution for those German sins here in Rome?"

"Oh, if that happens, surely the pope will realize his mistake. His scepter will sprout leaves." I laugh.

"Why do you laugh?"

"It's the only way of dealing with some problems."

He hasn't even smiled. "Play some more."

"Wagner?"

"Only if you must."

"You're from Vienna?"

"Yes."

I play the introduction to a song by Franz Schubert. Schöne knows the song, as I expected he would, and after a moment sings a little, in a gravelly baritone that sounds as if it has hardly ever been raised in song. *Du holde Kunst . . .*

> You gracious art, in how many dark hours,
> When I was caught in life's vicious circle,
> Have you made my heart warm with love
> And carried me to a better world.

We don't get much further into it than that.

"You're transported when you play," he says, almost enviously.

"Sometimes, with music like that, you don't feel you're playing it so much as it's playing you."

He looks startled. "You are a priest?"

"Yes."

"And you will teach classics here?"

"Yes."

"You don't look like a professor of classics."

"You don't look like a professor of fine art."

"I am not a professor. Just a teacher."

"Then that may be the only real difference between us," I laugh.

He scowls. "You may find that there are some great differences between us."

His look lets me know he means what he says. Maria has all but told me that he is a tormented man.

Near the end of the siesta, which I have not had the sense to avail myself of, three large chartered buses come down the palm-lined lane and turn the circle in front of the villa, salvos of student cheers issuing from the open windows. This sends us all scurrying out of our shuttered rooms to the front balconies to see the arrivals. They are the bulk of the student enrollment, almost two hundred of them, flown in from Chicago but educated in many places in North America. Catholic mostly, but other persuasions are represented.

Maria Parenti, who knows more about the yearly rituals than anyone at the school, says, with her glasses pushed up on her forehead, "Now, you watch. You'll be able to tell something of the personality of each of them as they step down from the buses."

And sure enough, here is a boy looking homesick already, there a girl tentative and worried about her luggage, there a thick-necked fellow striking a Roman pose—Mussolini, maybe—for the amusement of us who have come to watch, there a pair of girls anxious to be roommates. Here and there are the new American faculty members with wives and children, squinting in the sun, more exhausted by the journey than they had thought possible, but relieved and pleased with the look of the villa and eager for the new experience.

The villa *is* impressive—friendly and ready to accommodate us all. In a moment it is alive with voices and noises, with Pino and his fellow workers puffing under burdens twice their size, with the kitchen staff scuffling back to work, with the burly president in the thick of things, busy creating order out of all the chaos.

That night, looking almost Roman in his collar, he gives his opening talk to the students: The year will be different for them from any previous. It will be more elating and also more challenging. They will be free of many of the ties, obligations, and allegiances that may have inhibited them back home. They will form new friendships that will replace the old, and perhaps last all their lives. They will be beginning new chapters in their experiences. They will have, thereby, a duty to themselves.

The cultural riches that surround them in Rome they may find intimidating. They may find themselves, initially or in time, not responding to, even resisting, what they see and hear. They will have to make every effort to open themselves, humbly and receptively, to Rome, to Italy, and to Europe. To be ready to learn and grow and change. That is what the year is for.

The year will not help them toward upward social mobility, toward economic security, toward the fulfillment of any recognizably American dream. It will, if they respond to it, make them more adaptable, tolerant, and appreciative, with more joy in the beautiful, more respect for other opinions, and a greater ability to accept uncertainty, insecurity, and ambivalence as the givens of life.

The academic program is not designed to convince them that, as Americans, they are specially privileged, that the best things in life are theirs by birthright.

It might convince them that there is still much that can be done, even after the achievements of past civilizations, by a relatively new nation that has drawn its intellectual traditions and much of its human resources from an older world.

Immersion in the older cultures of Europe might also convince them that the minority cultures in their own country deserve respect. As Europe changed over the centuries, America will certainly change in their lifetimes. They should be ready. Ready perhaps even to initiate the changes.

It is not the usual introductory speech about regulations.

I look across the rows of upturned faces and wonder, Theophilus, how they—how I—will be changed by this year.

. . . Saints who have been changed from the evening to the morning.

2

O NE OF THE PLEASURES OF TEACHING here is living in
day-to-day contact with a practicing poet. Andrzej is a rueful,
witty, and impossible companion. I've found that he is almost
exactly my age, but instead of being born, as I was, in Detroit during
the Depression, he was born in Warsaw with a silver spoon in his
mouth and grew up in affluence. In his adolescence he lived through
some of the twentieth century's cruelest horrors. He survived. He says
very little about that. He studied (mostly theology) in Rome and published (mostly poetry) in Paris.

Together in the office we are working on the Englishing of his
poems. He provides me with a prose translation, which I am supposed
to versify or at least make into reasonably idiomatic and reasonably
poetic English. As I know next to no Polish, I often ask him the literal
meaning of his prose. I don't always see how his ideas are connected.
The meanings, the images, the sounds—none of these come clear to
a reader who has no access to the tones and the overtones the original words might carry for the aristocratic son of a centuries-old culture.

The poems are unembarrassed, full of recurrent images, and pessimistic. Amusing on the surface, they all end in death, some of them
in apocalyptic catastrophes. Change is of their essence: one strange
image passes almost imperceptibly into another, like the metamor-
phoses in Greek myths. One thing is always in the process of meaning,
even of becoming, another. *Panta rhei.*

Everything is in flux.

"How am I supposed to suggest that the electric eel in this poem is
in the process of becoming music?"

"Why is your mind so univocal? You don't *have* to suggest it. You
don't have to make everything literal and silly. Let the one who reads
discover for himself that a poem about an electric eel is not about an

electric eel. This poem is not about an electric eel. It is about every time you hope for something wonderful and something horrible happens instead."

"Well, I realize that the poem is metaphorical," I say, sounding very literal, "and that is as it should be. That's the chiefest thing about poetry."

He looks dubious about that statement.

"I mean, Robert Frost said the chiefest thing about poetry was that it was metaphor. Saying one thing in terms of another. But what we seem to get in your poems is the *process* of one thing becoming another. It's not just metaphor. It's a kind of metamorphosis."

"Call it what you like," he says. "Make a new word and call it metamorphoric if you like. It's not original with me. Any poet knows that metaphor is halfway to being metamorphosis. If something is like something else, the poet says, 'Let's make it *become* that something else . . .' But you don't have to understand any of this. Just make the English come out right."

"Do you want me to preserve your metrical schemes?"

"No. I don't see how you will be able to. It's not necessary."

"Do you want rhyme?"

"No. Blank verse."

I give him a blank stare. "But I can't understand any of this, in the prose you've given me. I don't know how seriously to take it. I can't get the tone of it. I don't know how it works."

He pretends to be exasperated, but his voice, accented like a middle-European viola, is imperturbable.

"Let your imagination go. They tell me you are musical. Well, an electric eel has the potential to become an instrument making music. Or it can become instead an unplugged extension cord, a thing alone, meaning nothing. A fish on a dinner plate can be an instrument sounding notes, or just a noteless staff, bare bones, limp fins, unsung scales. And, the world being what it is, the good possibilities usually go unrealized. We can do good things or bad things or no things in this life."

"I see." But I don't.

"Most of us end up dead without ever becoming what we could have been."

"I see. . . . Show me that in this poem."

An impatient sigh. "The poet gets invited out to a nice dinner and the dinner turns out to be a mess, as almost everything does in this life. And the poet transfers his feelings to the mess on the plate. His imagination goes to work on it. It becomes what he feels. The fish could have made music. It doesn't. It just issues a loud B-flat on the plate."

"How did you hit on those images?" My voice rises. "A flatulent fish perched on a plate. An electric eel balking on Bartok. An iced swan centerpiece drowning in diminished sevenths."

"It doesn't matter."

"Well, it matters to me. I've got to versify this."

"I don't remember. Fishes have scales. Electricity makes your turntable turn. A swan in myth and legend is always turning into something else, or something else is turning into a swan."

"Ah, that explains—"

"It explains nothing."

Better try another question. "Why do all of these poems end in apocalypses?"

"Because that's what the world is like. The fish flops. The swan melts. The electric eel shorts and burns out. That's what happens in this world."

"You really believe that?"

"Why do *you* have to know? All I'm asking you to do is put the damn things into English."

I give him as baleful a look as I can manage and, at last, he laughs.

The first week of classes isn't over before Andrzej and I are battling openly, if amiably, about poetry, which is also the concern of more than half of what I am teaching. My head is full of his images, the strange images that recur from poem to poem and seem to signify, in some way, his past experiences—though he insists they have no definable meaning. I'm about to turn a corner of one of the villa's long corridors when I hear him with a couple of students. I gather that they are two of his theology students, but it doesn't sound as if he's talking conventional theology with them.

"Everything," he tells them, "is full of gods."

I know the phrase. It has come down to us as a fragment, a mere scrap, from the first of the philosophers, Thales.

"Everything," he says, passing beyond Thales, "has a god, a secret identity, inside. The poet sees it. He sees what the thing really is, not what it appears to be. And that's what he tries to show."

Can I let him get away with that? That there is a god in everything? In poetry? It's a whole lot more than what he was saying about projecting his own feelings onto the subjects of his poems. I turn the corner and face him. It is a staged epiphany.

"Is that so? The poet finds a god inside the thing he's writing about, and shows that? I thought you told me that the poet transfers his *own* self to the thing, and shows the thing as himself?"

"Well, he does. That happens too. Both things happen."

The boy and the girl, whose names I do not know, watch us square off in some astonishment. The poet theologian explains.

"The subject of any poem has an inner reality—a god inside—and as a poet with a feeling for metaphor looks at it, it shapes itself into something like the god inside it. But of course the god inside things cannot be fully comprehended, and inevitably you invest what you're writing about with your own perceptions. If you know how to write poetry, that is."

"That's not anybody's idea of what poetry is!"

"Of course it is. What ode of Horace did you teach today?"

"*O nata mecum.* I like to start the course with it."

"The ode to the wine jug?"

"Yes."

"Well, then, that's an easy one. Horace makes the jug into himself, doesn't he? One stanza after another, he makes that jug into a little Horace—a little pot-bellied creature, a tippler, a gentle wrester of secrets, a playful conversationalist, a wise counselor, a witty worshiper?"

"You're making it sound like yourself."

"No, not like me!" I'd think him genuinely furious if I hadn't already sized him up. "Not like me! Like Horace. Horace, because he knows what goes on in poetry, transfers his own perceptions to something that can bear those perceptions. And the wine jug ends up like himself."

"And you end up like a flopped fish?"

"Yes. That's just how I feel with you around. When nothing happens right. But there's the other thing going on too in Horace's ode. He knows that there is something divine inside whatever he perceives, and because he's a poet he's got to let that out. The jug, like anything else, has got a god inside it. What does your Horace call it? *Pia testa.* Pious jug. And what does he tell it to do? *Descende.* Descend. And when? On a holy day. The jug is invoked exactly as a god is invoked.

In fact, if I remember rightly, the whole poem is constructed like a Roman prayer."

"It is." I am amazed at how he can quote so easily from memory in a field outside his professional competence. "But," I add, "Horace isn't saying everything is full of gods. He's only poking gentle fun at Roman prayer formulae, in a tipsy moment."

"He's also implying that there's a god inside the jug, making it what it is. And if you will read your way through all the odes of Horace with that in mind—that everything is full of gods—you'll see what Horace sees."

The girl, who has been listening closely, suddenly lets all the books fall out of her arms. She stoops to retrieve them and loses her glasses.

"Oh," says the boy. "Let me help you with those."

Andrzej and I hardly notice. I round on him, forgetting how the corridor will carry the words its whole length, how they'll increase in volume at the far end.

"Now wait! I've read my way through a lot of *your* poems, and I don't see them as full of gods. They're just full of you. Fishes, which you find appropriate surrogates. Birds that glare at you. The moon, which shows you no compassion. Always you. Those images tell me about you, not about the god inside them."

"Of course. I'm reassured when I look into the big eyes of a fish in an aquarium. They're peaceful and they don't threaten me. I don't like the beady stare of a bird's eye. I'm not reassured by the way moonlight shows me things differently from sunlight."

"Yes, and there are only three, or maybe four, settings in your poems. A dining room where everything disappoints. The empty street, a place to get lost. The sky, because flying over rooftops is a kind of escape. And the lake, which for you is as good a place to get lost in as the street, as good a place to drown in as the sky. And over the street or the sky or the lake the moon is floating, because in your poems everything happens at night."

"And the moon is unconcerned," he adds. "Don't forget that."

"He was just telling us about his new poem," says the boy, who has relieved the girl of most of her books. "It's about a man who goes fishing in the night, and throws a line into the sky, and catches the world's navel, and pulls. And the whole world collapses like a balloon."

"And," the girl adds, shyly from behind the glasses, "the birds flutter in their nests when the man goes out into the night, and fly up when the world comes loose, and in the end they cannot survive."

"And that," say I, "is revealing what night and moon and sky and birds are? Revealing the divinity in them? It's only telling what *you* are, and whatever thing is inside *you*."

"It's telling what the world is," Andrzej comes back immediately.

"It's telling what you think the world is. You think of the world, and our experience in it, in terms of deflation, drowning, failure, and confused survivors."

"Yes. That's my way of telling what the world is. Anyone's poems are about as good as the correspondence between what he sees and what is really there. Not what is on the surface. What is really there. The god inside things."

"And the god inside things is unconcerned? Destructive? Apocalyptic . . ."

By this time our excited voices—well, my excited voice echoing down the corridor—has drawn a crowd of student listeners, who keep their distance down the hall. Maria Parenti appears at the far end—large, frowning, sibylline, trying to look formidable, with her heavy glasses pushed up on her forehead. She starts moving toward us. Then, when she sees who we are, she thinks better of intervening. "Just an academic discussion?"

"Oh, yes, Maria. Nothing too important. We're sorry."

The two students are embarrassed. "I hope you're wrong about the world," the boy says to Fr. Zielinski. He is a wholesome fellow, struggling now to keep in balance the load of books he has retrieved.

"I know I'm right about poetry," Andrzej insists. "There is a reality inside everything. The poet sees it, and most other people do not. And the poet tries to describe it in terms that are real to him."

"I like that," says the girl, her eyes shining larger through the thick glasses. "I like to think that poets can help us see beyond what we normally see. I think what a person's life means can be conveyed more clearly in poetic images than in . . ."

The bell rings for a new round of lectures. "Come on," the boy nudges her. "These two aren't going to settle anything." She goes with him, clutching her share of the books. Their midwestern accents are as flat as my own. Their names, I discover later, are Ellen and Tim. They are theology students.

"The god inside everything . . ." I hear her say to him as they make their way down the long corridor.

3

To see rome from any high vantage point—from our roof, or the Gianicolo, or the Castel Sant' Angelo—is to see a red-tiled, sun-colored urban terrain marked by churches, crosses, cupolas, and domes. Bells ring above the muted sounds of human activity. Swallows circle through and over a slight but omnipresent haze.

To see Rome from the streets is to become aware of chipped ornamental façades, monumental gateways, excavated fora with stalagmite columns, noxious-fumed traffic, papal and fascist insignia, walls, fountains, cats, sewers, storefronts with torn posters, pine trees, sightseers seeking information in all manner of languages, thieves expertly going about their business, and, more conspicuously, the liveliest native population in Europe.

Rome mixes the beautiful and the ugly in about equal proportions. Even in the haze of summer, every impression is sharp and strong. On almost any street corner you can find something of antiquity, something Renaissance, something baroque, something of the mid-twentieth century's *dolce vita*, something of today's more anxious and violent manifestations. And on almost any street corner you will find one or two or perhaps even three churches.

The churches close for the siesta hours—from noon to four or thereabouts. Once open, they quickly fill with life, with kneeling worshipers oblivious of dutiful tourists, with mothers unabashedly breast-feeding babies, with whole families noisily lunching and officious sacristans sanctimoniously disapproving. The churches are damp and dimly lit, perhaps designedly so, for the accumulated dust ought not to be too obvious. They are, in addition, filled with the art of the last three or four centuries, and often of art from many centuries before that, ranging from the precious to the worthless, from—according to the unwritten Roman rule—the phenomenally beautiful to the atrociously ugly. But the atrociously ugly is often thought beautiful by the Romans, and in the atmosphere of the city it takes a strong man to say they are wrong.

To those who fill the churches, each domed enclosure is something like what heaven itself must be—abundant with things to delight. Nothing is self-consciously arranged, as in a museum. All the good gifts are poured out in earthy profusion. Every church is thought to be God's house, our Father's house, where we can content ourselves like his children, shelter ourselves from the sun and the rain, and pray.

Once opened, Rome's cold churches are no longer really cold. They are vibrant and warm as lit lamps. The enclosure of a Roman church seems almost miraculously to seal off the noise and distractions of the street, the better to present us with the noise and distractions of itself. There is a sense of being within a large but manageable space that shuts out a larger and not always manageable space.

And over all hovers the dome, spanning and guarding the space defined below. Sometimes, when rays of light penetrate the windows immediately below it, the dome can seem suspended in air, the saint or angel or dove within it floating protectively. Within these domed, enclosed spaces all the activity of the great city is turned mysteriously inward. The churches become places where you look into yourself with the assurance that, as within the church, so within the sanctum of your self God is present.

Manfred Schöne is one of the strong who can tell the Romans they are wrong about ugliness and beauty. He has no tolerance for any ugliness except that designed by an artist for his special purposes. He is meeting his class here in the Pantheon for its first lecture on art and architecture.

Some of the students arrive early and sit, exhausted from the September heat, on the floor, along the walls. There are no pews. The famous building, massively classic from the square outside, with an inscription that bears the name of the first Roman emperor's tough-minded general, Agrippa, is, within, an immense domed rotunda. Indifferent art stares from the niches along the walls, which also carry racks with the inevitable souvenirs and postcards. Not far from us an organist is playing "The Swan" from *The Carnival of the Animals*. All the tremolo stops are pulled out. The swan sounds like a defused electric eel.

"I hate this place," says one sprawled student, audibly.

He might well feel threatened and depressed by it, especially viewing it as he does at floor level. From the thick wall behind his back, the famous dome seems already to rise, curving by gradually perceptible degrees until it arches high overhead toward completion. And yet not quite to completion. The very top of the dome is open. A large round opening like an eye—called, in fact, the *oculus*—lets in bright sunlight from the very top of the structure. Just now, part of a cloud can be seen through it, sailing overhead. But the effect is spoiled by the artificial floor-level lighting provided for the paintings, by the organist and the postcard buyers. I too am slightly depressed. I have always felt disaffected in this best-preserved of ancient Roman monuments.

Schöne comes like a commander through the massive Roman doors, past the vendors and the groups of tourists just entering. He walks over to the organ and asks the player to stop. He has some kind of card that does the trick, but the force of his personality works equally well. He is handsome in a hard-bitten way, casually dressed, quiet-spoken. His English is idiomatically American, German in inflection. His eyes glower under heavy brows. If he disapproves of my auditing his class, he says nothing. He hardly acknowledges me.

He begins talking, quietly, directly under the *oculus*. The students along the walls gradually realize that the class has started and get slowly to their feet. They form a circle of about forty around him. Groups of tourists come and go. Some are unconscionably noisy. Some forsake their own groups and briefly join ours. Workmen busy themselves at one of the shrines along the wall, and the clank of their hammering is all but intolerable. The organist eventually starts up again, and the lugubrious swan reverberates again in the marble enclosure. There is no escaping these sounds. The round dome closes us all in as if we were under glass. But Schöne never raises his voice, never acknowledges the disturbances.

A few of the students, after fifteen minutes standing on the marble floor, look for something to lean against. There is nothing. They inch toward the walls. Some sit down with a sigh of relief, rub their shins or take off their shoes, and look around for the approval of the others. Schöne doesn't look at them. He keeps talking, quietly. Soon the sluggards are back with the group.

Schöne says none of the ordinary things about the Pantheon. He presumes that his students have done the advance work.

In the past I've shown people through the Pantheon myself, and I've always been careful to say the important things. A temple was built here by Marcus Agrippa in 27 B.C., to commemorate his naval victory in the name of Caesar Augustus over Mark Antony and Cleopatra at Actium. Virgil was writing the *Aeneid* at the same time, to commemorate the same pivotal event in history. Fifty years later, Agrippa's building was largely destroyed by fire, and what we see now was designed by the emperor Hadrian and finished a hundred years after the original temple. Hadrian was a man with a sense of history, and he kept Agrippa's name over the entrance. He called his new building the Pantheon—the temple of all gods. It was adorned by subsequent emperors, pillaged by invading Goths and Byzantines, consecrated as a Christian church to Holy Mary and All Martyrs (with twenty-eight wagon loads of martyrs' bones brought from the catacombs), restored and added to by various popes, and turned to a fortress during the city's Renaissance feuds, with some of its bronze melted down to make the canopy for the pope's altar at St. Peter's and the cannon for the pope's fortress at Sant' Angelo. After several restorations it was chosen as a last resting place for Italy's painters, notably Raphael, and for its nineteenth-century kings. This is the kind of history that can be applied, *mutatis mutandis,* to many buildings in Rome. Schöne says none of these things.

I've always been careful to tell people, after they'd moved around the great semi-globe which is the whole of the building's interior, that the height and diameter of the dome measure the same, one hundred and forty-two feet—hence the feeling conveyed so swiftly and surely to the viewer. That the circular opening at the top measures twenty-eight feet across, allowing rain and occasional snow to fall to the floor and drain off quickly. That the dome is larger than the dome of St. Peter's, or the one over St. Paul's in London, larger than any dome built anywhere in the world until our own century. That the circular wall on which it rests is more than twenty feet thick, to support the massive thrust. That this could be seen from the depth of the seven niches that punctuate its circumference. Schöne says none of these things.

Instead he conjures up how the building must have looked when new. The vast circle of the floor was highly polished. The walls on every side rose from the floor and, as much as the dazzled eye could detect, began an immediate curve inward toward a central point high in the air. They were sheeted in bronze, and they shone brightly as, forming one concave mass, they sloped upward. The spectator's eye followed while his jaw fell open, until at the very top the bronze stopped, or parted in a bronze ring, to form the *oculus.* And from that *oculus* there fell to the floor a cylindrical column of radiant light, slanted according to the position of the sun.

Schöne asks the class what they feel about the building, inviting them to think away all the modern distractions. The sense of the Pantheon as architecture begins to close in on them, and their wonder begins to grow. There are periods when Schöne says nothing and waits patiently for the students to react to what they see. They venture some responses. All admit to feelings of awe. Some admit that they find the building unsettling, vaguely depressing—and now they aren't thinking of the organist playing unsuitable music badly or the workmen clanking or the tourists noisily grouping or the hard discomfort of the marble beneath their feet. Though they have been standing on that unresisting floor for half an hour, they're wondering about their inner responses.

"Suppose you're a barbarian." Schöne doesn't raise his voice, but lifts his thick arms eloquently. "You're a German chieftain, captured and brought through the Alps to imperial Rome. You're dressed in an animal's skin, and your head and cheeks and shoulders and chest are as shaggy as the skin you wear, as bristly as the pines in your great forests on the Danube or the Rhine. You've been amazed at the sight of the pines of Rome, because you've never seen trees so immaculately trimmed, so gracious and so useless. You've always used your trees for shelter, to hide in, to make war from. But now you've lost your war, and you've been in prison for a week. You're wearing chains on your hands. The chains have been removed from your feet because you're to be brought before the emperor.

"In the streets the sun is blazing, blinding, inescapable. There's not a tree anywhere to comfort you. The square is full of people in peculiar clothes, shouting a peculiar language. You long to hear your own tongue spoken. You keep your head down, preserving your pride and your dignity. A clean-shaven soldier with a bronze breastplate lifts your chin and slaps your face for supposed insolence.

"You're brought to this building. Outside it looks to you like all the other buildings designed to intimidate in this strange metropolis. It has a triangular pediment resting on columns of some strange gray-red stone from Egypt—though in your simplicity you know only the strangeness. You can't read the letters inscribed across the entablature. You're forced up a great flight of stairs to get to the doors. (Today, as you've seen, the building sits below street level, but not then.) When you get to the brazen doors, they're as tall as the pines of your native forest. They open. Seven soldiers with an officer, clanging in bronze, lead you within.

"You don't lift your eyes, but as the doors ring shut behind you, you're conscious of sudden stillness and darkness. The sunlight and the shouting are gone. There's the smell of incense. Your name is called out, vaguely recognizable in the foreign tongue. In the darkness you see something like the reflection of your face in the polished floor beneath you. You lift your eyes, and you find yourself inside a kind of globe. The walls around you glow with burnished glory. Statues of Roman gods peer out impassively from their recesses. And enthroned above your head, seated in a column of light that slopes gently from some source outside your ken, is a radiantly beautiful man, with shining white clothes that seem to glow from within. He calls your name again. You answer in your own tongue because, though his face is stern, his eyes are kind and he seems immensely wise. You begin to realize that this is Hadrian, the emperor of Rome. You should hate him, but you are overawed. Your eyes adjust to the light, and you see that you and he are enclosed together beneath a great dome. You are on the floor of his world, surrounded by his subject soldiers, and he is at the center, radiating light. His Rome is the world, the world in which you stand, and he is the sun. He tells you in your own language to surrender, to submit to his power. He will be generous to you and your people. You submit.

"That is the effect this building is designed to have."

I too submit. Schöne may or may not be right. Hadrian was wise enough to know, with Confucius, that empires are made by force of arms and preserved by ceremony. He had a century-old mandate from Rome's greatest poet, Virgil, to "spare the submissive but to make utter war on the recalcitrant." He also wanted to rebuild the Agrippan temple as a kind of shrine to the empire and was enthusiastic about employing Roman engineering genius in new ways. He designed his own villa at Tivoli, with its miles of gardens, pools, and parks, in a way that anticipated some of the architectural achievements of seventeenth-century France and Italy. Here he designed a dome to inspire the central buildings in Constantinople, Florence, London, and Washington. And in Christian Rome. He was as humane a man as the world has made, charged with perhaps the heaviest office the world has known. Like his great predecessor Augustus, and like many of the popes who may be thought to have been his successors, he had the intelligence to use art, great art, rather than force, for his political purposes.

Schöne may be right. Or he may be reading himself, eloquently, into what he has made us all submissive to. But certainly he has articulated for me something I have vaguely sensed about the Pantheon since I first saw it. He has put my own feelings into words and made the facts and the feelings come together for the first time. The building *is* so constructed that on entering it you have the feeling you are in an enclosed world. It *is* possible that, when it was new, beautiful, and full of silence, a viewer was induced to think that what lay outside that rounded, enclosed space was unreal, unnecessary, unworthy of consideration, that the only real, necessary, and important thing was the will of the wisest and most beautiful of men, seated at the center of this prison-globe. It *is* possible that the dome was invented to prompt that overawed response. It *is* possible that this first dome rose directly from ground level so that a whole world would seem to be enclosed beneath its vaulted authority.

The time is almost up, but the class is far from over. Schöne leads us out into the sunlight. We proceed down the street to the left, to the right and left again. No explanation is given. I try to sort out my conflicting feelings about the building we have seen. Admiration for the stupendous feat of engineering. Wonder and even affection for a structure standing firm and majestic in the face of eroding centuries. But also, strangely, disaffection, because I feel at the same time less than assured, imposed upon, even slightly dehumanized the more I surrender to the demands the building makes.

Suddenly, turning the narrow streets, we are in front of the Palazzo della Sapienza, for centuries the University of Rome, now the national archives. We pass inside the gate and see for the first time a little baroque church rising in a series of charming arches and concave and convex curves to a kind of stone carousel, adorned with fantastic heraldic devices, capped with a carved lantern set with columns and imitation torches, lifting further in a fantastic little spiral to a crown, a small globe and, at the very top, an ornamental cross, outlined against the sky.

It is the kind of surprise Rome reserves by the hundreds for the curious tourist on foot. From the street no one would suspect that there was a church to be found beyond the palazzo walls. And what a church! The masterpiece of Borromini—Sant' Ivo.

Schöne rings for the porter, who is not happy about his sleep being disturbed until he sees who has rung. For all his Teutonic gruffness, Schöne can easily charm the people who are necessary to him.

We step inside. Like most baroque churches this one is astonishingly small within. There are pews, and we sink gratefully into them. And there is silence. Schöne invites us to sit for a few minutes and let the architecture work on us. Fifteen whole minutes pass. No one speaks. Hardly anyone stirs, until curiosity about the dome leads us, one by one, to rise and walk beneath it and stare upward. White and gold, it seems much higher than its exterior suggested, and there is a delicacy, a truly ethereal quality about it that is altogether different from the massive semi-globe of the Pantheon.

This dome is not rounded within. It is, at its base, a hexagonal shape in which three of the sides curve into concave semicircles, and the other three, alternating with the semicircles, have been shaped into convex, truncated bays. The six sides lift gracefully, adorned with stars, to form at their top extremities a circle surrounded by six winged cherubs. Six large windows around the base of the dome let in the light of Roman midday, so that the dome seems to be floating in air. Through its circle we look up into the lantern to a dim, angelic vision at the very top.

Then our eyes move down along the walls, which are interrupted by corners and curves formed by contrasting angles and arcs. While the dome is peaceful, the walls seem restive and troubled. No one pays any attention at all to the floor, but that is where Schöne, when he breaks his silence, directs our eyes.

The floor is a hexagon formed by two equilateral triangles superimposed, and shaped like a stylized bee. From this foundation, meant to indicate the heraldic symbol of the Barberini family, whose famous son, Urban VIII, commissioned the church, the walls rise and struggle—concave facing convex across the church—and finally soar to support the dome, which at its base is another stylized bee and at its top, a circle that reveals a distant vision.

The demonstration of technical skill in supporting the weight of the dome on such an intricate series of geometric rhythms is, in its way, as impressive as that accomplished fifteen centuries earlier in the Pantheon. And all those centuries between seem, in the little church, to come together: classic architecture is fused with Gothic in an extraordinary burst of baroque energy. Schöne remarks that Borromini drew some of his inspiration from the ruins of Hadrian's villa. You could swear that he knew about Notre Dame in Paris as well. But the impression is, nonetheless, completely Italian: Rome in a small space.

As the eyes travel upward from floor to suspended dome, the walls seem almost alive, so dynamic is the execution. But the overall feeling is, for all the physical energy, intensely spiritual. That is to say, we are led upward through a series of powerful struggles, and we come to rest in a perfect circle through which, with upturned faces, we glimpse a vision, altogether peaceful, of divine protection.

Schöne mentions, in response to our questions, that Borromini was making a personal and perhaps even a theological statement with Sant' Ivo. He was a tormented man, suspicious, neurotic, withdrawn. He was overshadowed by his rival Bernini, who was extroverted and extraordinarily successful. Borromini's enemies were saying that he had betrayed the classical traditions in which architecture reflected the proportions of the human body. And perhaps he had, for he was less interested in the body than in the mind—in solving geometric problems architecturally—and in the soul, molding mass and enclosing space to show how humanity must struggle to transform itself, must reach upward toward something more than human. Something more than humanism.

Borromini failed, as artists often do, in his private life. He killed himself. But his statements in stone are affirmative. His spirit is still with us.

Schöne doesn't have to draw his conclusion. The class is already suggesting it. The difference, the all-important difference, between this building and the Pantheon is that here the dome is lifted off the ground and made to float. Here the dome is not a structure imposed on the earth, made to overawe and subdue. It is a haven toward which one struggles upward from one's hereditary fundament, changing oneself as one moves higher and higher. Sant' Ivo is, equally with the Pantheon, a symbol of benevolent protection, of something wise and radiant set above us. But here that protective power is embodied in no earthly figure. Nor does it overwhelm and overawe. It draws the viewer upward, and in the process sets him free.

Christianity raised the dome off the earth, and in so doing changed not just architectural styles but human ideals and human souls.

That, I think to myself, is why I, why all of us with Christian conditioning, feel those strange feelings of disaffection in the Pantheon. We've come to think of the dome as something that should be raised and floated, suspended aloft. We feel uneasy inside a dome set on the earth. And that unease neither the Pantheon's harmonious proportions nor its present-day distractions can dispel.

Christianity's art as well as its doctrine affirms that the power that protects us is beyond us, ineffable, beautiful, worth all our struggling toward, worth transforming ourselves to ascend to. That the meaning in our lives lies not in humbled subservience but in rising through a series of transformations to meet that protective power.

Even if, to all appearances, we fail.

4

THE ROMAN AUTUMN IS RICH AND WARM. Back home the Watergate coverup trials are in full swing and, in an exclusively West Coast World Series, Oakland has handily defeated Los Angeles. Here, romances are blossoming among the students, and jealousies too. A little learning seems to be under way. Pino's coffees are fantastically popular, and a well-to-do Atlanta girl is determined to have her daddy buy her a cappuccino machine when she returns to the States. Her boyfriend suggests bringing Pino to Georgia and setting him up in business: "Can't you see the billboards? Pino's Cappuccinos!"

I help a student committee choose the top ten fountains in Rome, and there is a contest to see who can get to all ten first. Volleyball is the only sport on campus, and we on the staff go down in defeat before the students. The boys are unexplainably losing weight under a regimen of Italian cooking, while the girls are just as surely putting weight on—a cause, for them, of major concern. At Maria's matriarchal suggestion, they decline the almost unavoidable first course of pasta, eat more salad, go without the omnipresent sugared *cornetti*. But nothing helps.

The intense Roman sunlight is a problem for me. One day in the Forum the small print in the Blue Guide blurs before my eyes. I am fitted for my first pair of glasses, for reading only. They have their pedagogical value: I find I can relax a class almost automatically by removing them, make a class concentrate on the text again simply by putting them back on.

"Now you're ready to be advanced to full professor," smiles Fr. Costello the first time he sees me reading in my office with the glasses.

"I hope you're right," I say as I take them off. "I could use a raise."

He takes that statement for what it's worth. "I'm surprised, with all the reading you do, that you didn't need glasses before this."

"An optometrist told me, when I was in my twenties, that under normal conditions I could expect to need glasses when I was forty-two. He wasn't far off."

"After forty it gets to be a maintenance problem."

"What'll go next? Ears? I need my ears."

"Teeth, probably."

"You haven't lost yours." His smile is his trademark.

"I've been lucky. May I come in?"

"Sure."

He settles powerfully into a chair.

"I appreciated your help with the volleyball game."

"But we let you down! None of us was as good as you were. Johnny Hallagan didn't do so badly, but the rest of us—"

"Johnny's always there to help, great at games. You should have seen him play quarterback when he was in high school. He still keeps his helmet, like a trophy. He was even better at baseball."

"Shortstop?"

"Second base. But you're right to think of him as an infielder, a natural infielder. Small and plucky."

"Do you know what the eye doctor down the hill said when he fitted me for these?"

"What?"

"'You never could hit a baseball, could you?'"

"He said that?"

"Yes, and then he said, 'I see you play the piano.'"

"How did he know? I swear I told him nothing about you in advance."

"He could tell from the way my eyes function that I am used to reading two lines simultaneously—two lines of music. He also said that the way eyes read indicates something about the hemispheres in the brain. I wasn't ready to pay much attention to him until he started to tell me what I did right-handed and what left."

"*Questi Italiani!* So what *do* you do left?"

"I write left and do everything else right. I bat and throw right. I do everything right but write."

He laughs. "Is it too late now to start batting left and turn yourself into Babe Ruth?"

"Give me a little time with these glasses first."

"I will. Are things going well for you here at the school?"

"Oh, yes. I think I'll be able to put my enthusiasms to work for me here, all three of them—classics, music, and my priestly work."

"Are you pleased with the students?"

"So far, so good. I've got them from all parts of the States and a few from Canada. I'm amazed, though, that there's not a single black student in the whole crowd, when we have so many back in Chicago."

"I'm afraid that black students haven't shown much interest in coming here just yet. It's prohibitively expensive for most of them. But we'll be ready for them when they come."

"Then you expect that to happen?"

"Of course, in time. You and I may have come from poor families, but we grew up with a some awareness of who Virgil and Dante were. Not many black kids have had that advantage. But this generation of black students is more curious about European culture than their parents were, and we have every reason to expect that they will pass that interest on to their children. With any disadvantaged group, it takes a generation or two, after the escape from the ghetto, for a people to establish themselves in society and look to a wider world."

"It's interesting that blacks have taken that word 'ghetto' over from Jews. Jews, once the ghettoes were abolished, did great things in art and science."

"Yes," he observes. "It's a pattern with the Irish, too. All but silenced in one century, they practically took over English literature in the next. I think we'll see cultural achievements soon in some other groups that until recently have been, to a degree, ghettoized. And these are not racial groups. I mean homosexuals, who have often had to disguise themselves as what they are not in order to make their contributions. And women. They're half of the human race, and yet whole areas of expression have until recently been closed off to them. Two generations ago, you wouldn't have found many women on campuses like this one. Now let me ask you this. Do you think you'll be with us in Rome more than just this year?"

"I'd love to stay on, but if the president of our college in Toronto can manage it, I'll return to teach with my own religious community there. That's where I belong."

"He has to arrange it with the University of Toronto, is that it? Your college is part of the university?"

"Yes. It's something like the Oxford system, with federated colleges. I taught there as a priest for eight years in the sixties. But I've been teaching on other campuses for some time now, and in the interim there's been a moratorium there on hiring."

"How soon will you know if you'll be going back?"

"I hope by February."

"Meanwhile you have this year."

"Yes. I think it's shaping up as the best year I've ever had. It's not my first time in Europe. I had a summer scholarship to the American School of Classical Studies in Athens a few years ago, and we saw many of the famous archaeological sites. And I've been to Italy and Germany before. But to spend a full year over here, to have a whole year to see Rome, to be able to see opera the year round, here and farther north—all that is pretty exciting."

"Farther north?"

"In Germany, when I can get there. Do you know Germany?"

"Some of it."

"Opera houses?"

"Hardly. I was in three prison camps there."

"I never knew! Where?"

"One near Frankfurt. One near Nuremberg. And Dachau."

"Dachau!"

"I wasn't in the concentration camp, just our own compound. We prisoners of war had our own space, separated."

I can't say anything for a minute.

"I wasn't treated all that badly," he assures me. "In our case, the Germans respected the Geneva Convention. Being marched across Germany for days and nights on end was worse than the camp was—for us, anyway."

"So they treated you—"

"I suppose about as well as any prisoners of war could expect to be treated when the end was near, by the side that was going to lose."

"But I thought—"

"I'm not saying Dachau was any kind of picnic for anybody. It certainly wasn't for the Russian prisoners. They were separated off, and they almost starved. They weren't protected by the Convention. And the Germans detested them. '*Untermensch*,' they'd call them."

"And the concentration camp, where the terrible things happened—"

"That was wired off from us."

"Surely you knew—"

"We got to know what was being done over there. The word spread pretty quickly. About the experiments."

I sit there stunned. I can't even think about the concentration camp, so I ask, "How were you captured? Do you mind talking about it?"

"Sometimes it may be good for me to remember it. I was just a kid, on a B-17, on a bombing mission deep inside Germany. It was our very first mission, and we were shot down somewhere north of Frankfurt. The lead navigator in the squadron got his signals crossed and we flew right into range."

"When was this?"

"1944."

"You weren't injured?"

"*I* wasn't. The pilot crash-landed the plane, and the copilot was killed. He was half-dead from shrapnel even before the landing. Seven of us parachuted out. I was captured almost immediately."

"And they sent you to three different camps?"

"I escaped from the first two."

"My God, Jack! How far did you get?"

"The second time I almost got to the Swiss border."

"From Nuremberg? On foot?"

"That's right. It was a long haul, on back roads by night. But I was young, and the German farmers were decent men, I found. Many of them would give me food and let me sleep in the barn."

"They knew you were an enemy soldier?"

"Sure. I hardly knew any German."

"Do you think any of them reported you to the police?"

"I couldn't be sure of that. I don't think so. I hope not."

"But you were caught both times and eventually sent to Dachau."

"Yes. There was no escape from there. I was there till the American army liberated it. When Patton came in."

"How long was that?"

"About three months."

"It must have been terrible. I mean, when you saw the Jewish survivors."

"I didn't see much. None of us did till the liberation, and I didn't see much even then. As soon as I was given some decent food to eat I got terrible stomach pains and wasn't good for anything for a while. I thought I was going to die. I remember Patton came through and leaned over my bunk and asked, 'What's the matter with this man?'

When they told him, he said, kindly enough, 'You'll be all right tomorrow, son.' In a few days I was out."

"How did the others . . . how did Patton's soldiers react when they saw the camp?"

"Well, several other camps had been liberated already, so they knew what they were going to find." He pauses. "But there was no way of preparing yourself for actually facing it, when you saw the dead bodies and, maybe even worse, the prisoners who were still alive."

"Then you *did* see some of it!"

The memory of it takes hold of him.

"Luke, when I got to the other side of the wire, and saw them—so tiny and shriveled! Some of them were hardly recognizable as human beings. They didn't know what was happening any more. If they could move, they moved like robots. If they could talk, they gibbered and squeaked. As soon as we fed them, they started to die."

A pause.

"God only knows what they went through before I saw them. More and more now, reports are coming out. But who can say what it was really like?"

"Do you mind me asking questions?" I have to ask him that again.

"No, but I think that's all I can say about the prisoners."

"What about the Germans? How could they do such things?"

"Well, some of the prisoners were Germans too. Don't forget that. The camps had their share of German prisoners who had protested against the Nazis."

"Yes. I tend to forget that."

"We wondered how the guards could be so callous about what was going on. Near the end, some of them would come over to our enclosure and try to be friendly, recognizing us as some sort of superior species like themselves, I guess. They also wanted to surrender to us before the end came. They asked us to protect them. We didn't, of course. We just waited. The GIs who came in to liberate the camp saw more than we did. They just about went crazy. They wanted to kill the officers and guards with their bare hands. So did the prisoners—the ones who were strong enough. They wanted especially to kill the other prisoners who did the Nazis' dirty work for them. The German guards were locked up for interrogation and beaten badly during the questioning. Later they were made to dig the mass graves. And, as you probably know, the people from the nearby farms and the town of Dachau were brought in to see what had been going on."

"How much did the people know?"

"They knew as well as we did that the camp was a place of horror. They couldn't help knowing from the trains that pulled in with their human cargo. But they couldn't do anything, not any more than we could, I suppose. In the end they begged not to have to look."

"And all that we've heard about Dachau—experimenting on human beings, performing unnecessary surgery without anaesthetic, injecting prisoners with diseases—"

"All that's been documented. It happened in many of the camps. Hundreds of times over."

"And removing the skin from corpses?"

"Yes, they did that. It's peculiar how one perversity has come to be the symbolic horror. We find it horrible that people would even consider using human skin for gloves and slippers and riding breeches. But they were doing worse things with live bodies. The victims with good skin were quickly shot in the head and it was all over for them. I guess the skin thing was something we could deal with, so our reporters made a lot of that. But it was only one horror. How do you measure the total horror? The ovens of the extermination camps. The heaps of bodies. You can't."

"It's the most depraved thing in human history, and it happened in our century."

"If you read the official records, Luke, you will come close to going mad."

"How did you cope with it?"

"I saw as little of it as I could, and I got out. I've tried to forget, or at least forgive."

"Do you hate Germans?"

"I don't think so. You're never sure, after such experiences, about your feelings. I can remember the *Hitlerjugend* slashing at us with their knives when we prisoners were marched through the towns, so I'm not inclined, like some other veterans, to forgive the younger generation and not the older. But who knows? Their fathers and brothers may have been blown to bits, and their mothers and sisters were starving. The kids hated us. Maybe, as far as they could see, they were justified in hating us.

"How can you sort out your feelings?" he goes on. "At the time, you just saw the people as having made a terrible mistake. But you couldn't really equate the brutes you saw in the camp and the farmers who gave you food and shelter and asked no questions. You couldn't say they were all the same, and hate them all."

I venture the inevitable question. "But they were all obsessed by the same misbegotten idea, weren't they? They were all convinced that the Jews were responsible for everything that had gone wrong in Germany, and had to be got rid of."

"Yes. But that wasn't just a German obsession. I discovered soon enough that the idea was prevalent all over Europe—that the Jews had caused the wars and social injustices and economic problems. You heard it everywhere. They say you could even hear it in the camps from those who were suffering themselves. I heard it from the Russians at Dachau. I heard it from the decent people who helped me when I was on the run. One farmer's wife, a religious woman, was quite adamant on the subject. I knew enough German to understand her. 'We have to get rid of the Jews,' she said. She lived a long way from any of the camps and I hope she didn't know how it was being done. I didn't know myself, at the time."

"Well, maybe people all over Europe were saying that the Jews had to go, but it was the Germans who decided to do something about it. And God, Jack, what a terrible solution they devised! Europe loses millions of its finest people. A great city, Vienna, loses most of its intellectuals and artists and professionals. And Germany, in so many ways the most civilized land on earth, Germany loses its soul. If it could happen in Germany, and be done to God's chosen people, it could happen anywhere, and to anyone. I sometimes think that's what God was trying to tell us."

"Luke, I can't see God in any of this. Men did it."

"I have to respect your judgment there. You went through it and I didn't."

He says nothing.

"It has to have some meaning, Jack. It has to be seen as a terrifying demonstration of the capacity *all* of us have for evil."

"Yes, you may be right. Most of us who saw some of it and couldn't believe what we saw and got fighting mad about it eventually came away feeling not anger any more, but shame. Germany went on trial at Nuremberg. But what people all over the world began saying wasn't so much how inhuman the Germans had been. They were talking about 'man's inhumanity to man.' We *all* felt shamed."

"I can hardly bear to think of Germany as perpetrating the

depraved thing out of something deep within it, and within it alone. You know what I'm going to say. Germany gave us the greatest thinkers, scientists, musicians, and writers of the last three centuries. My ancestry is half German. Yours is Irish, I suppose."

"Irish, yes. We've had our own share of madness."

"I wonder about myself, because I'm part German and love the literature and am so moved by the music, especially Wagner. You know he was viciously anti-Semitic, and that his writings contributed to the spirit that eventually produced the Nazis."

"Yes, I've heard that. Well, none of us can escape our heritage. What we can do is try to see what there is about our own selves that might be wrong. We've got to rid ourselves of prejudices, and test our ideas rather than become obsessed by them, and try to build a better future. We can see that such things don't happen again. At least we can see to it that we're not the ones to do it."

"Americans?"

"Yes. I hope soon we can end this business of policing Europe and hurrying in to solve the problems of other countries when we don't understand them. I hope we can see the injustice of acting first, if not always, in our own interests. In Latin America, in Asia. But, just as importantly, we've got to respect every minority in our own country and, whenever the inevitable problems come, not look for any convenient scapegoats. We've got to solve our problems without self-pity and panic and a lot of mindless nationalism. And we have to tolerate dissent. The Germans were always strong on law and order. That was supposed to be their special virtue, devotion to duty. They were taught to do as they were told. And, heaven help us, they did. The Nazis were, after all, legally voted into power. Well, we have to learn from the Germans' terrible mistakes. By all appearances, *they* have."

"Do you think we in our generation are doing what we should?"

"Well, I hope at least that we're doing something here at the school. Americans really need some outside perspective on their country. I don't think the Germans had much of that before the war."

"What do you think of the church's record in Germany during the war?"

"Two thousand Catholic priests died at Dachau. At Dachau alone. And they were there because they protested. The church stood up to the Nazis better than the intellectual establishment did, better than the press and the universities and the cultural institutions and the judiciary."

"Well, when all those institutions lost their Jewish members, there weren't many left to stand up to anti-Semitism. The churches weren't decimated like that. They were strong."

"It wasn't long before the protesters in the churches, Catholic and Protestant both, were marked for extinction."

"Why didn't the Catholics who saw their priests taken away protest? Were they afraid, or were they naive? Weren't most Catholics, too, convinced by the anti-Semitic lies? I guess I'm asking—and I think I must ask—wasn't the church, too, responsible for the prejudice that made the whole terrible thing possible?"

"We can't be proud of the record. But as I said before, with something of this magnitude you can't begin to apportion the blame. Pius XII, working quietly, saved something like seven hundred thousand Jews. Even more, according to some Jewish historians. But everyone still wonders if he couldn't, by a public protest, have saved millions. It's impossible to say. With his first protests the Nazis simply stepped up the operation. The important thing now is not ever to let it happen again."

A long pause. I wonder if he came to my door purposely to tell me this.

"Thanks for telling me all this, Jack. Do you talk about it often?"

"Not very often."

"Has it affected you much over the years?"

"I guess you could say that's why I'm here, doing what I do."

"You went from the war right into the seminary?"

"I had to do what I could to make the world a better place."

5

OVER AND ABOVE OUR REGULAR TEACHING ASSIGNMENTS, Andrzej and I have begun joint-teaching a course we call "The Lyric Poem." Just because we want to. It's the sort of thing that can never happen at a large university, where such a suggestion would have to be passed by several committees, not to say departments, before ever being implemented. But here we can arrange for it on the spot. Every week for one three-hour class we discuss with the students a poem in a different language. The languages I don't know, Andrzej does. (But we figure we'll we have to rely on a dictionary completely when we read Li Po.)

With a last-minute go-ahead from Maria Parenti, we set up shop in a seminar room on Tuesday evenings. We require for admission at least a B-plus average, the writing of some poetry, and a working knowledge of two or more foreign languages. Given those prerequisites, we are not surprised when there are only seven in the class, seated at our round table.

Whatever the poem we choose for the week, we begin by reading it aloud in the original language, savoring the sound of it. Then we translate it slowly, sorting out the nouns from the verbs with the help of a dictionary at the center of the table. That much usually takes the whole of the first hour, and sometimes more. The etymology, evolution, and suggestive power of words can make it an interesting hour.

Then we talk a little about the author's background, and, finally, with about an hour and a half to go, we ask ourselves what the poem is all about.

So our method of procedure follows W. H. Auden:

(1) This is a verbal contraption. How does it work?

(2) What kind of a guy lives in this poem?

Today the poem is not by a guy. It's by the poetess Sappho, who lived on the Greek island of Lesbos in the sixth century before Christ.

It's composed in a meter which we still call Sapphic, very precise and formal, designed for singing, in stanzas with three long lines identical in rhythm and a short fourth line that picks up the sounds of the longer lines and rounds off the thought. Sappho wrote in other meters too, but this is the one she favored. She may have invented it. Poets in almost all European languages have tried their hands at it since. It is also a good meter for singing, and musicians have been attracted to it. Sappho's poems were lyrics, meant to be sung.

Sappho wrote about five hundred poems. But such have been the ravages of time and history that only one has come down to us intact. The rest of what we have is fragmentary. The poem we are going to read in class is a fragment, though virtually complete in thought. Some of its short lines are only partially preserved, and its fourth stanza is so mutilated we can only guess at its meaning.

Written twenty-six centuries ago, and lost for the major part of the time between then and now, the poem was found again only in the early part of the twentieth century, on a piece of papyrus in the sands of Oxyrhynchus, in Egypt.

I give each student a photocopied page. The Greek original is transliterated into roman letters at the top, and a close English translation is added below. This week it is my turn to chair the session. I read the poem aloud in Greek, emphasizing the metrical beat to drive the rhythm home.

First there are scattered comments about its sound being pleasing. But I can tell that most of the students are disappointed. It could be my reading, and I say so. I also say that music could have helped, that Sappho was associated with a special mode of music, the Mixolydian, which gave an urgent quality to her very personal and passionate utterances. In addition, ancient Greek was intoned when it was spoken. Though they are largely useless to us, we still write pitch accents over the words of ancient Greek—accents devised in the second century B.C. because the musical pronunciation of the language was even then being lost. Today we cannot hope to reproduce the effect of Sappho's musical speech.

I do what can be done. I sing one of the few bits of ancient Greek music that has survived. I even attempt to improvise a melody for Sappho's first stanza, using the pitch accents on the words. No one looks particularly convinced, but all are expectant as we begin our grammatical and syntactical pursuits.

"This doesn't look at all like the Greek I've studied," exclaims

Janet. "What's that *emmenai* that you say is the verb 'to be'?" Like most students who learn ancient Greek, Janet knows the Attic dialect used a century after Sappho, in Athens.

"This isn't classical Greek," I explain. "It's older. It's Aeolic dialect, and we're back a whole century before the historians and dramatists. We're almost two centuries before Socrates, in what is sometimes called the Archaic Age. We're not quite as far back as Homer, but in feeling we're closer to Homer than to classical Athens."

So the Greekless in the class don't feel as intimidated as they felt at first. Everyone is at some sort of disadvantage.

We spend our usual hour on the poem as a verbal contraption. We go at it hammer and tongs, passing the dictionary around and disputing the meaning of words. Then we approach it stanza by stanza to find what kind of lady lives in the poem.

> *oi men ippeon stroton oi de pesdon*
> *oi de naon phais' epi gan melainan*
> *emmenai kalliston, ego de ken ot-*
>   *to tis eratai.*

> Some say a host of horsemen, others of footsoldiers,
> and others of ships, is the most beautiful thing
> on the black earth. But I say it is
>   what you love.

I turn to Janet, the tall, self-possessed Virginian, an English major with several foreign languages, the brightest and best-educated student in the class.

"The language may be different from what you, with your knowledge of classical Greek, are used to, Janet. But the phrasing at least is classic. Sappho uses a trope which later Greeks were fond of using. That is to say, she provides three alternatives, then rejects them all in favor of a preference based on personal conviction. Can you recall any instance of that in later Greek?"

Janet thinks for a moment and coolly shakes her head.

Andrzej, of course, knows: "When Socrates' friend went to the oracle at Delphi and asked if anyone were wiser than Socrates, he got an answer in three sentences. Not in this meter, though."

"And that answer was . . ."

He has the Greek from memory and translates for us: "Sophocles is wise. Euripides is wiser. But wisest of all is Socrates."

"Yes," I come back quickly so as not to let him get the better of me, "and Socrates himself is supposed to have said, on another occasion, that some men want a good horse, some want gold, but that he himself wanted, above all, a good friend."

Unfortunately I can't quote the original Greek, so I don't come out ahead.

"Was Sappho the first to use this way of expressing preference?" It's Tim who asks the question. He and Ellen have felt that they had to take the course. It is, after all, partly taught by their theology prof. And by now they are used to the way Andrzej and I stage our encounters.

"No," I answer, "an earlier poet, a Spartan, says that some men are stronger than the Cyclopes, swifter than Boreas, handsomer than Tithonus—but none can compare with a brave soldier."

Tim looks up as if I'd been describing him.

"But what is special," I ask, "about Sappho's use of the familiar trope?"

A pause.

"She's a woman," Tim finally says, his black eyes lighting with a sudden thought. "She rejects what men would say are the beautiful things, especially men in an age of war—cavalry, infantry, navy."

"More than that," Janet comes back, "she's taking a subjective view. A relative view. The most beautiful thing is *whatever* you love. Anything you love." Even in the transliterated Greek Janet knows that the word split across the third and fourth lines, that *ot-to*, is an indefinite relative pronoun. "The most beautiful thing in the world," she says with a trace of southern accent, "is *whatever* you single out for affection."

Then Ellen, ever surrounded in class by her small library of books, pushes her glasses back—they'd been slipping forward on her nose—and, unlike the others, puts up her hand for permission to speak. "Shouldn't the emphasis go rather on the verb? It's the last word, after all. It should be important, and it comes in that last, short, indented line that, you said, rounds things off."

"All right, Ellen. If you emphasize the verb, what is Sappho saying?"

"The most beautiful thing in the world," says Ellen, "is not *whatever* you love. The most beautiful thing in the world is whatever you *love*."

Silence. We all know she is right.

"You make something beautiful when you love it," she explains.

"You make something beautiful *for yourself* when you love it," Janet insists, still sure of her pronouns.

"So," I attempt to summarize, "we've got three approaches to the stanza. Sappho could be speaking as a feminist—'You men say that ships and horses and weapons are the most beautiful thing, but I, being a woman say . . .' Or she could be speaking as a relativist—'I say it is *whatever* you love.' Or she could be speaking as someone in love—'I say the most beautiful thing is whatever you *love*.'"

Just when we feel we are ready to pass on to the next stanza, Joe, the quiet one, wants to know if there's any significance in "the black earth."

"Black, *melaina*," I say. "It's poetic but conventional. Homer calls the earth *melaina* dozens of times."

"*Rhee d' haimati gaia melaina*," Andrzej quotes from the *Iliad*, stressing the metrical beat. "'And the earth ran black with blood.' A great line. That quiet boy there is right. Something violent and Homeric *is* suggested when Sappho uses *melaina*."

Joe blushes, because rarely does Andrzej support a student in the discussions, and I concede, "I don't think violence is suggested, but Sappho does seem to be rejecting the ideas, not just of any men, but of Homer's warrior heroes, who were pretty well the only subjects of poetry in the past. Let's go on."

> *panchy d' eumares syneton poesai*
> *panti tout' a gar poly perskethoisa*
> *kallos anthropon Elena ton andra*
> > *ton panariston*

The thought overflows the stanza. We've got to go further:

> *kallipois' eba 's Troian pleoisa*
> *koude paidos oude philon tokeon*
> *pampan emnaste, alla paragag' autan*
> > _____*san.*

It is quite easy to make this understood
to everyone. For she that far surpassed
all mortals in beauty, Helen, deserted
    an excellent man,

her husband, and went sailing to Troy,
and of her child or of her dear parents
she never once thought. What led her away was

_____.

"You'll notice that I haven't suggested any critical emendation for the missing last line. I've just left it blank. I haven't suggested any translation there, either. But what can we make of these two stanzas?"

The class is tentative, so Andrzej makes a face. "I told you we'd have to bring in the *Iliad*. You see? When she adduces proof of her opening statement, she uses Helen of Troy."

"All right, what about Helen of Troy? What did she do that bears on this poem?"

"She left her husband Menelaus," says Tim. "Even though he was an excellent man. Sappho admits that. And she left her daughter—"

"Hermione."

". . . and her parents, without a thought. She sailed from Sparta to Troy."

"With?"

"With the Trojan prince, Paris."

"And you'll notice that Sappho doesn't even mention him."

"Because," says Janet, interrupting the exchange between Tim and me, "he doesn't mean a thing in himself. She conferred his beauty on him when she loved him. She made him the most beautiful thing in the world when she fell in love with him. That's why she had to go."

"What word, then, can we put—what word do we need—in the missing space?"

"I suppose, considering the opening stanza, it should be 'love,'" Janet says.

"Yes, I think that will do: 'Love led her away.' But, with all the myths to choose from, why take Helen of Troy as an example of the opening trope?"

"Because she's a woman," says Tim. And then, suddenly, "Because she was the most beautiful woman in the world!" A light dawns. He continues. "Hey, I see the way it works out! First Sappho says, 'The most beautiful thing in the world is what you love.' Then she says, 'Take Helen. Everybody thought *she* was the most beautiful thing in the world. But Helen herself didn't think so. She fell in love with Paris. And because she loved him, *he* was the most beautiful thing in the world for her."

"*Now* we're moving around in the poem," I say. "And I think we've shown that all three of our possible interpretations of the opening trope are true . . . all three at once. This is very much a *woman*'s statement, and it's very *relative* to her feeling, and above all it is designed to show that the real beauty in something or someone is conferred by the person who *loves* it, or him, or her."

"Paris isn't even mentioned," says Janet, "because he may not have been beautiful at all. It was Helen's loving him that made him beautiful. She could have chosen anyone for that. She is in charge of the situation, and I don't think it makes much difference what she chooses to love."

"I don't think we can say that at all," puts in Joe. "The poem clearly says she was led astray."

"It does *not* say that clearly!" Janet insists. "That's right where we've got that incomplete missing line."

Joe blushes again, grows still, and I have to strike off in a new direction. "Well, maybe Paris wasn't all that beautiful. Though in Homer he is. Homer is pretty explicit about his handsomeness. But about Helen and *her* beauty—what is the line, in English literature, that everyone knows about her?"

Several say it at once: "The face that launched a thousand ships."

"OK, Helen launched the whole Trojan War when she chose what she loved. When she ran off with Paris she set Marlowe's "thousand ships" in motion, and also all those horsemen and footsoldiers we get in Homer. And the ships and the soldiers were beautiful. Homer calls them beautiful when he sings about them. But more beautiful still, Sappho says, is whatever it was that was loved by the one woman who set it all in motion. So now the question is, Can't this poem, on one level at least, be about two different kinds of poetry? Can't it be about Homer, who writes epic, and about Sappho, who writes personal lyric?"

Several hands. Several voices. Tina with her slight German accent, and studious Jerry, and fresh-faced Asian Kim: "Lyric is better than epic. That's what she's saying."

Contributions from all seven start crowding in. We remind ourselves that Homer, in epic poetry, depicts the happenings at Troy vividly, almost as in a movie. He describes the action in detail, enthusiastically. He reports all the speeches, debates, and conversations. All the battles are marvelous to see. All the heroes are beautiful. Every piece of armor, every horse, every ship is contemplated with wonder. Homer himself stands apart, amazed at the wide world he sees. But he tells us nothing about himself.

Then we remind ourselves what lyric art is. We've read Frost and Propertius and Baudelaire. And now Sappho. The lyric poet, we say, knows and reveals himself. He is not Homer standing outside his world, watching in wonder. He is someone standing at the center of the world, feeling it personally, seeing it as his *own* experience. He does not tell us what other people say. He speaks in his own voice. He cares only about his own feelings. He or she, that is.

"It's a wholly different view from epic," I say, "and it was a new view in the century in which Sappho wrote, when epic was dying and lyric poets were writing their personal statements all over Greece. It was different and new. But," I ask, "does Sappho say it's better? A better way of expressing herself? Let's read on:

> _____ *ampton gar* _____
> _____ *kouphos ti* _____
> *me nun Anaktori* ___ *nemnai*
>   *pareoisas.*
>
> *<ta>s ke bolloiman eraton te bama*
> *kamarychma lampron iden prosopo*
> *e ta Lydon armata kai panoplois*
>   *<pesdom>achentas.*
>
> . . . . . . for . . . . . .
> . . . . . . lightly . . . . . . this
> . . . . . . has put me in mind of Anactoria
>   far away.
>
> I would rather look upon her lovely way of walking
> and on the bright radiance of her changing face,
> than on the chariots of the Lydians, and their arrayed
>   footsoldiers.

"We can't do much with that mutilated stanza," I say, "but by the last sentence it's clear that Sappho prefers, to all the panoply of war, a girl named Anactoria—the way she walks, the light on her face when her expression changes.

"Is she in love with another woman?" Quiet Joe asks the stunned question that inevitably comes up in any class on Sappho. The subject is no longer so hard to deal with as it once was.

"What we call lesbian today gets its name from Sappho—"

"I know *that*," say several faces. No one wants to appear naive.

"Sappho is called lesbian, not because she loved other women in a physical way but because she lived on the island of Lesbos. But two centuries after she died there were plays written about her in Athens, and then later, in Rome, there were references in the poets Horace and Ovid—all to the effect that she was lesbian in our modern sense. In fact, many of the fragments that survive from her output are love poems to young ladies. It's not surprising that the early church fathers attacked her."

"One reason why we have only fragments?" asks Tim.

"Yes, of course. It went on for centuries," says Andrzej, the anti-clerical cleric. "From the fourth, when a mob of Christian fanatics set fire to the greatest library in the world, at Alexandria, to the eleventh, when Gregory VII ordered public burnings of Sappho's works in Rome and Constantinople. Terrible, terrible."

I shoot a barbed glance at Andrzej, who is stealing my thunder. "I'm not sure we can say, any more, that it was 'a mob of Christian fanatics' that burned the library at Alexandria."

"Well, if her poems were burned, how did we get what we have?" asks Kim.

"Bits of Sappho were quoted in other authors that did survive," I answer. "In Longinus and Dionysius of Halicarnassus. Then in the last hundred years there were papyrus finds. Our poem was found only about sixty years ago on a papyrus leaf from the second century."

"And *did* Sappho love other women?" Tim is insistent.

"It's possible. It is also true that her closest rival in poetry was a man, on the same island of Lesbos, named Alcaeus. From the fragments that survive from him, it appears that he and Sappho carried on a running battle on several subjects. He calls her 'violet-haired, honey-smiling, and chaste.' None of that seems to indicate that she was homosexual. She was probably a married woman, and there is pretty solid evidence that she had a child, a daughter. While several of the poems *are* about lovely girls who came from across the sea to be with her, the presumption today is that they did so because their parents sent them. Her city, Mytilene, was a cultural center not just for the island of Lesbos, but for all the Greek world. Perhaps she ran a school for girls. If that seems too Victorian or otherwise improbable, perhaps she had something like a literary circle. In some of the poems the girls —Anactoria in this one—marry and move away to other islands and other cities."

Ellen puts her hand up. "Maybe Anactoria left her, as Helen left her circle of family and friends, for a man who came along, whom she loved."

"That's a real possibility," I exclaim, grateful for the suggestion. "Maybe Anactoria left Sappho's circle to marry a footsoldier or a charioteer. Maybe he was from Lydia, which Sappho mentions in the last stanza—it was a fabulously wealthy land across the Aegean, with mighty armies. We have another fragment from Sappho about a girl who went to live in Sardis, the capital city of Lydia. Maybe that girl was Anactoria. Maybe Sappho taught that music and poetry and such things as the girls were learning on Lesbos were beautiful things, and yet if you loved something more than these, that object of affection had to be more beautiful still—indeed, had to be the most beautiful thing on earth. Everything had to be left to follow it—or him."

"Sorry, that won't work," interrupts Andrzej, who isn't going to let me get away with all those maybes. "The girl that went to Lydia obviously didn't think much of her husband, if that's why she went there. She got lonesome for Sappho and the other girls. Especially a girl called Athis. You've got the whole collection there. Read the thing."

I find the fragment and read it:

> . . . in Sardis . . . often . . . she keeps us . . .
> how once we lived here, at a time when she thought of you
> as a goddess, and rejoiced especially in your music.
> Now she is shining among the women of Lydia,
> surpassing them as, after the sun sets,
> the rosy-fingered moon surpasses the stars,
> and sheds her light on the briny sea
> and the blossoming fields alike.
> She pours clear water to make the roses grow,
> and the delicate chervil, and the blooming honey-lotus.
> There in Lydia she wanders to and fro
> remembering gentle Athis with longing in her heart.
> And sadness consumes her.

"And these lines probably go with that same fragment":

> She cries aloud for us to come to her there.
> And the night carries what no one else can hear
> across the sea to us.

"It's beautiful stuff," says Tim.

"Yes, but you can push this business about leaving the finishing school and running off with a soldier too far," says Andrzej. "What about Wilamowitz?"

That draws puzzled looks.

"Wilamowitz," I say by way of explanation. "Ulrich von Wilamowitz-Moellendorff, the famous classicist who made things so difficult for

Nietzsche, when they were both young—just as Fr. Zielinski, bless him, is making things difficult for me here. Wilamowitz suggested that Sappho might have been a priestess."

"And he was right," Andrzej insists. "Most of Sappho's poems are *hymns*. They're epiphanies: the goddess Aphrodite appears in human form to Sappho when she prays. From all appearances, from the poems themselves, Sappho was no schoolmarm. She was a priestess presiding over a cult, a female cult, of Aphrodite."

"Yes, you and Herr Ulrich might be right on that one. The only complete poem we have by Sappho is a hymn to Aphrodite. There's also a fragment about an apple orchard and an altar wreathed with incense, and Sappho asks Aphrodite to come while the quivering leaves pour down sleep, to come and fill her golden chalices with nectar. She may indeed have presided over a cult, though the fragments don't imply that the other girls were worshipers. We'll likely never know much more about that suggestion. Nor do we need to suppose that there was any sexual intimacy between Sappho and the other girls mentioned in the poems."

"Except," quips Andrzej, "that there's almost always something like sexual attraction working in any good teaching relationship—or so your Greeks seemed to think."

I don't take him up on that. I want, in the time that remains, to tie the end of the poem to the beginning.

"I'd like to say a little bit, while there's still time, about the man who was Sappho's rival and fellow islander, Alcaeus. I don't think we can understand this poem unless we know something about him. Like Sappho, he seems to have invented a lyric meter—the Alcaic, named for him. Sapphic and Alcaic are the two most famous meters from the lyric age of Greece.

"The poetry of Alcaeus also survives mostly in fragments, and he too wrote about Helen of Troy. But, perhaps because he was a man, he saw mostly the externals about Helen: she was not chaste, she never bore a son, she was mad with passion, she followed a traitor across the sea, she brought destruction to chariots and flashing-eyed soldiers.

"Now, Sappho uses some of those same details in our poem, as if she were answering Alcaeus, insisting that, if you look deeply into the matter, you'll see that Helen simply followed what she loved. That is all a lyric poet should be concerned with.

"I want to read you one of the fragments from Alcaeus that I think

Sappho was answering when she wrote our poem. Alcaeus was a soldier and a patriot. He participated in revolutions against the local tyrants. He spent some time in political exile. He drank heavily, if we can take the fragments at their face value, and he loved and hated passionately. Some of his output was religious. But this, of all his fragments, is the one that bears most on our poem:

> The great house gleams with bronze.
> The whole roof is adorned with war's bright helmets,
> and white horse-hair plumes swing down from the
> helmets, adornments for the heads of men.
> Glistening bronze greaves swing on the pegs they conceal,
> greaves to ward off the strong arrow.
> And corselets of new linen and hollow shields are heaped up,
>   and behind them Chalcidian swords and full many straps and jerkins.
> These we may not forget when at last we stand to our task.

"Now, what we've got here is a man's fascination with the glitter and the movement of war. What is it that makes an army on foot, or a troop of horsemen, or a fleet of sailing ships beautiful? I'd say it's the glint of the armor as it catches the sun and sparkles, the radiance from the helmets and shields, the graceful movement of the ships. That's what anyone, perhaps especially a man, would respond to.

"And," I ask, working toward the final statement, "what is it in the girl Anactoria that Sappho loves?"

A pause.

"What does Sappho find in Anactoria that is better than sailing ships, and horsemen, and soldiers on the march?"

Finally an answer comes like an alleluia.

"Her lovely way of moving. Her radiance. The changing expression on her face." Ellen has forgotten her customary reticence. She hasn't even put her hand up. "Sappho loves in Anactoria the same things men love in the appurtenances of war."

"Good, Ellen! So the last stanza is a comment on the first, as—"

"But there is a difference in Sappho that makes all the difference! The fascination with war, the Homeric notion of it as a place where men win glory, is for Sappho an idea that has seen its time and gone. She will have none of it. Any value it might have had can also be found in loving, personal relationships. They are what count in the world."

"Now, wait . . ." Andrzej tries to interject.

But Ellen can't be stopped. "Anactoria is the perfection, the sublimation, of everything that Homer and Alcaeus and the rest admire in the panoply of war. It can all be found in this one radiant girl. And it's better there because it's concentrated and humanized."

"Good, Ellen!"

Even Andrzej decides to listen.

Ellen's glasses seem to be clouding up from her nervous expenditure of energy, but she's seeing into the poem as if she were Sappho herself. She takes her glasses off and keeps talking, *accelerando*.

"That's why lyric is better than epic. The best parts of epic are the lyric parts, the concentrated, human parts, the revelations of character. At the end of the *Iliad*, the man who couldn't understand his own feelings and almost goes mad with rage and grief learns tenderness and becomes a human being at last. At the end of the *Odyssey*, the man who had lost his way on land and sea finds it, finds *himself*, in his own home, in his own bed, with his own wife. Everything that is beautiful in the *Iliad*'s war and the *Odyssey*'s wandering is gathered together in those private moments at the end of each epic when the hero finds something to love. Isn't that what Homer says at such great length? Well, Sappho says the same thing simply, in just a few lines, and you never forget it. I love her."

Suddenly, Ellen is embarrassed, because she has let so much emotion escape, and because she has gone on so long, and because she is right and thinks maybe somebody else ought to have been. But we have all noticed how, when she was speaking, her whole person was in movement, and her face underwent subtle changes, and radiance played upon her.

All of us, I think, love her at that moment. She is beautiful. For a moment, she is the most beautiful thing on the black earth.

6

OCTOBER. The students seem enthusiastic about their work. I have, in addition to the year-long seminar I'm teaching with Andrzej, three one-semester courses, two of them with small enrollments. There are four students reading Plato in Greek and five reading Horace in Latin. But I have over thirty for Greek drama in English translation. So all told I reach many students in the classroom and, I hope, a few more outside.

I learn from class to class. The students are teaching me. Not so much by what they say as by what they prompt me to think. They come to the classics from their own major interests—psychology, sociology, poetry, philosophy—and their fresh perspectives invite me to reassess what I know.

I also learn, wonder, and reassess outside the classroom.

Rome's opera house is not one of the great theaters in Europe, either for its architecture or its acoustic properties or its administrative proficiency or the general quality of its productions. It is only a little more than one hundred years old, younger than most of the works it presents. It was restored under the Fascists and still reflects some of the hardheaded philistinism of Mussolini's era. When productions are bad, they are treated by the public with perhaps more scorn than they deserve. At other times, depending on the many imponderables that affect a performance of this most complicated of the performing arts, productions can be very beautiful indeed. In Italy, on the rare occasions when every talent responsible for an artistic enterprise responsibly contributes, the result cannot be duplicated anywhere else.

The opera tonight, the season's opener, with a prestigious cast, is *I Puritani*. It was composed, in the last year of his short life, by Vincenzo Bellini, an elegant Sicilian who, along with Gioachino Rossini and Gaetano Donizetti, composed the elaborately embroidered, fiercely demanding operas we call *bel canto*, for the beautiful singing they require. In ten years of composing, Bellini produced eleven pieces for the stage. That might seem a prolific output by today's standards, but it hardly matches the records of Rossini, with twenty-five operas in his ten-year Italian period alone, and many more besides, or of Donizetti, who in a twenty-five-year period wrote close to seventy operas and six hundred other works.

Bellini's specialty was the long, languorous vocal line spun out over a succession of slow orchestral arpeggios. His music is one of the touchstones of nineteenth-century Romantic expression. His style influenced Walt Whitman's poems and Chopin's piano pieces, especially the nocturnes, and was admired even by Wagner, who had little use for opera from south of the Alps but found Bellini's melodies pure and full of genuine feeling, always an expression of the words that inspired them. It was Wagner's disciples and successors who dismissed Bellini, after the opera house orchestra had expanded to twice its *bel canto* size and operatic voices had become less flexible and florid, charged as they were with the task of surmounting great waves of orchestral sound. To appreciate Bellini today a listener may have to feel his way back past more than a century of operatic development. It is a challenge worth accepting.

I met a millionaire in Texas once, a self-made man of humble origins. I was teaching his son in high school, and I mentioned opera in class. "My daddy," said the boy, "has all them operas at home." This was in the early fifties, when far less opera was available on radio and records than is the case today. I wasn't inclined to take the boy's *"all them operas"* at face value, but I accepted an invitation to hear *some* opera at the father's home, and he and I listened for the better part of a Sunday undisturbed except for periodic telephone calls from his business associates. For hours there was no sound except the singing and the occasional ring of a well-aimed chew landing in an expensive spittoon.

The Texan had some fifty recorded operas, complete and mint-new on long-playing records, lining his shelves. Someone had told him, after he had made his money, that opera was one of the good things in life. He had promptly driven to a record store, filled his car with every complete opera they had in stock, returned home, and started listening.

He played through those operas without any advance information on what was and what wasn't a classic. His instincts were, I think, sound. He decided that the real classic was *I Puritani*. I didn't tell him that he was wrong, that—as was true at the time—whole decades could roll by without a single performance of *I Puritani* anywhere in the United States or anywhere in the world outside of Italy.

I didn't tell him because, after all, he was right. He saw more clearly than the impresarios of the thirties and forties. Since then *I Puritani*, when there have been singers for it, has drawn full houses and brought audiences to their feet.

In Rome, the houselights dim. The orchestra begins edgily with a rush of chords and ominous kettle drums. Then there is a hymnlike passage for French horns, instantly evocative of a past age of more formality, perhaps of more moral conviction, than our own. The curtain rises amid this same musical atmosphere, strangely tensed. The scene represents a fortress near Plymouth. The male chorus, dressed as English Roundheads, takes up the hymn tune and follows it with a martial anthem.

> I hear the chorus, it is a grand opera,
> Ah this indeed is music—this suits me.

Gradually the opera's mood establishes itself, even with the wrinkled, waving scenery and the rich but ill-fitting costumes. The defects are soon forgotten or overlooked, as the music takes command. A bell chimes, and three offstage male voices surround and support the clear tones of a soprano yet unseen.

Then we hear the first solo aria. The baritone stands center stage. He is a stalwart young man. Bellini surrounds his song with delicate orchestral effects—gently plucked strings and chattering woodwinds—and yet the effect of the song is noble, innocent, and virile. It is the song of a strong-willed soul in a strong-limbed body dressed in the delicate satin and lacework of another time and place.

The orchestration thickens, and the tempo picks up as the baritone is swept into a florid and passionate declaration. His feeling is flung in formal patterns across the auditorium, and the growing excitement of the audience is palpable, as the verses of Walt Whitman surface again in my memory. For Whitman this passion stronger for the constraints put upon it awakened quick responses:

> It glides quickly in through my ears,
> It shakes mad-sweet pangs through my belly and breast.

That is what I feel in the upper gallery of Rome's opera house this night, at one with the poet who heard the same music in a Manhattan theater a century before. The music reaches swiftly through the ears to the heart. I feel the sincerity, the passion of the melodies—bass and soprano are singing now—as they form a paradigm of human sentiment. I also feel the excitement of the risks taken by the singers, the triumph of the challenge met, the physical tingle of the sheer sound of it all. I am convinced that passion such as this ennobles as it enflames.

The action moves to the great hall of the fortress. Bellini's orchestra begins a series of arpeggios, and the tenor—an unromantic figure to look at—begins his aria. He sings as, perhaps, an angel might. The whole house is hushed, throat-caught, hanging on every liquescent note raised and floated out over the rhythmic accompaniment.

> A tenor large and fresh as the creation fills me,
> The orbic flex of his mouth is pouring and filling me full.

We relax only when the other singers and the chorus give the tenor a pause in which to gather his strength. The music exerts a gravitational pull on us. We are flowing, without resistance, along a vast Bellinian arc.

The honey-throated hero repeats his song, reaching into his uppermost register with breath-taking ease. The soprano wafts her finest, most silvery tones over the swaying choral song, and the music builds to its climax. We surrender to the irresistible force of it all. We feel that for a few moments we are in touch with the mystery of our own lives. (Whitman called his most operatic poem "Song of Myself.") Though that mystery is unexplained to us, we hear it and it touches us.

> It wrenches such ardors from me I did not know I possess'd them . . .
> I lose my breath . . .
> At length let up again to feel the puzzle of puzzles,
> And that we call Being.

When the music stops, the tense house explodes in shouting and applause. We are celebrating a ritual, but with what, or whom, are we communicating?

> All music is what awakes from you when you are reminded
>   by the instruments,
> It is not the violins and the cornets, it is not the oboe nor
>   the beating drums, nor the score of the baritone singer singing

his sweet romanza, nor that of the men's chorus, nor that
  of the women's chorus,
It is nearer and farther than they.

What, then, is it that awakes the response in us? Here in the theater
the acting is crude. The melodramatic happenings are unconvincing.
The plot bears no relation to history. Events happen at random. Yet
everything is true, as everything about a myth save the literal facts is
true. This is not the world of human affairs. It is both nearer to and
farther from human experience than they. This is the inner world of
the soul, where the random and the capricious constantly surprise the
reason. This is also the outer world of the cosmos. The cadenzas and
sustained high notes are hurtling meteors, galaxies, planets in orbit.
Bellini shapes into abstract patterns the beauty and terror of the
unknown within us and without.

Myths are equally true of the inner world of the psyche and the
outer reaches of the heavens, and opera is an expression of myth. It
began as an attempt to depict myth on the stage, and it has always
concerned itself with the soul within us and identified that with the
workings of the universe beyond us. (Whitman named another operatic poem "Song of the Universal.")

Now Bellini's Puritan girl, thinking that her Catholic chevalier has
deserted her, has gone mad. Her song seems to express the sadness of
all human suffering, of helplessness in the face of adversity. The music
penetrates the literal meanings of the text and the stage action and
reveals that all of what we see actually takes place within us who listen.
A hundred years ago it sent Whitman out of the opera house to write
his ballads of the self and the universe:

Haply what thou hast heard O soul was not the sound of winds . . .
Nor vocalism of sun-bright Italy . . .
But a new rhythmus fitted for thee,
Poems bridging the way from Life to Death, vaguely wafted in
    night air, uncaught, unwritten,
Which let us go forth in the bold day and write.

It was Italian opera that made him pray his secular prayer:

Give me to hold all sounds, (I madly struggling cry,)
Fill me with all the voices of the universe,
Endow me with their throbbings, Nature's also,
The tempests, waters, winds, operas . . .

On stage, the baritone and bass join their voices to pledge their loyalty. A trumpet leads their strong voices onward, and I feel the exhilaration of being carried away by a power beyond my power to control:

O trumpeter, methinks I am myself the instrument thou playest,
Thou melt'st my heart, my brain—thou movest, drawest, changest
    them at will . . .
Vouchsafe a higher strain than any yet,
Sing to my soul, renew its languishing faith and hope,
Rouse up my slow belief, give me some vision of the future,
Give me for once its prophecy and joy.

In the last act the tenor and the soprano have their greatest moments, their voices blending, soaring, leaping to stratospheric high notes and making them ring like silver bells, he leading her out of her madness and despair, she trusting and following. An ensemble builds up in which, in the manner of opera, the various characters voice their separate sentiments at once, each contending with the others in melodic lines that explode into high notes. The whole auditorium seems to be throbbing with the steady, cumulative effect of the voices and orchestra, till the tenor, now supremely confident, reaches an impossible, shining F above high C. The audience erupts volcanically.

O glad, exulting, culminating song!
A vigor more than earth's is in thy notes.

A fanfare of horns and trumpets heralds the unmotivated and altogether improbable solution to the plot. Enemies are reconciled, suffering is transcended. The soprano ends the evening with a sustained, squarely placed, joyous and altogether triumphant D above high C.

War, sorrow, suffering gone—the rank earth purged—nothing
    but joy left!
The ocean fill'd with joy—the atmosphere all joy!
Joy! joy in freedom, worship, love! joy in the ecstasy of life!
Enough merely to be! enough to breathe!
Joy! joy! all over joy!

The curtain falls. The house lights come up. We in the audience have no more constraints placed on our enthusiasm, and now we vie with one another, one section of the house with another, in our shouting and stamping. When the lights in the house begin to go out, we finally move to the exits, emotionally spent, moved as in some religious experience by the genius of a composer, by the prodigious skill of four solo singers, by what the music has shown us of ourselves, by the force with which it has lifted us out of ourselves. Bellini told his librettist, as they wrote *I Puritani*, that opera "must make people weep, shudder, die through the singing."

In the Roman night, the memory of the music fades in my ears.

The aria sinking,
All else continuing, the stars shining . . .
The love in the heart long pent, now loose, now at last tumultuously
    bursting,
The aria's meaning, the ears, the Soul . . .
The strange tears down the cheeks coursing . . .

Is it only that I have surrendered to the music? Or have I come, in the course of surrendering, face to face with something, someone, deep within me and at the same time infinitely beyond? Is that what great art is for, that encounter? Is it meant to change me?

7

THE WARM DAYS CONTINUE. Students are busy learning Italian, but keep in touch with American pop music via a high-powered radio station in Luxembourg and with world news via the old GI newspaper, the *Daily American*. The economy is in decline back home. It looks as if Lieutenant William Calley, convicted of the My Lai massacre, will be released. Muhammad Ali has regained his world heavyweight title. At the movies, the *Godfather* sequel is reported better than the original.

In Rome, I head down the hill every free afternoon to the center of the city, guidebook in hand, to search out the wonders. It is my ambition to see, this year, every sight that gets a star in the Blue Guide. It isn't long before I've seen a hundred of the churches. Sometimes I'm accompanied by a student or two. Often that student is Tim Brannigan. Tim of the flashing eyes, Homer would say.

Tim, I've discovered, knows Rome better than any of the others, having already spent a full year in the city with an Italian family. He knows the Raphael frescoes in the Villa Farnesina, and the Fontana delle Tartarughe, and Borromini's miraculous Carlino, which like Sant' Ivo rises in a series of daringly executed geometric designs to float a rounded dome over a small space. These are things the casual tourist doesn't see.

Though I'd known Tim, inside and outside of class, as bright and promising, he made no special impression on me until he came to my office for some help on a piece for a course in communications. He had heard that, during the heyday of university film courses, I had taught one or two on the history and the aesthetics of film. He was set to write a paper on editing techniques and wanted to know about Sergei Eisenstein's *Potemkin*, the silent Soviet film made in 1925.

I was surprised that he hadn't seen it. Eisenstein, commissioned by the Soviet government to make a piece of inspirational propaganda, recreated a mutiny aboard a czarist battleship and the events that followed. In editing his scenes he evolved techniques still in use and still unsurpassed—*Potemkin* has several times been voted the greatest film ever made.

There are a dozen or so facts about *Potemkin*'s editing that anyone involved in film can give you straight off. I hadn't concerned myself for several years with movies, as I prefer to call them, and I was at my desk with an administrative problem when Tim knocked at the door. Impatiently, without inviting him to sit down, I said, "I haven't much time right now. When is the paper due?"

He hesitated, more than a little embarrassed. "Tomorrow."

"All right. Here is the general idea."

He stood in the doorway as I hurried over the details.

"Now," I said almost as a challenge, though actually this is an old pedagogical device, and a good one, "can you tell me what I just said?"

He proceeded to give me the material back, not only correctly, but more concisely and more convincingly than I had given it to him. He had immediately assimilated a mass of fact and opinion, sorted it out, and reordered it. I was astonished, not only by his quick intelligence and the way his features revealed the mental processes at work but also by his modesty and his eagerness to learn. There wasn't a trace of superiority, which, in the circumstances, he might have been entitled to show, and not a suggestion of wanting to score me for my impatience. Only enthusiasm and quick, grateful responses.

This was a student from whom I could learn.

I pushed away from my desk, invited him to sit down, and swiveled around to face him squarely.

He was nineteen, from Chicago, Irish and Italian ancestry. Dark, tousled hair, thick eyebrows, clean-shaven face with signs of a heavy beard. Intense black eyes. He carried himself like an athlete, which, to some extent, he was. He didn't settle into the chair but leaned forward eagerly.

We talked a little about movies, then a lot about him. He had only an average track record academically, but he was more intelligent than I. He wanted someday to make movies.

Why?

Because he wanted to help people to understand their problems. He wanted to give the hopeless like those he knew on Chicago's

South Side something to hope for. He was saddened at the amount of money his country spent on defense, wishing some of that could go to help the poor of the world. He knew the facts and figures on the matter. He knew the neighborhoods of Chicago and had seen the slums of Naples. He knew his congressman back home. He had headed a high school deputation to ask for better public housing. He thought some of F.D.R.'s policies of the thirties could help alleviate the unemployment problems of his generation.

He had helped with retarded children in his neighborhood, sacrificing his Saturdays. Evenings he had worked in a supermarket to pay for his tuition. He had played varsity basketball in his Catholic high school. He also played, inevitably, the guitar. He sang his own songs.

He was the oldest of five children. His father was a machinist who made a fair amount of money at his trade and was outspoken at union meetings. Sometimes his father antagonized union leaders as well as management. His mother worried. She was Roman-born and religious. Tim too had a religious bent. More than that he was, I quickly gathered, in love with religion. Jesus was the model for us all. Jesus' words were life-giving. Jesus' love, refracted into a million loves throughout the world, was the ultimate answer to all questions.

He responded to Italy and Italians. "Something atavistic there," he smiled. A year ago he had come over on a student charter, sold the return ticket, sought out his mother's family and, with their help, had found a job in a trattoria. After a year of that, he was ready to take some courses and work in the accountant's office at the school.

We talked about *La Strada* (his favorite movie) and *Grand Illusion* (mine), about the Sistine Chapel and the statues in the Museo delle Terme. He knew the Orpheus and Eurydice relief in Naples, and the big mosaic there depicting Darius and Alexander at the Battle of Issus. He knew the frescoes by Fra Angelico in San Marco in Florence, and the Giotto ceiling in Padua, and the Ca' d'Oro in Venice.

I reflected, after a half hour's exchange during which we prompted each other to more and more enthusiastic appraisals of the things we had seen and loved, that this was the most appreciative and intelligent conversation I'd had with anyone at the school, that this was in some ways the most admirable person, and the most congenial—and that I was old enough to be his father.

This boy might have been my son.

Most priests, when they reach the age of forty, wish they had children. Perhaps most unmarried men do. You're told as you prepare for ordination, fifteen years in advance of your fortieth year, that this will be the case. But you still aren't prepared for the ache of the realization when it comes. Here was a boy closer in many ways to what I am now than I was myself when I was his age. And potentially he was much more, with hopes and dreams I would like to have as my own.

Had I married, I might have had a son his age. Though chances are I never would have been so lucky as to have a son like him.

He may have wondered why, of a sudden, the bottom dropped out of our conversation. I hoped he thought it was because I had to get back to my desk.

Actually, I was filled with new feelings I didn't know how to deal with.

He saved the moment. "Hey," he said, "this essay is due tomorrow. I've got to get out of here."

But that was weeks before. On this feast of All Saints, after early Mass, Tim and I take bus 47 down the hill, then bus 64 from the Vatican to the train station. From the upper level of Rome's most famous public conveyance we see, successively, St. Peter's, the Castel Sant' Angelo, the Tiber and its bridges, St. Philip Neri's Oratory, Sant' Andrea della Valle, and the Piazza Venezia fronting on the Capitoline and the Forum. Then the bus veers upward on the Quirinale and threads a slow passage along the busy Via Nazionale until it circles triumphantly around the ostentatious Piazza della Reppublica, where a massive hero stands in the midst of a circular fountain strangling a great fish to send a jet of Aqua Marcia high in the air. Rome is not subtle in its public displays. The fountain stands where once was the exedra of the Baths of Diocletian, where once the world's athletes struggled with animals before roaring crowds.

We pull to a halt before the station, with perhaps one hundred other buses, and make our way on foot through November's vendors of roasted chestnuts, lottery booths, tourists, and pickpockets and stand in separate lines at the ticket windows, so that whoever gets with painful slowness to a window first can buy for both. Elbowed and elbowing, each of us arrives simultaneously with the other at a separate window. We laugh and hurry with the tickets to the train for Naples.

There was no need to hurry, The train is, as usual, a half-hour late leaving the station. By the time we pull out, the second-class compartment is full, with eight of us occupants filling the eight seats and two small children now on, now off one lap or another. Even the corridors are lined with passengers leaning on the half-lowered windows. Four of those seated with us are men over fifty, and they begin an animated political conversation. The two-hour trip takes longer than two hours and is not quiet.

In Naples a blustery rainstorm has filled the station with more than the usual number of importunate gypsies. Near the Piazza Municipio we get a double room in a small pensione, with a patch of pollution-shrouded Vesuvius visible from the window. We are lucky enough to get a couple of gallery tickets for that evening's opera, Verdi's *Don Carlo*, and we call in at the various tourist offices—CIT, Ente, Amex, and Cook's—to ask about trips to the Virgil places. We are told that there are no excursions until the spring, and even then the trips won't stop at Cumae, which I most wanted to show him. It looks as if, for Virgil, we'll be on our own—which we half expected would be the case.

The San Carlo in Naples is one of the most beautiful houses in Italy, with good sight lines, acoustics that favor the voices up top and the orchestra on the main floor, and elegant décor climaxing in a casemented, frescoed ceiling that appears, from below, to have the softness of a cloud. All classes of people fill the seats. We are with the fanatics up near the ceiling. Even when the performance starts, the buzz of conversation fills the theater, rising from the lower boxes to the upper reaches where we sit. It drops to a hush only for the famous moments. Fortunately there are many of those in *Don Carlo*. They spill over the battlements of the Escorial in glorious profusion. The genius of their composer, Giuseppe Verdi, blazes throughout the four acts at white heat, illuminating Schiller's tangled, powerful, not always historical recreation of events in Spain during the reign of Philip II.

On Verdi's stage, five characters act out great public and private events interdependently. Each character is in some way strongly tied to, even in some way in love with, the other four. No one of them is complete until seen in complex relationships with each of the others. One of the characters, the Princess Eboli, sings a Moorish "Veil Song" in which her prismatic relations with the others—and by implication theirs with her—are subtly suggested. The "Veil Song" is one of Verdi's additions to Schiller. His version of the story is a series of revelations, unveilings. With his powerful music, his pessimism, and his compassion, Verdi turns Schiller's drama of ideas into five interrelated tragedies.

I am most moved by the tragedy of young Rodrigo, the Marquis of Posa, a kind of proto-Protestant at the Catholic court. Friedrich von Schiller made him a figure, in a sixteenth-century setting, of eighteenth-century ideals of tolerance, political and religious freedom, and universal brotherhood, though he gave him an ambivalent moral sense. But in Verdi he seems as straightforward and unambivalent as the two cornets that adorn his soldierly death. He is, ironically, the only man at the Catholic court in whom the Catholic king can confide, a kind of surrogate son to him. And that, for reasons I can now begin to understand, is why Rodrigo affects me so deeply.

Tim, for reasons I was later to understand, is more moved by the relationship between the powerful king, Philip II, and his flesh-and-blood son, Don Carlo. They clash in their public lives, because the father wants to punish Protestant Flanders and the son wants to save it. And they clash in their private lives, because each is in love with the new queen, Elisabeth of Valois. Young Carlo has an almost Oedipal love for his stepmother and an almost Oedipal hatred for his father.

But the scene that keeps an audience, even the noisy Naples audience, hushed and awed is the scene between King Philip and a sixth character, a small role but an unforgettable one—the Grand Inquisitor. Powerful, blind, and intransigent. Catholicism at its most fanatical and frightening. The absolutism I pray we have put behind us forever.

The king asks his Inquisitor if he can condemn his own son to death. The Inquisitor says that God himself did no less.

The Inquisitor then asks for the death not just of the son, Don Carlo, but of the surrogate son, Rodrigo. Sonorous brass chords emphasize the terror.

So the surrogate son, Rodrigo, must die, but the flesh-and-blood son, Don Carlo, survives—perhaps to make a better world. He is saved, on the opera's final page, by a mysterious figure in the robes of a priest.

On the way to the exits, with Verdi's music still ringing in our ears, we begin to piece together the ironies of the story.

"So who is it at the end who comes to save Carlo from the Inquisition?" Tim wonders. "Who is the priest who comes out of the tomb to take him away?"

"I'm afraid Verdi never made his mind up about that," I answer. "Some people say it's a terribly weak, melodramatic ending, that it trivializes the whole opera—that figure from the tomb. There was no such rescue in Schiller, let alone in history. But neither Verdi nor Schiller was writing history. Schiller wanted to express new liberal ideas. Verdi wanted ambivalences."

"Ambivalences?"

"Well, the saving figure at the end could be a supernatural mani-festation—the spirit of Don Carlo's grandfather, Charles V, risen from his tomb. Or it could be Charles alive—there's a hint in history that he did not die when his subjects thought, but lived on for years in seclusion, in a monastery. I think that Verdi wanted us to ask at the end whether history was propelled by political power or by more than natural forces."

"But he never made up his own mind?"

"No. Not about history, and not about God either. He was an agnostic. He didn't know if God existed, or whether, if he existed, he was good or evil. Verdi was also of two minds about the church. He hated its triumphalism, and there's no question that it *was* an oppres-sive force in the Spain of Philip's day, and a reactionary one in the Italy of Verdi's day. All the same, Verdi had a chapel at his villa at Sant' Agatha, and he prayed there. His last pieces were a 'Te Deum' and a 'Stabat Mater.'"

We've made our way out of the theater and into a rain-washed night, confronted almost immediately by a small army of beggars—an old gypsy man with only half a face, an emaciated woman with a baby in her arms, some dangerous-looking *giovanotti,* some pathetically dowdy streetwalkers. We give the gypsy woman some of our lire. A big policeman in fancy dress scolds us for that and asks us to move on. We feel helpless to do anything.

"Here in Naples you can feel some of Verdi's pessimism," I say.

"And his compassion," Tim adds, quietly correcting me, for that, powerless though we are to do anything, is what we feel. "I want to do something with my life that will help people like those people."

We head down the street as the crowd thins out. Tim changes the subject back to where it was before. "It would be a really good opera if it weren't for that ending."

"The figure from the tomb is a pretty crude device, all right. But it says what Schiller didn't say. It preserves the flesh-and-blood son so that the death of the surrogate son is not in vain. In a way it's like the whole opera—untrue to history, but true, in the most important ways, to life. True to the uncertainties and ironies."

"But aren't Verdi's operas hopeful? Weren't they taken as rallying cries for the new Italy? I thought Verdi was loved in Italy for his patriotism. And loved all over the world for his sympathy with suffering people."

Walking through the streets of Naples, with visible evidence of two hopeful centuries in decline, the questions cut right to the heart of Verdi's operas.

"In some of the operas he pretty well abandons hope for despair. In *Il Trovatore*—a profound statement, though you may have heard people saying otherwise—there is no indication that Verdi sees any sense in human suffering. He's saying, 'In the end, life means nothing.' His wife, Giuseppina, said he was happier believing that. Once when she talked about God he laughed in her face and called her mad. When he wrote *La Forza del Destino*, for Russia, he had the hero, crazed by sudden terrible revelations, leap off a cliff renouncing God, screaming 'Let the whole human race perish!' And that's the way the opera ended! He had to soften that for Italy. The hero was a priest, and he dies calling on hell to open its mouth and swallow him. Verdi had to change that."

"Maybe he changed the ending because he didn't really believe it."

"Possibly, though later, when he turned his hand to Shakespeare's *Othello*, he made his Iago equally nihilistic. Verdi's Iago says, in defense of the evil he plans to do to the Moorish hero, 'After death there is nothing.'"

"What could have made Verdi so bitter?" Tim turns to face me as we walk. "I mean, there's so much compassion in the music."

"His own life, especially his young life, was full of death. When he was in his twenties, he lost his wife and two children to fever within the space of a few months. He narrowly escaped death himself when he was a baby, and a Russian regiment was massacring the women and children in his village. His mother climbed to the belfry with him in her arms, and escaped the sabers. Something like that happens in *Il Trovatore*. The year before he wrote *Il Trovatore*, his mother died. His librettist died in the midst of writing it. When it appeared on the stage, he wrote, 'People say that it is too sad, that there are too many deaths in it. But death is all there is to life. What else is there?'"

Tim is silent when he hears that. We turn a corner. He says, "I still have the feeling, from the music, that he thought that our suffering ennobles us. Maybe his universe is cruel. But his suffering people— they touch our hearts."

"Of course you're right. The suffering figures in Verdi sing for all of us."

We head down a long street. I introduce a subject that Verdi's music always brings to mind. "There is a figure that keeps appearing in Verdi's operas, one after the other. The father. A patriarch, something of a symbol for Italy itself. Maybe even a kind of figure for God. He's often a terrifying figure, but he loves his children, and weeps with them. You know *Traviata, Rigoletto, Boccanegra*?

"I've seen *La Traviata*."

"Then you know that the music Verdi gives those fathers in the scenes with their children, or their surrogate children, is the best music he ever wrote. Full of tenderness and understanding. The fathers sing '*Piangi, piangi.*' They weep what Virgil calls the 'tears of the world.'"

"Did Verdi have any more children, after the first two died?"

"None that we know of. His private life is something of a closed book. I sometimes think that, through his long life, he sought out subjects where he could speak, through his music, to the children he lost and the children he never had."

Late as it is, and November-cool, a long-lined song with distinctive Neapolitan cadences comes, now from the occasional window, now from a rooftop, as we walk the wet streets. Was it Spanish or Moorish influences that brought that strain to this Mediterranean seaport with its wide bay and its extinct volcano? A city where the threat of violence seems to flicker around every darkened corner, where there is much poverty, where one always has the sense of many lives having passed into history?

The streets are lit by rainy moonlight. The moon is unconcerned.

"Verdi asks whether anything in life is really important, except for our compassion for one another's sufferings."

That night I think I hear Tim crying in his sleep.

8

"**A**RT THOU SLOW TO PRAY?"
Early the next day, All Souls' Day, at a small, enclosed side altar in a Neapolitan church crowded with images and candles, I come to say the three Masses that a priest says on this day for the dead. Tim is with me.

The darkness of the place is almost oppressive. The small tabernacle gleams fitfully with what looks, in the surrounding dimness, like the gleam of gold. I open the gates of the enclosure around the altar, gates once meant to keep out uninitiates, and approach the altar, chalice in hand. Tim kneels reverently on the unyielding stone step. At the offertory he pours the wine streaming into the cup, and at the communion he takes half of the consecrated host hesitantly in his hand. The missal provided is in Latin. Through three Masses, we pray in that language for the souls of the dead, especially for the departed souls in his family and mine. For my father, dead now for eight years.

Then, in our hardiest all-weather clothes, we try our luck getting to the Virgil places—the two cliffed temples at Cumae and the cave of the prophetic Sibyl below. It is, for me, a return visit to a remote and sometimes dangerous region, reached by a clanking train trip underground and a very slow bus, requiring a pilgrim's determination and some direction from the local residents. The last is not always immediately forthcoming. Neapolitans look after themselves and their families first and—smiling to make you understand—last and—save in remarkable circumstances—only. That is simply their way of survival.

So it is close to noon when Tim and I arrive at the lonely site, above sea level, of the two ruined Cumaean temples. The sun is high overhead as we start across the volcanic landscape toward the sky. The spaces are free even of the gypsies they sometimes shelter. When we reach the temples, the sea churns below us.

The first temple we see is dedicated to Apollo. It was immortalized by Virgil halfway through his *Aeneid*. His hero Aeneas mounts this height from the side of the sea, with his close friend Achates, and they stare in wonder at the temple's gold-blazoned doors. On them is depicted the death, in myth, of a young prince, and the fateful chain of other young deaths precipitated thereafter. Much of this mythic past is to happen again in Aeneas's future. He will lose seven surrogate sons.

The golden figures, Virgil says, were made by the artist of all artists, Daedalus, who came winging his way across the sea to this height, with his only son, Icarus, both of them on wings of the father's devising. And on that skyey voyage Daedalus lost his son to the sea. Young Icarus, in the exhilaration of flying, flew too close to the sun's rays. The grief-laden father wanted to depict that young death, in addition to the other youthful deaths, on the doors. But he could not steel himself to do so. Virgil, writing as if the dead son were there before his eyes, says:

> You too would have found a place of honor in this work,
> Icarus, had your father's grief allowed it.
> Twice he tried to fashion your fall in gold.
> Twice his fatherly hands fell from the task.

Tim and I stand at the spot where, Virgil says, Aeneas and Achates once stood. The golden doors are gone forever, but Virgil's words are engraved in Latin on a plaque nearby. I translate them for Tim. Clouds begin to gather overhead. The wind picks up.

"So this temple was consecrated in memory of a son who died?" asks Tim, the wind catching his hair.

"Well, all we really know is that the temple was built in honor of Apollo, the god of poetry and prophecy. It was Virgil, a poet and a prophet, who, much later, wrote of the father graving the doors here and grieving at the death of his son. I think that, halfway through his epic of past hopes and sorrows, Virgil wanted to plant a prediction of something that had already happened in his own day. He was writing the *Aeneid* for Augustus, who never had a son of his own but adopted his nephew, Marcellus, a young man full of promise."

"And Marcellus died?"

"Yes. He was Augustus's heir, and the hope for the future. He would have been the second Roman emperor, and he might have changed the face of Europe if, as Augustus hoped, he had lived to extend Roman influence east of the Rhine. That was the next frontier to be crossed. But the Germanic tribes were never to be romanized. Europe was never to be unified. Wars were to be fought across that German river for centuries in Roman history and for centuries after. The adoptive son who might have made the difference died at nineteen of undiscovered causes.

"My age."

"Yes."

Only the Tuscan sea speaks for a while.

Then he asks, "Why does Virgil say 'twice'—twice Daedalus tried to fashion his son's death on the temple doors, and twice he couldn't bring himself to do it?"

"I don't know. I've wondered often. It's meant to tease us out of thought."

"Maybe it's that Icarus dies in myth and Marcellus dies in history. What we see in art happens in our own lives."

He is probably right. He faces into the wind.

"That's good, Tim. Art is often prophetic."

There is a pause, till I explain a little. "Virgil's art certainly is. Through the centuries Europeans regarded him as some sort of prophet. They thought he had predicted their own histories. What he writes about in the last books of his epic—the loss in war of the young men whose good qualities might have been used to build the peace— that surely is prophetic. We mightn't have had to fight World War II if the best of French and German manhood had not been killed off in the first war and had survived to build a peace."

Tim says nothing to that. It's not part of his past or his memory.

"Virgil lived just before the birth of Christ, didn't he?"

"Yes, and in one of his early poems he was thought—by Constantine and St. Augustine, by Dante and Alexander Pope—to have predicted, with his usual ambiguity, the birth of Christ. He also made a pre-Christian virtue a recurrent word, a key word, in the *Aeneid*— *pietas*. It's close to piety and it's close to pity, but not quite either of those. It's more like duty, devotion. A father's devotion. Virgil uses it often to describe the bond between father and son. He calls his hero *pius Aeneas* and *pater Aeneas*. So far twelve of the popes, those perennial Roman fathers, have taken the name Pius."

Tim looks up at me. "Aeneas had a son, didn't he?"

"Yes, just a toddler when he escaped from Troy, and not quite old enough, at the end of the poem, to fight in his father's wars. He's not as important in the *Aeneid* as all the other young men who become like sons to Aeneas. One by one, as Aeneas fights his way to the founding of Rome, they die. That becomes one of Virgil's main themes. In order for any progress to be made in history or in human lives, there have to be sacrifices. The innocent must suffer. One man dies in place of another. Virgil weeps in *pietas* for the young men who lay down their lives for the future of Rome."

"That sounds like one of the few bits of Virgil I know—*lacrimae rerum.*"

"Yes. The sadness in everything, the tears shed in the course of human history. The *Aeneid* isn't so much about the Trojan War as it is about all the wars fought by the Romans in their history. It's a massive metaphor for all wars and what they do to men. 'Of arms and man I sing.'"

We climb farther up to the temple of Jupiter, the sky god, the god who, for Virgil, directed all of history with his utterance, his *fatum*. The god who, for Virgil, had determined that Rome would be the center of the world at the central point in history.

The temple, reduced today to little more than its foundations, is a long way up from the sea. Overhead the wind is driving great scudding clouds. God's power seems, at this point in history, much more imposing than these remnants left in his honor by past conquerors, these pagan temples that, centuries after Virgil, were used as Christian churches—and now lie in ruins.

"So this is where it all began for Rome!" Tim exclaims.

"Virgil would have it so. This shoreline is where Virgil has his Aeneas, the father of the Roman future, come first to land in Italy. After losing his helmsman, Palinurus, to the sea."

"Palinurus?"

"Yes. It's the most beautiful passage in the whole epic. The sea, which has already claimed most of Aeneas's fleet off the coast of Africa, demands that, when they near the coast here, one life be sacrificed for the safe passage of the rest. So the god Somnus passes a dewy branch across the eyes of the helmsman of the lead ship, Palinurus, and he's lulled to sleep and falls into the sea—and the ship sails on of its own. Palinurus is faithful to father Aeneas to the end. He tries to resist his fate. He hesitates just before he falls."

Tim has his usual flash of recognition. "Maybe *that*'s why the hands of Daedalus fell twice when he tried to depict the fall of his son into the sea. Icarus dies in myth and Palinurus dies in Virgil's narrative, and both of them signify the death of Marcellus in Virgil's own time."

He is probably right. He has the sun on his shoulders. "Virgil certainly is complicated, layer on layer," he says.

He scans the coastline. "Why did Aeneas have to land here first in Italy? Why didn't he head straight up the coast to the Tiber?"

"Because his dead father appeared to him in a dream and told him to come here first, to have his mission confirmed by the Sibyl. Besides, Aeneas wanted to *see* his father again. The Sibyl could help him with that. The entrance to the world of the dead was here, at Cumae. Come on—let's go down to the Sibyl's cave. It's really something."

We descend from the temple heights down the cliff to see the miraculously well preserved place of prophecy. What we see matches what Virgil saw in his own day and magnified in the telling:

> Into the flank of the cliff was carved a massive tunnel. A hundred corridors led into it, with a hundred doors. And a hundred voices would rush back through it—the oracular responses which the Sibyl interpreted.

Tim and I stand at the entrance where Aeneas and Achates stood and look down a triangularly shaped cavern cut into corridors that were once sectioned off by doors and illuminated by slitted windows cut laterally in the walls. Few archaeological sites convey so real a sense of mythic awe. We make our way silently past what was once an enclosure keeping out the uninitiates, and proceed through the length of a cave, through its successive corridors—not Virgil's one hundred, but to an awed initiate long ago they might have seemed like the mythic hundred, as he saw door after door open before him and a sudden flash of daylight from the windows illuminate the darkness of each successive chamber, until the Sibyl was revealed in the farthest chamber. I remember what Virgil said:

> They made their way forward, and the Sibyl's voice cried, "It is time! Ask to know thy future! The god—look thou!—the god is upon me!" The presence of Apollo was breathing round her . . . "Art thou slow to pray, Trojan Aeneas? Art thou slow?" she asked. "The house is full of thunder, but its great responses will not reveal themselves until thou prayest." Icy terror shot through the sturdy frames of the two Trojans, and father Aeneas poured out prayers from his very heart. . . . Then the hundred mighty doors opened of their own accord down through the cave, and a wind swept forward the Sibyl's responses.

"And what," Tim asks, "did the Sibyl prophesy?"

"That Aeneas's past would also be his future. That the gods would test him as they always had. But that he must not lose heart, but must press on bravely. He was called to found Rome. To be the father of a new race."

"And did he get to see his father?" Tim's voice echoes in the cave.

"Yes. It's a moving passage in Virgil. 'Let me see my father. Show me the way to him.' Halfway through the *Aeneid*, at its great heart, Aeneas pours out streaming offerings of sacrificial wine, descends to see his father in the world of the dead, and there his father shows him all his future sons—the famous Romans, from Romulus onward, who will change the course of history."

Tim looks into my eyes. "I guess most of the heroes in myth are looking for their fathers, aren't they?"

"Or looking for themselves, which in myth is pretty much the same thing. That's a kind of archetype in hero myths: finding your father is finding yourself."

The cave is suddenly silent.

"Let's go back up into the light."

The sun and the wind from the sea are like a sudden blessing. I point inland.

"The entrance to the world of the dead was a long way over there, across a forest, near a volcanic lake. The Sibyl tells Aeneas that, to see his dead father, he will first have to find and pluck a golden bough in the forest:

> There lurks here on a shadowed tree a bough of pliant leaves and stem, sacred to the goddess of the nether world. All the forest, all the valleys round conspire to hide it in darkness. And only he who has plucked from its tree the golden spray can pass beneath the hidden places of earth.

"The Golden Bough!" Tim exclaims. "I've heard of it! It's like the Holy Grail, like the Blue Bird. If you find it, it's the answer to all you need to know in life. It's like finding yourself. So Aeneas finds it . . ."

I look straight at him. "When he is burying another surrogate son, lost to the sea."

"It all doubles back on itself, this Virgil poetry! Another surrogate son?"

"Yes, the trumpeter, Misenus. Aeneas found his corpse and buried it on a flat mountaintop over past the lake. It's still called Mount Misenus. And for the lost helmsman there's a promontory farther down the coast still called Cape Palinurus."

"Twice the father's hands—"

"—fell from depicting the son's death in gold, yes."

"The trumpeter has to die for Aeneas too?"

"I think so. The helmsman dies so Aeneas can reach this shore, and the trumpeter dies so Aeneas can find the bough—and he does. Following two white doves, he presses on into the forest and sights a gleam, not quite a gleam, of gold. It looks like mistletoe, clinging to its tree with glistening fresh leaves and yellow berries. And you're right about the bough being like the Holy Grail. Only those who are called to find it can find it and make it their own. The Sibyl tells Aeneas that, if he finds it and is truly called to his mission, the bough will come willingly in his hand. But if he is not called, nothing—not even a sword—will be able to sunder it from its tree."

"That's like the Holy Grail, all right. You have to be called. *You* don't find *it*, *it* finds you. And so the bough comes willingly for Aeneas, like the Sibyl said it would?"

"Not quite. It hesitates in his hand. Just for a moment."

"It hesitates?"

"Yes. It's another of Virgil's mysterious little touches. In most of these questing myths the talisman the hero seeks has an intelligence of its own. Here it's as if the Golden Bough is not quite certain that Aeneas is called to fulfill his mission."

"But he does, doesn't he?"

"In the old legends, yes, but not in Virgil's poem. At the end, Virgil leaves the matter open. The bough was right to hesitate."

Tim is silent again. Then he looks at me again and asks, "Did Virgil have a son?"

"No, he never married."

We proceed along the path once walked by Aeneas and the faithful Achates. In the *Aeneid* they have a long conversation which the reader is not allowed to hear. Tim and I talk about our Virgilian and Verdian visions, about the sadness in the world, about our uncertain futures. We were not destined, walking that day in the November sun and wind through the desolate Virgil places, to find the Golden Bough. It still awaits him whom fatherly love and human loss might guide next to the tree hidden somewhere in the forest.

9

I T IS ALMOST WINTER IN ROME. Mount Soracte, seen from the roof, has early snow. And we have rains.

The results of the first tests dismay the students. In Connecticut and Carolina they almost invariably got As. Here many have received, or rather given themselves, Bs and Cs. Some have received failing grades for the first time in their lives. There are tears. Feelings of humiliation are compounded by homesickness. In some cases, long-standing resentfulness of parents is directed against the teacher who seems to serve *in loco parentis* and has given them a lower mark in Greek Tragedy than they have ever received in anything before.

Jennifer sits down anxiously in my office. Her usually pretty face has lost its composure. The lovely eyes are swollen, the lower lip trembling. "You ought to mark us easier over here, because we spend our weekends sightseeing."

"I know you do. I'm away most weekends myself—longer, perhaps, than anyone else. There's so much to see. But, if you're not learning—"

"I'm learning about Europe when I spend the weekends away. Seeing for myself is more important than anything I'll read in books."

"Then why not spend the year traveling? You could get a refund on the second semester's tuition, work a little to support yourself, and resume your college career in the States next fall."

"I can get the money from home if I want to. That's not the point. The school promised us a year that would allow us both—sightseeing and studying."

"Yes, that's right. And the one should complement the other."

"Well, I don't want to spend all my time reading and writing essays. I want out of your course."

I sign the paper she slides across the desk.

Bergan slouches in the chair with his right ankle perched on his left knee, the foot pivoting in a series of challenges. His eyes are glazed again. He's been on something more potent than marijuana.

"I've had lousy teachers before, but never one that was unfair."

"Tell me how I was unfair."

"I'll *show* you. This is an A answer."

I read the answer. "That is a straightforward, commonsense answer. In my book it rates a C."

"Cheesh!" His hands rise in theatrical exasperation. "A lousy C!"

He points at the answer. "Tell me what's wrong with that?"

"There's nothing wrong with it. Everything there, except for the grammar and spelling mistakes and the punctuation, is correct."

"And that's a C?"

I reach for the school's handbook and read: "C. 70-80. The student shows a grasp of the fundamental materials and is making satisfactory progress."

"So what's an A answer?"

"I wish I had one here to show you. I've handed the papers back."

A pause while he glowers.

"Bergan, an A answer interprets the material. There might be a flash of insight, something I didn't see myself, even after years of teaching. There might be a quotation from the play under discussion or a comment from some critic in the field or, even better, some comment from far afield, brought to bear on the question. There would be more detail than you provide here, and the answer would be written with power and persuasion."

"And it would say what you said in class."

That makes me red under the ears. "Your views don't have to coincide with mine. I said as much when I gave out the topics. An A answer usually differs from my own views. That's why I always welcome one. I don't know all there is to know about Aeschylus and Sophocles."

"You don't?" He is sarcastic.

"I'd be foolish to think so."

This is getting nowhere.

"Who got an A in the class?" This is issued as a challenge.

"Let's not bring anyone else into this. You can find that out easily for yourself if you look around the room sometime. See who is learning. Judge from the questions they ask."

"Is that how you judge? Do you set us all up in advance? Do you like the ones who respond to you?"

I pause. "I think any teacher can tell fairly easily who the good students are from their reactions. They don't have to say anything. Their eyes and their faces show that they understand. They know when I'm not being entirely serious. They're excited about discovering. They're moved by the feeling in what we read. They don't take a lot of notes, but balance what I say against what they read in the recommended books."

"Yeah. They're acting, that's all. You're fooled by their acting."

"Come on! Anybody can spot a phony after a while."

I oughtn't to have said that. He explodes. But he stays in the class, and eventually Fr. Costello gets him off his habit.

Margaret has failed outright. It is a dismal paper, dutiful but, even when it addresses the question, hopelessly inaccurate. Margaret hit her stride in grammar school; she was an A-student then. In high school things started to pass her by, but she got through. Here she is out of her depth. It is a common enough pattern, but often very difficult for anyone who must live through it. Though failure is no longer new to Margaret, she thought she would do well in my course.

"I love the plays. I really do."

"And that's the important thing, Margaret. The plays are more feeling than thought."

"I thought I said good things about Antigone."

"You told me how you felt about Antigone. You may have felt her sorrows more than Aristotle did. But you didn't address the question."

"Oh, all my professors are saying the same thing. I thought you would be different."

She cries. She looks smaller, older than her nineteen years, as she slumps in the chair across from me.

"Margaret, you've failed this test. Let's be honest and say so. You haven't spoken to any of the issues in the play—I should say, to any of the issues we discussed in class or any of the issues critics have discussed in books. And you haven't written an answer that reads intelligibly. But you've succeeded in feeling the power of the play. You haven't failed there."

"Couldn't you give me marks for that?"

"No. That isn't what I, or the school, or universities anywhere ask of a student in a course like this. It *is*, though, what a playwright or an actor would welcome from someone watching the play. A good response. A catharsis."

She seems only vaguely to remember the word. There is a long pause. "I can't seem to pass anything any more. I'm failing everything here."

"Well, Margaret, this school isn't the whole world, and failure is no disgrace. Failure is how we come to know our limits. It's part of being human. We all fail, though most Americans don't want to admit it, because we're so success-oriented. Actually, we can learn more from failure than from success."

That doesn't seem to help.

"Do you think I should go home?"

"I think you should stay here until Christmas. Finish the semester and learn all you can. Attend all the classes and listen, both to your professors and to the other students. See if what they say is what you might have said, but don't be afraid if you have different ideas, and don't be afraid to ask questions."

Minimal response. I try another tack.

"Did you look at the handout I gave you the first week? You should find something there for extra reading, something to start you thinking. There are a lot of ideas in the plays, and one of those books might start you thinking for yourself."

It is the wrong tack. "What do I tell my father if I fail my year?"

"Tell him you *have* learned something. Tell him you've seen some beautiful things in Italy and read some Greek plays, from centuries ago, that you really loved. I hope you can tell him too that you're at peace with yourself."

"He'll know I've failed, though."

"Oh, admit that you've failed, if you have. It's only hurting yourself to pretend you've succeeded where you haven't. But keep your self-respect. Tell your father you've failed academically but you've found other things that are precious to you. If he doesn't understand, and he may not—Is he paying for all this?"

"Yes."

"Well, he's got some right to be upset then. But tell him *you* think the semester was a success. And if he doesn't understand, at least *you'll* know, and *I'll* know, where you have succeeded."

"I wish I could get a C or a B on some course."

"Margaret, it's more important, believe me, to do what you can the best way you know, and to be comfortable with who you are. Some people get As in college and fail in life."

I am hoping she'll smile and say thanks and leave me to my work. But she just sits there, waiting for my next move.

I move. "I saw you at the Pasquino last week. Do you like movies?"

"Yes."

"Do you like Deborah Kerr? Did you see *The Sundowners? The King and I?*"

"*The King and I.*"

"Do you know that Deborah Kerr was nominated six times for best actress and never won? Do you know what she said? I would love to have won, but I didn't, and I'm not bitter. I was brought up by a mother who would tell me, when I'd say 'Not fair, mummy!', 'There is no such thing as not fair. Life isn't fair.' Well, maybe it isn't. That didn't stop Deborah Kerr from giving wonderful performances, and it shouldn't stop you."

Margaret doesn't look altogether convinced, but she thanks me.

10

H AS ANY PLACE IN THE WORLD seen so much history as Rome? Does that long history mean anything to us today? On the ninth of November, the feast that commemorates the dedication of the great church of San Giovanni in Laterano, I meet a group of students there, in the Lateran, for Mass. They have lived in Rome long enough to grasp what I mean:

Most people who have been to Rome have special memories of St. John Lateran. Mine is of almost being run down by a bus in the square outside. There is usually a little danger, a little violence, in what people remember of this church. Nero first took the property away from the Lateran family when they plotted against his life. Constantine got possession of it when he married, and he built the first church here—over the barracks of his private bodyguards. Subsequent structures have had to face complete or partial destruction by earthquake, fire, invasion, and plague. But the church always rose again.

The popes were crowned here until about one hundred years ago. That proto-Mussolini, Rienzi, last of the tribunes, bathed in the Lateran baptistry before he summoned the rulers of Europe to kneel before him. (He was later murdered on the capitol steps.) That proto-Luther, Tannhäuser, was refused absolution for his carnal sins in the Lateran square. (He later won forgiveness, when the pope's staff sprouted blossoms as a sign of God's mercy.)

The Lateran has housed five ecumenical councils and has seen historical events to make us proud and, in some cases, ashamed. It saw the proclamation of the doctrine of Transubstantiation and also the beginnings of the Inquisition and of the Crusades. Francis of Assisi came here for permission to found his Franciscans. Dante sang how beautiful the building was in the holy year of 1300. Not much later, Petrarch wept over its ruins.

The Lateran today is under constant repair. It has been called the loveliest and also the ugliest of Rome's basilicas. Augustus Hare thought it "hideous." But its doors are the very doors of the Senate House of Cicero's day. It has paintings by Giotto; its design is by Borromini; its colossal statues by Bernini and his pupils. It has the tomb of that most powerful of all popes, Innocent III, and also that of Martin V, who ended the great schism by returning here from Avignon. The well and the cloister outside are, by common consent, the most beautiful in Rome, with cosmatesque mosaics and sculpted birds and beasts that look as if Picasso might have designed them. The church also has its share of things less convincing to our Picasso age: the heads of Peter and Paul preserved in silver reliquaries and, nearby, the steps Jesus ascended to be judged before Pontius Pilate. Legend says they were brought here by that first archaeologist, St. Helen, to be a staircase for the popes. Now pilgrims ascend them daily on their knees, to see the "Holy of Holies" at the top—a painting of Christ that legend says was begun by St. Luke and completed by angels.

Finally, in all that traffic, noise, pollution, and purse-snatching outside, there is the obelisk—the tallest in the world, fifteen centuries older than Christ, brought from Egyptian Thebes to the Circus Maximus to this historic place, virtually timeless, battered, and no doubt in the past blood-stained, but still proud.

In our century, Pope John XXIII loved St. John Lateran above all other churches, in spite of its ambivalences, and he asked to be buried in it. But the private wishes of popes are hardly ever respected, and he was buried with his more modern peers in the Vatican. For centuries, Christians used to speak of "the Lateran" as we today speak of "the Vatican." Even today, St. Peter's in the Vatican is not the cathedral church of Rome. This church is. St. John Lateran. *Omnium urbis et orbis mater et caput*—the mother church of Rome and all the world.

And why do I say all this today, and why are we celebrating the feast of a *church*? Of a building that has known so much glory and sometimes something less than glory, that seems an impossible Roman mixture of the sublime and, if not the ludicrous, at least the questionable?

Because St. John Lateran is, perhaps more than any other building on earth, the Church. And, my fellow Christians, we too are the Church. Its stones are both hideous and glorious, and have been for centuries. And we, with all our virtues and vices and our potential for good or for ill, we are the *living* stones that build up the church here, this day, in this century. We share human nature with Constantine, Francis of Assisi, Dante, Bernini, and John XXIII. We have been baptized into the same immense body of believers, with its long, glorious, and inglorious tradition.

It is a privilege and a burden to have to bear the weight of all that tradition. But the Catholic Church has always based its faith not just on the Bible but on Tradition as well, and her places of worship have reflected that. They are full to overflowing with memorials of the past, some of it great art and some of it the worst kind of kitsch.

How much simpler and purer is the feeling we get in a strict Protestant church in Stockholm, or in Mississippi—completely bare of ornament, with nothing but a pulpit and the Bible and places to sit. Some Protestant churches have their traditional glories—the crypt of St. Paul's in London, or the poet's corner in Westminster Abbey—but these are monuments to national achievement and empire rather than a reflection of the Tradition that, with the Bible, is a part of faith. Most Protestant churches are simple and uncluttered. They reflect one valid view of the church, where the individual is alone with God, who speaks through his Word. What the Lateran reflects is something else: Tradition in the technical sense—the continuous handing down of the faith from century to century, where nothing beautiful is discarded and all experience is relevant to faith, because God speaks to us, not just from his own book but also from our art and our history.

What you sense here in the midst of St. John Lateran is something more than the sanctity of the Word. You sense that the church has, for twenty centuries, in exaltation and depression, meditated on the significance of the Word and again and again understood the message in new ways, each of them related to the new situations that have arisen in human events.

And Tradition, insofar as it reflects new insights into the meaning of the Word, actually adds to the Bible. The Bible reveals more of itself when mediated by the Church Fathers, the Scholastics, the councils and, especially, the saints.

The business of the recent council was not to divest the church of its Tradition but to renew the church in its Tradition and, understanding its significance in new ways, to look to the future. So our postconciliar church is less aware, say, of its seventeenth century and more aware of its first, tenth, twentieth—and thirtieth—centuries, of what it has been, is today, and will be tomorrow. It is still in the process of renewing itself.

It is more difficult to be a practicing Catholic these days. But it's also more of a privilege, because we are living in one of the pivotal periods in the history of the church—when, after four centuries, the opposition of Catholic to Protestant has at last begun to give way, when the Bible is being restudied in the light of new scholarship, when Jewish and Islamic and Buddhist and other traditions are coming to mean more to us, when women are coming into new prominence. It is a privilege. But a lot of believers are, frankly, confused and alienated.

So I'd like to say to you this morning, young men and women:

love your church. And learn, in your studies in philosophy, history, sociology, theology, literature, music, and art, to love it more and understand it better. For you are its living stones.

It needs you, because you are a part of it, and it is not perfect. It never was, nor did its Founder every say that it would be. In fact, He likened it to a field sown with both wheat and weeds, to a net full of fishes good and bad, to a tree that grew from a tiny seed to harbor all kinds of birds in its branches. The church is imperfect because life is imperfect. But it is a precious part of your experience. He said it was a field that contains a pearl of great price.

The church is with you at all the important moments of your life, with its sacraments—baptizing, confirming, forgiving, nourishing, marrying, giving the last rites. It will still be life-giving long after we here are gone, and it will house your children and your children's children. But *you* are the living stones today. You build the living church with your lives. And you can build, as St. Paul says today, in gold and silver if you choose—or else in wood and straw.

Did you know that the very last words of the Second Vatican Council were addressed to you, the new generation? Here is what Cardinal Agagianian of Armenia and Cardinal Gracias of Bombay and Cardinal Ritter of St. Louis read out on that last day: "Lastly it is to you, young men and women of the world, that the council wishes to address its final message. For it is you who are to live in the world at the period of the most gigantic transformations ever realized in its history. It is you who are to form the society of tomorrow. We exhort you to open your hearts to the dimensions of the world, to heed the appeals of your brothers, to place your youthful energies at their service. Resist all selfish feelings. Refuse to give free course to the instincts of violence and hatred which beget wars and all their train of miseries. Be generous, pure, respectful, and sincere, and build in enthusiasm a better world than your elders had. The church looks to you with confidence and with love."

If there is anything to be added to that today, it is what is written over the entrance to this church of St. John Lateran: *non est in toto sanctior orbe locus.* In the whole world there is no place holier than this.

That is said not just of a historic church in Rome but of you that are within it now and are part of it all your lives. For you are the church's living stones.

Tim sees me in the office later that day.

"I couldn't help thinking, during your sermon, that my children might be living in a very different Catholic Church from the one we have today."

"I hope so, Tim. I hope it's a lot better church than the one we have today."

"It still needs to be transformed, even after the council?"

"It does, just as it has been transformed often in the past. I hope I didn't give the impression that everything in the church's Tradition is good."

"No, you certainly didn't."

"I didn't go into the matter very far. You can only say so much in a single homily. But Tradition is an ongoing process. It doesn't just preserve the past, and it doesn't stand still. It prepares for the future. It lets go of what can no longer be thought right."

He looks surprised. "But can something be thought right and then be wrong?"

"If it was wrong all along. That has in fact happened often, in human history. Our understanding of things is almost always partial, and we're slow to learn and slow to let the old ideas go. I suppose the most obvious single instance is our understanding of slavery. It was thought for centuries to be an economic necessity, essential to the survival of society, defended by the classical Greek thinkers and, following them, by theologians in the church. It's almost incredible to us today, but for centuries it was an accepted idea."

"Until we got machinery—electricity and automation—to do the work."

"Yes, and then with the Industrial Revolution came a new kind of slavery and a new set of moral problems. I think the popes were ready with some better responses then. Meanwhile, some of the old defenses of slavery were never officially repudiated until just a few years ago. We've been too slow, in the church, to let go of what can no longer be accepted."

"My mother used to say that the Catholic Church never changes."

"Well of course that's not quite right. The church claims to keep unchanged the faith and morals of the Gospel. And in order to keep those unchanged, in a world that is forever changing, the church itself has to change, to rethink and reassess. Protestants were right to speak of reformation and to work for it. I'm not condoning everything they did, of course, or everything we did to them. But eventually, as you know, the seventeenth-century church was reformed, partly in response to and even partly along lines suggested by Protestant reformers. And we're going through more reforming today."

"But aren't some of the teachings irreversible?"

"Yes, there are defined doctrines, as we call them. But even there, the formulation may be partial. Who is to say that the whole truth of a matter can be preserved in a single definition? Even defined doctrine can be rethought and restated, and should be. In theology, as in the arts and sciences, there is ongoing research. There must be. We know so little and have made so many mistakes."

"But the Church is guided by the Holy Spirit—"

"Yes, that's true—I don't see how we would have survived the centuries otherwise. And the church has also been fortunate in its 'living stones.' I hope it will prosper in the future, with Tim Brannigan's children as its living stones in Chicago, in the next century."

He doesn't blush. He is serious. "Well, Father, they'll be Catholic no matter what, because my parents' families were always Catholic."

"That's not reason enough, Tim. They'll be born into the church, and have no say in the matter. But please God they'll stay in the Church because they find goodness and truth and beauty there. Part of that will be your responsibility."

He agrees. He is clearly in love with his faith. It is easy to imagine him in the future, with his loving wife, loving his children.

11

I WOULD LIKE TO TALK A LITTLE about the three vows, Theophilus. The promises I've made to God. The traditional three, the hallmarks of a life in religion.

I've taken them not because I am a priest but because I am a member of a religious community. An ordinary priest, under the present dispensation, vows only chastity. Even that one vow is only a matter of ecclesiastical discipline, though traditional for many centuries and obligatory since the Council of Trent. Sometime in the twenty-first century the obligation of priestly celibacy will almost certainly be lifted. The three vows are not a part of the commitment of an ordinary priest.

But a religious, be he priest or not, is another case entirely. By definition he is one who takes the three formal vows. He promises his God poverty, chastity, and obedience. He promises freely, and he undertakes the pursuit of the three virtues he has vowed in common with others like him.

He promises, at first, only for a time—and eventually, for all his life.

Before I made any promises at all, I had to spend ten days as a postulant, seeking admission to religious life, and then spend a full year as a novice, learning to love God and to live with my brothers in religion. In the years following World War II, I was one of a group of teenage boys and slightly older ex-GIs seeking admission. We spent the ten days searching our souls in silence and playing baseball cheerfully after meals to break the tension.

Some pulled out during that period. They knew this was not for them. The rest of us, on the tenth day, put on, over our T-shirts and jeans, our new religious clothes—simple clothes, in keeping with the simplicity of our active, versatile teaching community. Now we would be novices for a year. It was a very happy year.

I remember working out my own symbolism for the three bits of clothing I put on. The black cassock, which covered me from its V-shaped neck to the tops of my shoes, folding double across my chest to provide pockets for pencils, notes, chalk, and other appurtenances of teaching, seemed by its very color to express renouncement and, enfolding me as it did, complete dedication to my work. It was the poverty I would someday embrace, which would someday wrap me round.

The cincture, a broad belt of black Belgian cloth pulling the capacious cassock tight around my waist, girding me for work, was my chastity.

The collar, the white round of linen set in the V at the neck, the smallest item but, symbolically enough, the hardest to get used to, was my obedience.

There is always great joy in religious communities on the days of investiture. No one can live alone. All of us need affection and comradeship and a sense of belonging. In religious communities, the joy comes in being able to share, with others of one's own age and outlook, a common purpose that all regard as the highest purpose—to grow to be like God.

All the teaching, all the other work of a priestly ministry—which for the novice may still lie years in the future—all of this is secondary to, and flows from, the common commitment to becoming like God.

"Be perfect as your heavenly Father is perfect," Jesus said to those who first undertook this life. And as guides to perfection he gave three counsels.

To be poor. To the young man who wanted to know more before committing himself, he said, "If you will be perfect, go, sell what you have and give to the poor, and you shall have treasure in heaven. And come, follow me."

To be chaste. "Not all can accept this teaching," he said, using startling metaphoric language: "There are eunuchs who have made themselves so for the sake of the kingdom of heaven. Let him accept it who can." Then he called the little children to him and said, "Of such is the kingdom of heaven."

To be obedient. "The Son of Man has not come to be served but to serve." And again, "Learn of me, for I am meek and humble of heart. Take my yoke upon you, for my yoke is sweet and my burden light."

When Peter exclaimed, "Behold, we have left all and followed you.

What then shall we have?" Jesus answered, "Everyone who has left house, or brothers, or sisters, or father, or mother, or wife, or children, or lands for my name's sake, shall receive a hundredfold, and shall possess life everlasting."

The kinds of religious communities have varied considerably over the centuries. In the East, Basil saw them as combining prayer and the intellectual life. In the West, Benedict equated prayer and hard manual work. Their followers preserved much of the literary heritage of Greece and Rome and reworked the ravaged landscape of feudal Europe. Francis saw God reflected in the utter simplicity of nature and taught such simplicity to his followers. Thomas Aquinas said that neither the active nor the contemplative life represented completely the teaching of Jesus: the ideal was a dynamic fusion of the two. In our century the shining ideal of possessing nothing, helping freely all who ask, and living in utter simplicity is practiced by the brothers of Charles de Foucault and the sisters of Mother Teresa of Calcutta, while the call to respond intellectually to a world charged with the evolutionary power of God has been answered by, among thousands of others, the Jesuit Pierre Teilhard de Chardin.

I like to think that my own small community, named for Basil, has drawn inspiration from all of these.

At the end of a year with a kind novice master who believed in these ideals—and who knew Latin and Greek and music—I took my first vows. I renewed them every year. After three more years praying, working, studying Latin and Greek, and listening to music, I took vows that would bind me for life.

Assumed voluntarily, practiced with love, in common with one's brothers, poverty is honorable, chastity childlike, obedience liberating. There is nothing negative about the vows. It is not a matter of doing without—do not make a fortune, do not raise a family, do not insist on your own pride of will. It is not a matter of frustrating basic drives, avoiding responsibility, withdrawing from life. It is a matter of affirming life, saying to the Author of life in an overflow of generosity and love: "I love you and I want only you. Not possessions, not other affections, not even my own will."

I was more content, I think, during that first year of religious life, than I've ever been at any other time. All I thought of was religious life. It was the beginning of the adventure—possessing and being possessed by God, loving and being loved by him, trusting him, immersing my will in his—that has been my experience ever since. I felt, with Thomas Aquinas, that the promises I made made all of my actions, thereafter, holy things. Everything I did was dedicated, consecrated.

It was beautiful but, human nature being what it is, Theophilus, it has not always been easy since.

The room down the hall, the other side of the big window, belongs to Johnny Hallagan. He's poor, chaste, obedient, and he's full of joy. Not just a sense of well-being or of ordinary happiness, but of something abundant and overflowing. Joy.

Johnny may be teaching history on the university level, with a book and several scholarly articles to his credit, but essentially he's a child-like man. His soft eyes light at any experience that presents itself. He is enthusiastic about everything—sunshine and rain, baseball and books, classical and popular music, old people and little children, Europe and America.

His cheerfulness is not loud. He's quiet most of the time, content with the happiness of whatever occupies him at the moment. But the quiet joyfulness speaks. To be with him is to be happy.

He has had his share of troubles. He grew up in Philadelphia during the Depression. His father was out of work for some time then and was killed in a factory accident when he was still in his twenties, leaving a wife and three small boys. One of Johnny's younger brothers died fighting in Korea. His mother suffered a long, painful death from cancer. His confreres saw him quietly accept this, shoulder the responsibilities, give comfort where he could, and carry on with his work.

Johnny is positively liberated by the vows he took years ago. He accepts everything that comes his way as a part of God's love for him, as mysteriously joyful or sorrowful, as an invitation to respond, learn, and grow.

He has no possessions except for what he uses for his work. He listens a lot and reads a lot. He is at home with ideas. *They* are his possessions. He turns them over and over in his head, examining them from every angle. He'll discuss at great length, but he won't argue. He knows he can't and shouldn't agree with everyone, nor they with him.

He has no children and no wife. But he loves. He shares his time with anyone who cares—and hundreds care. He spends an immense amount of time helping other people. *They* are his children. One student at the villa was taken to the hospital and kept saying over and over in near-delirium, "If only Father Hallagan was here . . ." Well, Father Hallagan was with him at that very moment, looking after him until he came to, and for many hours afterward. Johnny is gentle and tender with people as perhaps only a man sure of his manhood can be.

He has no ambitions apart from knowing and loving. Perhaps that is why he is so much at peace. As a department chairman and an academic vice president, he has known something of the uses of power. In those positions he was hard-working and fair, and he handed over the reins to his successor in due time with no fanfare. To do what God asks of him, *that* is his only ambition, and of course it is a great, searching ambition.

Poor, chaste, and obedient, Johnny is alive to the real wonder of the world. God made him that way. But I think, Theophilus, it was the vows that kept him that way. The promises he made out of love.

In the room past the window, I ask Johnny about the practice of poverty, which is going to be a problem for me in the next three months. I am going to begin using the rail pass that will speed me on long weekends to the other cities of Europe.

"It's my opportunity at last to see a lot of opera, Johnny. This year in Rome, taking trains to points north. I'll be spending money I made by writing pieces about opera, and I've got my superior's permission to use it. But it's more money, I think, than a man who professes poverty should spend."

"Yes," he says as he looks into my eyes, and I know that it is more money than *he* would spend, "poverty is always easy to keep when God gives us only a little. The problems start when he gives us a lot. You've been given a lot."

I don't think he means, by that, a lot of money. "You mean, a love of music."

"And a talent for it, and for spreading the love of it. You know what a talent is, Luke. You know better than I, with your background. Isn't it a Greek coin worth a thousand dollars? Before Jesus, that's all it was. But when he wanted to make the point that it was criminal not to use our natural gifts, he gave the word a whole new meaning. The Greek coin became a symbol for a natural gift. And both, he said in the parable, are to be invested."

"And so I should—"

"Put your talent to work. Use it to enrich other people's lives, and your own, by telling about what you discover in all those opera houses north of the Alps."

I still feel I have to make excuses. "I won't be spending all that much. I'll be sitting up top in those houses. Or standing."

"Good. You'll stretch your money farther that way, and go more often. But don't count the cost too closely. The vow of poverty is supposed to free you from all that—all that worrying and hoarding. The music is the real treasure, isn't it?"

"Yes."

"You're not investing in material things, comfortable things. 'Store up goods for yourselves where the moths and thieves can't get at them.' I think that means store up in the heart and mind and imagination. Right?"

"Yes."

"A chance like this might not come again, Luke. I hate to keep quoting from the same old source, but he said the first and last words on these matters. The vows are only ways of practicing what he preached. And he preached, 'Be not solicitous.' You haven't spent your life amassing money, you haven't been preoccupied with it, and now he's rewarded you, like the lilies of the field."

"And all the people who haven't professed poverty but are born into it or forced into it? What about the ones who haven't got any money and could use the money I have?"

"Well, that is the real problem, isn't it? You can always give the money away. Send it to some relief fund, some charity. That might be the better thing."

"I mean, poverty was first embraced by monastic orders as a formal protest against existing social conditions."

"Yes, and against excessive wealth owned by priests and bishops."

I study the floor.

"On the other hand," he says, "I don't think what you're going to spend is excessive, and you're going to be spending it, eventually, for people who want—perhaps need—to hear what you're going to say. So try to consider all the sides of the question. It was, after all, Judas who objected when the repentant woman lavished her expensive ointment on Jesus, 'This might have been sold for much and given to the poor.' Jesus knew that some gestures, even some expensive gestures, were necessary. He didn't rebuke the woman. He defended her. He knew that she needed to make the gesture, spending the money on what was important to her and would honor him. That changed her whole life. Now, maybe, a little spending will be good for you."

"Well," I laugh, "I don't think I'm faced with a life decision here." He had been waiting for the laugh.

"You're not. But this *is* the chance of a lifetime for you, isn't it? Look. I know enough about music to know that it can fill a music-lover with joy and that it can also, if he listens to it humbly, make him more compassionate. It can teach him to accept darkness and pain. It can deepen his awareness of the things that really matter. It can change him if he needs changing. You, more than anyone I've ever met, find God in music. And God finds you when you're listening to music. Well, he called you into religious life for that reason—to meet him in the way most suited to you. Keep this operagoing on a personal basis, something between you and him. He'll look after the rest. Trust him."

He's said more, perhaps, than he knows, or than I know at the time.

"Thanks, Johnny." I get up to go.

"Do you think you'll see *Four Saints in Three Acts* somewhere up north?"

It's uncanny that he should ask that.

"Not very likely. It may be the best American opera, but they know it even less over here than we do back home. Do you like it?"

"Like it? It's the story of my life. We did some scenes from it in college. I played the trumpet. A muted trumpet."

"And which saint's story is yours?"

He remembers the names. "How about St. Stephen the garden inside and outside? Or St. Ignatius silent motive not hidden? How about all the saints who have been changed from the evening to the morning?" (Actually, with his Philadelphia speech patterns, he has said "How about awl the saints.")

Virgil Thomson's opera could, for awl its apparent eccentricity, be the story of Johnny's life. Set to a cock-a-hoop text by Gertrude Stein, it is about—if it is about anything—the absolute craziness and joy of giving yourself to God in religious life. With a kind of cubist's perspective, it tries to show religious experience on several different planes at once. It has one more than three acts and has many more than four saints. It sets Catholic mysticism to Baptist Bible songs, and turns sixteenth-century Spanish ecstatics into exuberantly happy twentieth-century American blacks.

"Four saints prepare for saints it makes it well fish. You can get high on that," he says.

"Not over here. There are some good things you get only in America."

"Just as surely as there are some good things over here that are best seen from an American perspective. Well, Luke, if you can't see *Four Saints* for me, see some Handel if you can."

"Yes, now *that's* a possibility. They do him in Germany."

"They should be doing him everywhere. His operas, I mean."

"Right. Beautiful stuff. I'll see some Handel for you."

His eyes are shining with excitement about what I, not he, will see. He contemplates my good fortune, as he does every good thing, with childlike wonder.

He puts me in mind of an old saying: "A man comes of age when he assumes responsibility, and becomes a man when he recovers his childhood."

12

N O CHILD IS SO HAPPY AS I when the weekend comes and I can board a train for the places north of Rome. Today I bring a suitcase to class, and at the first bell I leave immediately for the station. Today I will head past Italy's greatest cities and through the Alps. It is mid-November, and the opera season in Germany is in full swing. I'm tingling with excitement.

The railways of Western Europe offer a card that lets you board any of their trains, save the privately owned lines in the higher reaches of Switzerland, without buying another ticket. You put down a hefty sum at some travel agent's office in the United States before you leave, heftier as you opt for one or two or three months of train travel. My card, with a big red three, has set me, or rather my religious house, back a tidy sum. My superior said, "Use it a lot, and see all you can."

It is easy to make the pass pay several times over its original cost. But its greatest value is not the saving, or the convenience of boarding a train without having to wait in line at the ticket window, or the comfort of riding first class and often, as you travel effortlessly through the night, of having a whole compartment to yourself for sleeping. The greatest value is the spontaneity it allows you. With Europe's wonderfully fast trains (wonderfully fast, that is, if you have the wit to board the right ones), you wing your way easily in any direction you please. If it is raining in Venice when you arrive, you can board a train almost immediately for Ravenna, where it is not raining, see the mosaics, and then return to Venice when the city is freshly washed and gleaming in the sun.

It's senseless to schedule your pleasure, to plan your enjoyment. Some of the time you may have to, to find any relaxation at all, and then you take your chances. The rail pass lets you be spontaneous about it. The joy of experiencing Europe is increased many times over when the experiences are allowed to come the only way true pleasures can come—of themselves, unexpectedly, without forcing, as so many blessings.

The train pulls out of the Stazione Termini. Soon it is winding past Mount Soracte. When Horace saw the mountain from a distance, he told the boy at his side to take full advantage of what every passing day would bring, for life was short. Another poet, an American, said, as he set forth:

Henceforth I ask not good-fortune, I myself am good-fortune,
Henceforth I whimper no more, postpone no more, need nothing,
Done with indoor complaints, libraries, querulous criticisms,
Strong and content I travel the open road.

Walt Whitman's song is the great hymn of the traveler, and it also applies, as I'm sure he meant it to, to the man who voyages innerly, summoned by the sense of surrender and abandonment to love:

You road I enter upon and look around, I believe you are not all
    that is here,
I believe that much unseen is also here.

The Germans call what I feel wanderlust. It may not be essential to everyone's well-being, but I'm convinced that it is essential to mine. Riding the rails past hill towns, along rivers, through forests and mountains and great cities, I am fulfilled. I eat next to nothing and sleep less, because I need less. I have wings. When I am alone I sing. I pray. Myths and legends crowd my mind, as do old history and geography lessons appropriate to the villages and valleys. When I am not alone I converse with my fellow travelers in as many languages as I command.

Sometimes the conversations can become quite intimate, my being a priest. Traveling with only one other person in a compartment for several hours prompts you to be more confiding than you would be in almost any other situation: the world is passing by outside, and you are face to face in a closed space with someone who, when the final destination is reached, will vanish into a crowd, in all likelihood never to be seen by you again.

Europeans are sometimes surprised to discover that Americans know the difference between Fribourg and Freiburg. They don't expect us to know that Wroclaw was, before World War II, Breslau. They are surprised to find an American who knows that Nice is Greek for "victory" and that the city across the water, Antibes, was once

Greek Antipolis, the "opposite city." They are surprised to find a priest who reads the sports column in *Time* and knows the Botticellis in Florence too. And they want to talk.

Often, of course, you needn't talk, but simply watch the castles and cliffs go by and smile quietly at the lady who knits or the businessman who quietly folds his newspaper and says nothing. Europeans respect your privacy and expect you to respect theirs. But signals, quietly given, are unmistakable. A proffered piece of station-bought chocolate or a question about arrival times, just to see if you know the language, can initiate a conversation as stimulating as any you have with your closest friend. What you feel, speeding across a continent with nothing to pressure you until your arrival time, hours in the future, is a kind of surrender to the present moment, a self-abandonment that releases you from the prison you have made for yourself of your own inhibitions during a day-to-day clocked existence. The spontaneity is more rewarding for having the terminal point set. Disembarking, saying last farewells to people who may now know more about you than your closest friends, and who will now drop out of your life forever, you feel strangely at peace with yourself. And the city you are put down in, however unfamiliar, never seems hostile.

On this trip, which inaugurates my three months of travel, I have hardly had a moment to myself from Rome to Florence to Bologna to Milan. There have been animated, friendly conversations in Italian and English every lap of the way. Now the train from Milan to Monaco, which is what the Italians call Munich, is as quiet as the first was unquiet. Through the night I sleep stretched out on the six seats pulled forward to make an improvised bed, waking only to peer out from under the blanket of my black wool-lined raincoat at the white masses of the Brenner Pass, or to show my passport to the officials who apologetically open the door and flick on the overhead light.

"To discover myself in the objects I see." That is why Goethe traveled. Andrzej, a poet too, and a thinker—and a man who might have quarreled even with Goethe—would say, "To discover myself in the objects I see, and to meet God in them." But then, I think as sleep overcomes me, Andrzej travels no more than he has to.

Munich, a bombed-out disaster area when I first saw it years before, is now the favorite city of many tourists. Its churches and museums, royal residences and opera houses, restored to their original glory, convey the feeling of a prosperous and spirited nineteenth century alive in and enlivening a newer century of glass and chrome and bright-colored pedestrian malls. Bavarian atmosphere, simple and often simpleminded peasant atmosphere, is all-pervasive. You find it in the banks and galleries and concert halls as well as in the restaurants, hotels, and beer cellars. Peasants and burghers are still to be found in Munich, but they no longer crowd into clanging old streetcars as they did when I visited here ten years back. A gleaming underground railway now speeds them quickly across the city and its suburbs.

November is a brisk, bracing month in Munich. From the onion-shaped towers of the old cathedral the distant Alps show white against the sky. And two small, Greek-style museums face each other across the Königsplatz. Newly reopened, they house one of the choicest collections of antiquities in the world. The Antikensammlung displays Greek vases and miniatures. The Glyptothek has mostly sculpture, lovingly assembled in a series of smallish rooms surrounding a courtyard.

In the Glyptothek, archaic youths from the sixth century B.C. greet the visitor first, larger-than-life and rigidly stylized as if they were just emerging from their red or white stones. At first they look like nothing much more than superimposed blocks and cubes. There is only the merest suggestion of physical development or detail, from the formalized braids on the massive heads to the firmly placed, equally massive feet. But eventually one senses an almost imperceptible quickening that passes though the center of the body, caused by one foot thrusting slightly forward. Each figure is tensed with some force which seems at that very moment to be gathering within. The body is poised to spring into life. The great staring eyes have not yet reflected the world's gleam, but the face is already lit in an inscrutable smile—the famous archaic smile found on Greek statues long before the classic age. The smile of consciousness.

These *kouroi* are the first large-scale figures in the history of art to stand free. And they are smiling.

Then suddenly, at the end of the corridor, you see the Barberini Faun—a life-size, michelangelesque figure sculpted almost four centuries after the smiling archaic youths. Now the Greek figure is as fully developed as any hero from the Italian baroque. But he is a half-beast sated with indulgence. His face is twisted in pain. Perhaps the expression reflects a disturbing dream. His right arm is sprawled languidly over his head, his limbs slightly convulsed. You would say that the spirit that animates his body is at the point of leaving it, and the impression is all but confirmed as you move around the figure and almost see the painful breathing. The spirit is forsaking the debauched flesh.

The juxtaposition is startling: in archaic Greece, the dawn of a civilization—freshness, quickening, promise; in Hellenistic Greece as reproduced by imperial Rome, unavoidable signs of the end—surfeit, decadence, collapse.

What the Glyptothek shows after that is a succession of pieces from the high period in between. Man moves from nature to culture, shapes his individuality, achieves greatness, loses touch with the sources of his strength, and declines.

There is, in the room beyond the Faun, a head and torso of Diomedes, a Greek original in a wondrous Roman copy, triumphantly surviving the ravages of time even though some barbarian from some invasion has mutilated the face. There is an archaic torso of Apollo, headless, limbless, yet full of the most vibrant life. There are poignant grave markers—aristocratic ladies saying farewells to their husbands and children as they prepare for death.

Above all, at the midpoint of the collection, there are the smaller-than-life sculptures of gods and heroes fighting at Troy. They are pre-classical Archaic warriors, shattered but still beautiful, idealized yet delicately individuated and vital, standing erect or poised or crouching or lying, depending on the position each once occupied under the sloping sides of a temple pediment on the Greek island of Aegina. Each of the heroes reaches his moment of Homeric glory in fulfillment of the will of Zeus, who decrees life for some, death for others, suffering and glory for all. Trojan Hector outmaneuvers his Greek opponent. Ajax smiles a last archaic smile as he succumbs heroically to his great death. All the warriors seem filled with the glory of God.

The sculptures are spectacularly displayed—now correctly positioned, in accord with recent archaeological scholarship, from the markings in the bases. How the eye delights as it travels across the nobly aspiring figures, and how the heart searches itself, remembering its own meanness, its hesitations and anxieties and fears! The spirit of Greece seems, in these moments, the force of life itself.

Perhaps it is right that these pieces rest in Germany, brought here by Bavarian kings. For Germany's poets more than any others have felt the force and bewailed the loss of the gods that once quickened Greece. Even Germany's crusty old scholars reflected wistfully on a time when man was *in* nature and not opposed to it, when he was acted on by spiritual forces—gods—within and without, permeated at the great moments in his life with the strength that sustained the universe itself.

God within him and without. Breathing life into man and at the same time lifting him out of himself. That is what we sense most in Munich's Glyptothek. It is the spirit of an age in Greece earlier than the age of Pericles, earlier than the fully shaped, classical bodies appeared, and the unsmiling faces. This Archaic art is humanity new-born, still feeling the force of the god within. It is innocent and full of promise. No wonder it smiles.

There are no opera tickets available at the Kasse any time during the day, but minutes before starting time I buy a low-priced place from a German student on the street, check my coat as ordered, and hurry to my place high in the gallery, close to the gilded proscenium.

Munich's National Theater, newly restored after its demolition in the war, is the most resplendent theater in Europe. It was the scene of the first performances of Wagner's *Tristan* and *Die Meistersinger*. This evening's opera is by a native son, Richard Strauss, with a text by the Viennese poet Hugo von Hofmannsthal. *Ariadne auf Naxos*. It is an opera within an opera. It climaxes when a mythic drama is performed simultaneously with a harlequinade. In effect, it sums up the whole history of musical drama from its baroque beginnings through Gluck, Mozart, Italian bel canto, and Wagner to Strauss. It is a reminder that opera, a metaphor for life, has survived by transforming itself, in moments of crisis, into something new.

Strauss wrote ingenious music for Hofmannsthal's text, but he admitted to his librettist that he didn't understand what *Ariadne* was supposed to mean, and Hofmannsthal had to explain: "Whoever wants to live must transform himself. From our childhood, and even in the time before birth, there is in the depths of our nature a bond between us and something unidentifiable, everlasting. In life those depths may close within us. At death, we hope, they will reopen. But before that, a gentler force than death can unlock those depths. Love can permeate them. If love takes hold with all its power, then the deepest depths of our soul are released from paralysis, and the world is restored."

This twentieth-century opera was composed by a German, a son of the most civilized and most barbarous nation our age has seen, to the words of a poet who was part Jewish, from the people who suffered most and also—in Marx, Einstein, and Freud—most profoundly changed the century's notions of itself.

"What *Ariadne* is all about," its librettist said, "is whether to hold fast to that which is lost, to cling to it even to death, or to live, to live on, to transform oneself."

"*Ich bin ein anderer, als ich war,*" sings the young Greek god at the end: "I am another person from what I was before." And he takes his Ariadne, transformed by his love, to the stars.

The last visit I pay in Munich, the next morning, is to the concentration camp at Dachau. The sun is red on the grey expanses. It is a chill morning, and I don't stay long. I don't tour the compound or see any of the exhibits. I don't even think much about Fr. Costello, who survived his ordeal here. I do the one small thing that can be done. I pray quietly in an open space, that God will give peace to all those who died. Those who dealt out the deaths I leave to his judgment, not mine.

But I ask him, too, to give me some understanding of why it happened. I ask that Europe may renew itself, and that people of all races and lands may learn what we must from this tragedy, which humbles us all.

13

THE FIRST TERM IS HURRYING TO ITS END. Tim's paper on movie editing gets him a mark which surprises his instructor, an unimaginative sort. Ellen sometimes seems to have all the books in the library piled here, there, on every windowsill. Janet, reading Plato with me and three other students, sails through the Greek as if it were English and doesn't wonder much about what it all might mean.

Reading Horace in Latin class—with a fairly ordinary class, where neither Tim nor Ellen nor Janet is there to enliven things—we've now studied a score of the odes. The pot-bellied wine jug with (perhaps) a god in it, the vision of Sappho and Alcaeus in the next life, still writing poetry and still in competition, the view of Mount Soracte shining in deep snow, the transformation of puckish Horace into a swan so he can take Pindaric flight to higher poetic regions—we've read them aloud in Latin for their sounds, tried to fit them, sometimes, to tunes of our own devising, translated them into English, and asked ourselves what they might mean beneath their polished surfaces. Whether the ode under consideration is eight or eighty lines long, we devote a single class to it. So we get to say much more about the shorter ones.

Today's is only sixteen lines long, printed in Latin quatrains that make a varied pattern on the page. And it's about poetry. We translate:

> *O fons Bandusiae, splendidior vitro,*
> *dulci digne mero non sine floribus . . .*

> O fountain of Bandusia, more glistening than glass,
> worthy of sweet wine, and of flowers too . . .

First I have to fill in the background briefly. "Horace addresses the source of the spring that waters his Sabine farm. He calls the spring

Bandusia, which seems to be a romanization of the Greek *pan-dosia,* 'all gifts.' The fountain, he says, is like crystal or glass. It is translucent. But it also reflects light—that is what the Latin adjective *splendidus* implies.

"He speaks, as we soon discover, on the day before the Roman feast of fountains, the Fontinalia, pouring a libation of wine into the waters in honor of the god who lives at their source and casting a garland of flowers on the stream, to be swept away. Can we say anything about those two sacrificial offerings?"

All volunteer quick answers: "Wine and flowers—they're his two usual symbols."

"His recurrent pattern."

"His life images."

Yes, in reading the odes, we've established a liquid-vegetative pattern as a dominant motif in the poetry of Quintus Horatius Flaccus. Rivers and trees, wine and roses, ointment and garlands are almost invariably mentioned in association and appear to be images of life for him. Young saplings and clear-flowing streams suggest youth; the sea and the forest lashed by winds image the crises in our lives; frozen rivers and snow-bent trees are reminders of old age, even as ash trees and cypresses and the streams of Lethe and Acheron are images of death. The wine and flowers given to the fountain of Bandusia here are, then, not just ceremonial offerings. They are somehow intended as a pattern for human life.

We move on:

> *cras donaberis haedo*
> *cui frons turgida cornibus*
>
> *primis et venerem et proelia destinat.*
> *frustra. nam gelidos inficiet tibi*
> *rubro sanguine rivos,*
> *lascivi suboles gregis.*

> Tomorrow, my fountain, you will be presented with a kid, a male,
> whose forehead, with the tips of horns emerging,
>
> foretokens both love and war.
> In vain. For he will stain your icy
> waters with his red blood,
> that offspring of the frisky flock.

"Tomorrow. The poem is written for the eve of the feast. And the ceremony will include, on the morrow, an animal sacrifice. A kid, presumably from Horace's own flock, will be slain, and its hot blood commingled with the fountain's cool waters."

Some of the students find that distastefully strong. I hasten to support them: "You're right to feel that way. At this point, the crotchety Scotsman A. Y. Campbell, a good Horatian, said, 'Ugh! Who wants to drink of the fountain of Bandusia after that?' We have to feel our way into Roman sensibility here. Augustus, the first Roman emperor, was striving—by law and by the persuasive powers of his artists Horace and Virgil—to encourage his people to rework the devastated Italian countryside and to restore something of the old rural values that had once prevailed among Romans. They, like us Americans, were a rural people who, after a couple of world wars, became increasingly urbanized. Augustus hoped to solve his urban problems—violence, overcrowding, crime, poverty, and war guilt—by moving people to the country and inaugurating development programs to help both them and the land. And he saw as an aid to this a return to the old Italian worship of the divinities that lived in streams and groves. Country people in Italy had never quite abandoned nature worship, and blood sacrifices were a part of that.

"So Horace will sacrifice a kid, the most promising in his flock. A sacrifice is nothing if it does not hurt. The god of the stream that irrigates his farm and makes it fruitful deserves to have the offering that promises most."

They still feel sorry for the kid. We concern ourselves with ablatives of means and comparison, datives of reference and indirect object. Then we move on:

> te flagrantis atrox hora Caniculi
> nescit tangere, tu frigus amabile
>   fessis vomere tauris
>   praebes et pecori vago.

> The savage season of the flaming Dog-Star has
> no power to touch you. You offer loving coolness
>   to plough-weary oxen
>   and the roving herd.

"Even in the hot season—August, when Sirius the Dog-Star rises— the fountain on Horace's farm is always cool. When the sirocco blows across the Sahara and north to Sicily and the boot of Italy, withering the trees and wearying the limbs of man and beast, the fountain is always cool, providing relief for cattle and sheep."

Some of the students have in fact felt the effects of the sirocco that term.

"Now, in the last stanza, the poem takes an upward leap, and I think Horace demands that we see it as meaning both what it says and something more."

> *fies nobilium tu quoque fontium*
> *me dicente cavis impositam ilicem*
> *saxis, unde loquaces*
> *lymphae desiliunt tuae.*

> You too will become one of the famous fountains,
> as I sing of an oak tree planted on caved-out
> rocks, from which your speaking
> waters leap down.

We declaim this stanza in the meter and then fit it to a little song, noting how in the delicate Asclepiad verse the word for "rocks," *saxis*, is so stressed as to produce an onomatopoeic splash, and also how Horace uses that most liquid of letters, *l*, in combination with the thinnest of sounds, *i*, to produce sound effects at "famous" and "oak tree" and "leap"—*nobilium* and *ilicem* and *desiliunt*. Romans could trill their *l*'s as we can our *r*'s, so in Horace's day the "speaking waters," the *lymphae loquaces* in the last stanza, would trill along liquidly.

But, it's now time to ask, what does it mean?

"We suppose, from this stanza, that Horace's fountain falls across a kind of grotto, or rocky cave, where a small oak is kept alive by the waters, even though it is grounded in less than favorable earth. Some Greek and Roman oracles were situated at caves over which water fell. The roar of the waterfall would echo around in the cave and issue out of it, as if the water itself were speaking. But what is unusual here, as Horace comes to face his own waterfall?"

A pause. Then a perceptive answer. "Here it isn't only the roar of waters echoing back from inside the cave. Horace speaks first. '*Me dicente*,' he says. Then the waters take his words, echo through the cave, and speak back to him."

"Very good. I really like that! Now we're ready to see this as more than a simple nature poem. As meaning more than it says. In what form is it cast?"

No response.

"Remember Horace on the wine jug? Did you ever read Catullus on the sparrow?"

"Is it a kind of hymn?"

"That's it. The poem makes use of a prayer formula that Catholics will still recognize in the three formal prayers of the Roman Mass, and everyone will know something of from the prayer Jesus taught when his disciples asked him how to pray. 'Our Father, who art in heaven, hallowed be *Thy* name. *Thy* kingdom come. *Thy* will be done.' Here it's 'O fountain, *you* will be presented, *your* waters, no power to touch *you*, *you* provide, *you* will become one of the great fountains.' What are the famous fountains of antiquity?"

"The fountain of the Muses?"

"That's one. The Pierian spring. A symbol of learning. Do you remember what Alexander Pope said about it?"

They don't.

"He said something that we who are learning should take to heart:

> A little learning is a dangerous thing.
> Drink deep, or taste not, the Pierian Spring.

Any other springs? From Keats? From his *Ode to a Nightingale*?"

"Something about a beaker from the warm south."

"Right. A drink from Italy or Greece."

"With beaded bubbles winking at the brim."

"Good! And that drink is from . . . ?"

Silence.

"The Hippocrene," I answer. "The fountain that sprang from the rock when that symbol of poetic flights of fancy, the winged horse Pegasus, dashed his foot on the earth. Any others?"

No one knows.

"There are quite a few—Dirce, Arethusa, Egeria with her oracular powers. And half way up Mount Parnassus, near the oracle of Delphi, there is the Castalian spring. Parnassus you must know as a symbol of learning. Old grammar books used to be called 'Steps to Parnassus.' And the Castalian spring, like the Blarney Stone I suppose, gives to whoever drinks from it the power to speak poetry, only poetry, forever after."

"Did you drink from it?"

"Of course. Ten years ago, half way up Parnassus, under a million stars."

I see a few dubious glances exchanged.

"So Horace's fountain will become like all those famous fountains, a symbol of inspiration, oracular wisdom, poetry. Now let's start at the beginning again, and see whether this little poem couldn't really be, on a metaphorical level, about Horace's poetry, about the collection of eighty-eight odes he was about to publish.

"'O fountain of all gifts': his art is a source of all manner of blessings to Horace.

"'More glistening than glass': his poetry lets light in, and reflects it. Horace sees himself in his poetry better than in a mirror.

"'Worthy of sweet wine, and flowers, too': Horace's life images. Writing the odes was, for Horace, worth dedicating his life to.

"'Tomorrow you will be presented with a kid, the tips of his horns just bulging from his forehead, foretokening love and war. In vain': Horace might have had a career, like any other promising young Roman. Though his father had been a slave, and he had no important connections, Horace had risen rapidly in those dangerous times. He was put in charge of a contingent at the Battle of Philippi, a battle you will remember from the last act of Shakespeare's *Julius Caesar*. The young Horace fought there with Brutus and Cassius against Antony and the future Augustus. Fortunately, Augustus pardoned him and, recognizing his genius, commissioned him to write for him. Horace could then have had a successful career, marrying and producing sons and rising up the military-political ladder like other young Romans. He showed the promise and he felt the itch. But he gave all that up for his art. He lived content with very little. He virtually retired from public life to write. He produced no children. He poured his hot Italian blood into poetry's clear stream."

Some look as if they'd received a revelation. Others look skeptical: "Did he plan all that and put it into the poem?" It is an inevitable question, and there is no answer for it.

"Have you ever asked a poet that question? He'll likely tell you, 'I didn't plan all that consciously. But if you find it there, it's there.' He may smile when he says it, but he's serious all the same. He knows that he works intuitively. He plans his words and his sounds. He has his supply of faithful and congenial images. But his ideas—he doesn't start out with ideas, and he doesn't put them deliberately into his poem. A good poet will tell you that. Let's read on."

"'The savage season of the flaming Dog-Star has no power to touch you.' That is to say, 'You, my odes, will survive in and out of season. Come harsh critics or devastating changes of fashion, you will remain untouched.' Isn't that how we define a classic? A work of art that survives all cultural changes. Through the Middle Ages and the Renaissance, through the Enlightenment and Romanticism and all our modern 'new criticisms,' Horace's odes have always been there, meaning different things to different ages, but always speaking. We can't be sure that what we're saying about this ode today is the last word on the subject. What we say may match our sensibilities today. But if this ode is really a classic, it will mean something else in the next century, just as it meant other things before. All the same, it does begin to look as if this is more than just an ode to a fountain.

"'You provide loving coolness for plough-weary oxen and the roving herd.' A humbling bit, that. What do you suppose it says?"

"Horace's odes provide refreshment for ordinary people."

"Yes. I don't suppose we commoners, Horace's readers, can really object to being called sheep or oxen when he has already cast himself as a sacrificial goat. Still, it's a little disappointing, don't you think?"

"Do you mean, poetry should be more than just refreshment?"

"Yes, that's what I find insufficient."

A hand goes up: "Isn't he saying more? Isn't he saying that art gives *meaning*, not just refreshment, to our lives?"

"I'd like to think so. Tell me more."

"It's like, well, many people have work that doesn't satisfy them, lives that are pretty dull. They need something beyond their ordinary lives, and art can give it to them."

Another hand. "I think a lot is implied in the adjective *amabile*, 'loving.' Art provides something loving."

"Yes, there's a song by Schubert that makes that affirmation. Now we're at the heart of the matter, surely. At the heart of this ode. So, help me, tell me . . . why do we need art? What is it for? Is it a luxury —or is it essential?"

Many answers. "It's essential." "It's not." "It expresses beauty, and you can't live without some beauty in your life." "But you don't have to get it from Horace's odes." "You can get it from rock." "Rock is art." "It is not." "You can get high on rock." "So what?"

"Well," I interrupt, "you've got to find *something* in your life to pull you out of yourself. You've got to transcend yourself in some way, some of the time. And that might be why we need art."

14

G OD SPEAKS TO US THROUGH WORKS OF ART. On a Sunday in Germany, when opera performances can begin as early as five in the afternoon, many of the houses perform Wagner. On a Saturday in Rome's Stazione Termini, I sit in a compartment waiting for the train to start, and my hands actually tremble with excitement as I open the pages of *Die Zeit* to see what Wagner operas are playing this Sunday north of the Alps: *Tristan* in Bielefeld, *Parsifal* in Düsseldorf, *Meistersinger* in Mannheim, *Lohengrin* in Detmold, *Walküre* in Wuppertal. An astonishing array of performances! And I've got the long train ride to Milan—or even to Basel, in Switzerland —before I have to reach a decision.

The train pulls out of the station, and our first-class compartment is filled. There are six of us in the provided seats and, beyond the open door, many more standing in the smoky corridor. This part of the *carozza* is supposed to be for *non fumatori*, but Italians pay little attention to signs.

I begin talking with a volatile Venetian, and soon we are joined in the compartment by a laid-back black dude, still in his twenties, born in Boston and working as a disk jockey (rock and jazz records) for RAI in Milan. The conversation shifts from Italian to English and back, with periodic silences. We pass through da Vinci country, with pines and hills like the backgrounds in his paintings. The dry November air makes each distant object—castle or cupola or square farmhouse— stand out with three-dimensional boldness. When we stop in Florence and Bologna people come and go, and in quiet moments I tinker with an article on Horace. But my thoughts are full of Wagner.

Before we reach Milan, I've opted for *Parsifal*. I'll be heading down the Rhine—north, but downstream—to Düsseldorf. Perhaps, given the itinerary, I should be seeing one of Wagner's *Ring* operas instead, as the action of that massive cycle takes place up and down the

Rhine. But the *Ring* is now easier to come by in North America, while *Parsifal*, Wagner's last and in many ways most beautiful work, is still something of a rarity in America, outside of New York. *Parsifal*, as much about the Holy Grail as Virgil's book 6 is about the Golden Bough, *Parsifal*, partly inspired by Wagner's sojourn in the Virgil country around Naples—*Parsifal* it shall be.

The disk jockey says, smiling knowingly as we pull into Milan, that he has heard it, and that it's not as demanding as some of the music he plays.

In Milan's chilly station there is scarcely time for me to board a train for Switzerland. Soon I am asleep in the comfort of a first-class compartment, sitting alone save for a tall, bespectacled woman of indeterminable age and nationality, occupied with a book of poetry. Whenever I wake she is there, silently reading.

I wonder, half-dreaming, where she might have boarded the train and how old she might be. Though it is no business of mine, I seem to be counting the years of her lifetime till I fall asleep again.

Finally I'm brusquely awakened by the customs and immigration officers. Then massive Alps surround the ageless woman and me for close to three hours. She never speaks. For a while she sleeps, with her overhead light turned off. Her breathing is heavy.

The mountains are all but invisible in the night, but powerfully present to me in the silence of the compartment. Of all composers, Wagner captured the majesty of mountains, dimly glimpsed, in his music. *Parsifal* is set in mountains, though they are legendary mountains more easily identifiable with Spain than with Switzerland.

Parsifal is Wagner's long, slow, delicately nuanced retelling of the legends of the cup from which Jesus drank at the Last Supper. The legends appear in literature in Chrétien de Troyes, the first poet of courtly love, and Wolfram von Eschenbach, the Bavarian minstrel Wagner put on the stage as a character in *Tannhäuser*. The *Perceval* of Chrétien and the *Parzifal* of Wolfram are long poems packed with incident. Wagner condenses this wealth of mythic material into three deliberately paced acts that together form a vast symmetrical pattern. *Parsifal* is both a light work, with transparent textures, and a dark work, with terrible ambivalences. A work that ponders what the Grail legends might have meant before the Christian poets sang them. A work that ponders what lies deepest in the soul. And it is set to magisterially slow, surpassingly lovely, profoundly introspective music.

There is a moment near the start of *Parsifal*, in the prelude, when

a high solo trumpet, surrounded by three oboes, sings out over shimmering arpeggios in the violins. A silvery trumpet that makes in sound
a kind of stained-glass-window effect—mysteriously transparent, mysteriously muted. Debussy, unsympathetic to much of Wagner, nonetheless said that *Parsifal* was "lit from within" and "one of the
loveliest monuments of sound ever raised to the serene glory of
music." Another anti-Wagnerian, Nietzsche, when he first heard this
music, said that it cut through the soul like a knife. Anyone who has
heard that silvery trumpet will know what Nietzsche and Debussy
meant. Anyone who has heard that trumpet has, to my mind, already
caught a glimpse of the Grail.

My window is opaque, and I can see the outline of my face in it.
Beyond the glass, mountains, gorges, and waterfalls are invisibly
present.

Parsifal begins high in the mountains, in a forest near the castle of
Monsalvat, where the cup from which Jesus drank at the Last Supper,
and the spear that pierced his side when he hung on the cross, were
brought by angels in a vision to a wise old king. These sacred objects
once summoned knights from far and near to the castle, to do good
and just deeds. But when the old king's son, Amfortas, inherited the
kingdom, he lost the spear in battle. He forsook his vow of chastity
and yielded in love to a mysterious temptress. So his enemy, Klingsor,
found it easy to wound him in the side with the spear, and then to
carry the sacred weapon across the mountains to heathen lands.

So the cup and spear that should be inseparable have been separated. And the young king Amfortas suffers from a wound that will
not heal. A wild rider, an ugly woman speeding from beyond the
mountains, brings him a magic herb. She is Kundry, a kind of sibyl.
Wise, as her name implies, but the bough she brings does not help.

Then an innocent boy follows a white swan to the Grail's lake and
shoots an arrow through it as it circles above. The knights have been
promised that "a pure fool" will someday heal their wounded king.
But the boy, when questioned, knows nothing, not even his own
name. He sinks into a sleep, the first of his transforming experiences.
The swan, as always, is a figure for transformation.

I drop off with thoughts of the swan until, with a start, we pull into
Basel. The woman with the book is gone. She must have left the train
sometime when I was asleep. Basel is the university town where

Nietzsche was given a chair in classics at the age of nineteen, and from which he traveled to the Lake of Lucerne to visit Wagner and learn from him. That was years before they came to disagree—violently on Nietzsche's part—over *Parsifal*. Eventually, *Parsifal* became for Nietzsche "an evil work, an attempt to assassinate basic human ethics, an outrage on humanity."

We move into Germany. The immigration officers pass through quickly and quietly. Now I am in my ancestral land, speeding through the darkness with the low hills of the Black Forest on the right and the Rhine to the left but beyond my sight. I sleep for another hour, stretched out and covered with my black wool-lined raincoat. I wake as the dawn lights Germany's forests, lightly dusted with snow.

In Wagner's opera, a kindly old man takes the innocent boy through the mountain forest to the castle of the Grail. The boy exclaims that he is walking without seeming to walk, moving without seeming to move, and the old man, whose name is Gurnemanz, explains, "*Du siehst, mein Sohn*—you see, my son, time becomes space here."

The forest trees in Wagner's forest become the soaring vertical lines of the Grail's temple. Bells toll, and light falls on the assembled Grail knights from the dome high above the boy and the wise old man. A musical phrase—the "Dresden Amen," which Wagner must have remembered from his boyhood in that city—sounds throughout the castle. The boy who has pierced the swan with his arrow watches the knights reenact the Last Supper, watches them eat the bread and drink the wine, which, as the old tales have it, the Grail provides of its own power. They do this in memory of him. Amfortas is in their midst, wounded in his side, bewailing the loss of the spear. "Have mercy on me," the young king cries, "you merciful God!"

The boy understands nothing, but suddenly feels the pain of the young king's wound in his own side.

In the bright early morning, we pull into Mannheim. I have a little time to stretch my legs, buy some coffee and a *Käsebrot,* and board one of Germany's elegant Intercity trains. I settle down to just a little more slumber, and some dreams.

To find the Holy Grail, what does it mean? What is the cup in the shrine in the castle in the forest set in mountains? What is the spear that has been lost? Who is the young king wounded in the side? Who is the boy who feels the young king's pain? Who is the wise woman with the herb? Why is it that, if you go questing for the Grail, you will almost certainly never find it? Why does the Grail alone decide who will find it and who will serve it? Why could Virgil's Golden Bough be found only by, come away in the hand only of, the one who was called? Why the doves leading the hero to the Golden Bough? Why the swan circling over the Grail's lake? Why . . .

In Act II of *Parsifal*, the nameless boy travels to the castle of the evil Klingsor, hears from a beautiful woman there that his name is Parsifal—pure fool—and rescues the lost spear. The beautiful woman is the wild rider of the first act, Kundry. She has lived, like a sibyl, for age on age, in many incarnations. The kiss she gives the boy is intended to destroy him, as it did Amfortas before him. But he is not destroyed because his heart is pure.

It is a sunny, almost warm winter day as the train speeds past Worms and its great medieval cathedral and the vineyards that produce the wines named for the Virgin Mary. Soon we have reached the great river where another forest innocent, Siegfried, followed a woodbird and passed through his adventures.

The Rhine! No river has more wonder about it, at least for me with my part-German ancestry and my feelings for Wagner and myth. The river has been called the soul of Germany, and the first sight of it this morning is a heart-leaping moment.

We begin our trip up the west side of the Rhine, with a window view of the hills on the opposite bank, the turrets, castles, and crenellated walls. The river rushes, wide and proud, under its many bridges, alive with boats and barges flying many different flags. Like me, it has just descended from the Swiss Alps, though it has passed between the Vosges of France and Germany's Black Forest on a route different from mine and will head beyond my destination through the Low Countries before it finally sweeps into the sea. It is surely an international river, and yet it is Germany's own. Roman Catullus, the first to mention it in the literature of the West, called it the "Gallic Rhine" in the year Caesar crossed it with his legions, and Frenchmen have fought Germans across it for centuries. Yet Germany has claimed it, if not always in war, at least in story.

Germany keeps watch on the Rhine. A hymn of that name, sung by bards in the centuries when Gauls from the opposite side constantly threatened the German Holy Roman Empire, is perpetuated today on the pedestal of the massive monument, Germania, which I see looming from the top of a snowy ridge. The Germania is phenomenally ugly, I'm told, when seen close up. But from my window she is a small dark angel, dramatically poised in the morning light. I can't see the smaller embodiments of war and peace that stand at her feet. I only see, gleaming in the sun, the blue coverings on the vineyards that begin marking the terraces down the slopes she watches over.

Kaiser Wilhelm thought himself and his country invincible when he dedicated the Germania. He was surrounded by the kings and lords and princes of Germany after winning the Franco-Prussian War, in the year Wagner died. Nothing seemed beyond the powers, then, of the kaiser's land. Yet in a quarter century another Wilhelm drove the world to war, and Germany's armies retreated from the Rhine and left it to France. The monument stayed, though, and watched as, another generation later, two great armies clashed across the river again. The German high command remembered what the Romans had done twenty centuries before. They kept the Rhine as a barrier and destroyed the bridges across it. All save, inexplicably, one. And they lost the war.

The sun climbs. On an island in the river is the little Mouse Tower, flying a flag to direct the barges as they travel downstream. And on the bank is the town of Bingen, home of the wise abbess Hildegard, home too of the cruel bishop who, if we can believe the story, had to flee to the tower set in the Rhine where, *horribile dictu*, he was eaten alive by a plague of mice.

The train, in its progress along the river, passes a succession of amiably dilapidated half-timbered German towns, each of them taken more than once by French armies, now bustling with their vineyards. On another island in the river is a castle like a floating white ship, the fourteenth-century Pfalz, once the customs house where even Marie Antoinette had to stop as she traveled from Vienna to Paris to be its queen.

But almost immediately the train has passed that turreted island, and the castles have begun in earnest—ruins perched on top of every second or third hill, the cliffed fastnesses from which, when the Rhine was the main trade route between the Alps and the sea, feudal tyrants would descend on the river traffic to exact their various tributes violently. The castles have been crumbling since Louis the Sun King of France ordered their destruction. The train speeds on as the gorge narrows.

We are overtaking one of the *Schnelldampfer,* the ships operated by the jaw-breaking Köln-Düsseldorfer-Rheindampferschiffahrtsgesell-schaft. I think I can spot on the deck the *Köln-Düsseldorfer-Rhein-dampferschiffahrtskapitän!* Warmly dressed people are waving from the ship, and, on the far shore, motorists are speeding along the river-side highway.

Finally the river turns, the gorge closes to its narrowest point and the water reaches to its lowest depth. The gray-green surface churns. On the opposite bank, and not so far from my window, the Lorelei comes into sight—the cliff on which the river's siren combed her golden hair, sang her song, and lured knights to their drowning in the depths below. In those depths lay once the Rhine gold—the purest of all natural substances, guarded, in Wagner's *Ring,* by three Rhine maidens. He who stole it, first foreswearing love, would have power over all the world.

Our train whistles through a tunnel, and soon the Lorelei rock is gone like a dream.

More towns and castles. St. Goar, named for the hermit who came to know the river's secrets and guided travelers through its dangers. Rheinfels, once strong enough to withstand eight thousand soldiers. Castle Cat and Castle Mouse and the two fortresses of the Enemy Brothers—all with their romantic, violent legends. Boppard, where a faithless lover was challenged by an unknown knight in armor, won the duel, and then discovered, when he lifted the helmet from his opponent's head, that the knight he had vanquished was the girl who had always loved him.

The river makes a great S-shaped turn. Barges going upstream make slow progress chugging against the current. Even those that, with us, are heading downstream move more slowly than before. Marksburg, greatest castle of them all, passes by, lordly on its lofty cliff, while, on our side of the river, the train speeds beneath Gothic Stolzenfels.

We reach Koblenz and stop briefly where the Rhine is joined by the Moselle. Roman soldiers once saw the two rivers flowing together here and gave the town its name—*Confluentes.* My grandmother's family, who came from the banks of the Moselle, must in their day have looked on the confluence.

In the compartment with me now is an old Pater. He is dressed almost as a layman, German-style, and it is only when he starts recit-ing his *Stundenbuch,* his Book of Hours, that I realize he is a priest.

We talk only a little, then he bends his aged head again over his illuminated pages.

At this point, where Roman and German cultures meet and to some extent merge, I think again about the Grail legends.

At the end of Wagner's opera, Parsifal makes his spiritual journey, carrying the spear that had riven Christ's side, and also wounded the Grail's young king, back to the land of the Grail. He lifts the helmet from his head. He has grown older. The sibyl-woman who had tried to destroy him is now penitent at his feet. The kindly old man who once took him through time and space to the Grail castle now weeps with joy to see that the spear has been brought back, that the Grail will be whole once more, that the young king who has longed to die will now be healed of his wound.

We pass Andernach, Remagen, and Apollinariskirche: the castle of Charlemagne, the church of Catholic pilgrimages, and the site of the bridge that in the Second World War took the Allied armies into Germany's heartland. The train presses north and leaves the river for stretches. Then on the right is Drachenfels, the rock where Siegfried of the *Nibelungenlied* slew the Rhineland's dragon and thereby enabled the townsfolk of Cologne to hew the stones of their great cathedral and the villagers of the area to crush their bright red grapes into Dragon's Blood wine. And on the left is Bad Godesberg, Wotan's mountain and so perhaps the site of the magic fire in Wagner's *Ring*. It is also where, in 1938, Neville Chamberlain was humiliated by Hitler. We halt briefly at Bonn, where Beethoven was born, and then the land flattens out quickly, and I sit back from the window.

History and legend, music and myth. Wagner's last act begins in my imagination to recapitulate the first. His musical themes and mythic images regather and regroup. Once again, through a subtly changing landscape where time becomes space, Parsifal makes his way back to the castle of the Grail. Once again the bells toll, and light falls upon the Grail knights from the dome high above them. Once again the ceremony of the bread and wine is reenacted. Once again the silvery trumpet sings its song, and "Dresden Amens" rise from the worshipers. But this time, wise old Gurnemanz does not lead Parsifal but follows him. This time, the ageless Kundry enters the castle to see the mysteries and, after centuries of reincarnations, finds release in death. This time, Parsifal brings the lost spear, touches the wounded king with it, and heals him. This time it is Parsifal, no longer a boy but a man, who elevates the cup.

His face shines like a saint's. With the cup he traces a benediction in the air. The music of Act I, the silver trumpet, sounds again. The voices of innocent boys float an ethereal high A-flat across the space enclosed beneath the dome.

Cologne's cathedral vaults onto the horizon. The crowning glory of the Rhine, marking the place where the Romans built their *colonia* two thousand years ago. Thrusting skyward after six centuries of construction, spared in World War II by British precision bombing that leveled almost everything around it, the great Gothic prayer still stands, in wintry awesomeness, as we pull into the station alongside it. It is a reminder at once of the age of faith that made the Rhineland something more than a riverbed of Germanic myths and legends, and also of a time when French influences were freely felt in this Roman colony which the Germans call Köln and the rest of us Cologne.

"Be healed, purified, and absolved from your sins," sings Parsifal to the wounded Amfortas. "And blessed be all your suffering, for it gave me the strength of compassion, the power that comes from learning."

My maternal grandfather came from Düsseldorf, and in a few minutes we are there. I take a tram from the station to the old part of the city, and at St. Lambert's near the opera house I concelebrate Mass, speaking with other priests the words that change the bread and wine into his body and blood, wondering if one time my forebears might have worshiped in this very church. I inquire of the pastor after Mass. He consults the parish records. There is no entry. He generously gives me something to eat, a kind of *Brotabend*. Düsseldorf in my grandfather's day, he tells me, was a collection of village parishes. Many records were destroyed in the war. Hundreds of thousands went to America at the turn of the century. I may never find out much about my German ancestry.

The new opera house, set beside a now leafless park, has good acoustics and sight lines and is much too small to meet the demands of this expanding city with its thousands of opera lovers. Today's *Parsifal* has long been sold out. There are only about ten minutes to go when, shivering with the cold but with the Irish luck I inherited on my father's side, I get a cancellation.

My heart is pounding as the conductor draws the first quivering measures of the prelude from the orchestra. Then, after a hushed silence, that silver-edged trumpet floats that same melody through the stained-glass softness of the woodwinds and strings. The music is full of wonder and hurt and the need for healing. At the start of the second act, the swirl of strings is truly terrifying, and the scream of the clarinet anticipating Kundry's scream is an intimation of evil. Finally the last act gives me, for a long hour, the unearthly feeling of floating outside of time in an immense space, bathed in spreading light, suffused with the presence of the mystical, healed of my hurt.

The singing is, as so often in German houses, variable in quality but powerful in effect. It is often said that Wagner wrote badly for voices. But his works were written with these small houses in mind. And in these small houses, given a conductor who knows how to use the orchestra to support the voices rather than cover them, the singers can project their vocal lines effortlessly for hours over the ever-shifting orchestral textures. Düsseldorf's Parsifal is a young American with the naive and childlike quality essential to the role, with a small but clear voice. The German Gurnemanz has a sound like black velvet and sings with quiet authority through his long narratives. The Kundry is Italian, the Amfortas French, the Klingsor Greek. Such is the nature of opera in performance. The stage director "paints with light" in the style familiar all over the world since Wagner's grandsons evolved the neo-Bayreuth style. The theater here also has a never-fail method of enabling characters to walk to the back of the stage and disappear into a field of light. It is perfect for Lohengrin, for Palestrina in Hans Pfitzner's opera, for Tadzio in *Death in Venice*, for every symbolic character who leaves the world mysteriously. In today's *Parsifal*, the hero comes and goes like an apparition, and the Grail castle becomes the inner keep of one's mind or heart or soul.

At the end I'm hardly aware of people applauding and then moving up the aisles. I'm the last to leave the theater, the music streaming through me. Late as it is, and November cold, I sit down in the deserted park beside the theater and, with my head in my hands, let the emotions subside. For more than five hours I've surrendered to *Parsifal* without holding anything back, yielding from moment to moment to each detail of the score. The music has carried me out of myself. Now I have an overwhelming feeling of clarity and peace.

After midnight, I walk to the station, buy some provisions, and take the Holland-Italian Express—not a very modern train, but one in which first-class compartments are unoccupied all through the night. I pull six seats forward and have, at no cost, a much larger sleeping area than I'd have in an expensive couchette. But, even with a wool-lined raincoat for a blanket, I do not sleep. A hundred memories of the music keep me awake.

In the dark the Cologne cathedral appears again, bathed in spotlights that make it mysteriously gray-green in the black night.

What am I feeling? Perhaps something akin to what saints and mystics call ecstasy. In the presence of great music the listener is lifted out of himself and sees his own experience—indeed, he may have the feeling that he sees all experience—at a higher level of awareness. Put in touch with a power greater than himself, he feels something, perhaps, of the boundless peace of the power that sustains the universe.

He feels at once infinitely small, in the presence of such immensity, and at the same time as great as all the world. Wagner has his characters sing of this. In the midst of *Tristan und Isolde*, in a moment of ecstasy, the lovers sing, "I myself am the world." In the midst of the *Ring*, in a moment of self-revelation, the father-god who tries to understand the mysteries of his world, whose mountain I have just passed in the darkness, says to his consort, "You only understand what you see. My mind is reaching out to possibilities that have not yet come to be."

The train hurries through the night. In my ears the silver trumpet sings its long melody over and over. The "Dresden Amens" lift heavenward.

"You see, my son, time becomes space here."

It was when burying his trumpeter that Aeneas found the Golden Bough.

Into the Rhine gorge the arching span of the trumpet melody travels with me, carries me out of myself while I am still conscious of myself.

I myself am the world described in *Parsifal*. The thought is with me as I finally drop off to sleep, passing under some Rhine castle: I myself am the castle in the mountain forest. I myself am the shrine that is reached while walking without seeming to walk, while moving without seeming to move. I myself, beneath the dome where the light floods in, am the cup and the spear. I myself am the "Dresden Amen," the silvery trumpet and its luminous song of longing. I am both the wounded king and the healing boy. I have within me the potential of the evil enemy. I also am the ambivalent woman and the wise old man. I am them all, and I am called to transform, purify, and heal myself.

15

I T I S A D V E N T . On the eighth of December, as Fr. Costello asked me to do, I meet a group of students in the massive church of Santa Maria Maggiore. It stands on a hill where once rose a temple to Juno Lucina, goddess of childbirth, and after that a fourth-century church to Mary the Mother of God. It preserves better than any church in the world the proportions of a Roman basilica, and its famous mosaics depict scenes in Mary's life. One of its loveliest legends tells how Mary caused snow to fall in August, to cover the hill and outline the structure of the building to be built in her honor. But like other Roman sites, sacred and secular, it can tell tales of terror as well, and they are better documented than the legends.

Devotion to Mary, the mother of God, is quiet today. That is fitting. The Bible begins and ends with the woman and the serpent, but most of the books in between are silent about the archetype of the feminine. The few references to Mary in the New Testament are vivid and touching but also riddled with problems. Mary is, will be, and should remain mysterious.

A little Jewish girl, she said in effect, "I understand nothing. Let it be done." And with those words she gave the consent of the whole race to the process of its redemption.

And she had a Son. The only son who ever chose who his own mother would be. As God, that Son was born of the Father before all ages. As man, he was born of his mother in a moment of time.

Was there ever another of our race so blessed, so chosen, as she?

The feast of the Immaculate Conception always falls within the season of Advent. We gather for Mass in one of the smaller chapels of the great church, and after the Gospel I speak to the group:

In the Annals of the Celestial Empire of China we read how, in the twenty-fourth year of Tchao Wang, of the dynasty of Chou, on the eighth day of the fourth moon, a light appeared in the southwest, that illuminated the emperor's palace. The emperor asked his sages what it might mean. And they showed him books in which this prophecy signified the appearance of the great saint of the west, whose religion was to spread into their own country.

A century after that, farther to the west, in the land that today once again we call Israel, a procession of prophets prophesied, watching, waiting, and longing, in such passages as these: "Behold a virgin shall conceive and bear a son, and he shall be called Emmanuel." And again, "Come, O Lord, do not delay. Set free your people Israel." And again, "Prepare the way of the Lord. Every valley shall be exalted, and every mountain and hill brought low. The crooked ways make straight, and the rough ways smooth. Make straight in the desert a highway for our God."

A century after that, farther to the west, in classical Greece, Aeschylus, in his *Prometheus*, sang: "Look not for any end to this sorrow till the god appears, to accept on his own head the punishment for your sins."

Four centuries later, westwards further still, here in Rome, Cicero, reading the books of the Sibyl, about a king we all must recognize in order to be saved, asked "To what man, to what period of time, do these prophecies point?"

And in the Augustan age, at the very end of the centuries before Christ, when all the world was at war and was soon to be, for the first time in the memory of anyone alive, at peace, Virgil, echoing the words of the Old Testament, sang how a golden age was about to dawn, at the moment when a long-awaited infant son, sent down from heaven, would smile at his chaste mother.

Incipe, parve puer, risu cognoscere matrem.

The time was near. It was just a generation away. And Mary was immaculately conceived. In the womb of her mother, St. Anne, she was spared the flaw we all inherit. One of us was spared the destructive fault the human race has known. That was because her baby flesh was eventually to be the flesh the human race would provide for God's own Son. That is what we celebrate today—the last of all the wonderful preparations.

And finally he came. In the fullness of time, when the nations, watching and waiting and longing, were at last at peace, when Mary was ready, he came. And his coming is the central point of our history, so that for centuries thereafter we have dated events on this planet from before and after it happened, that first coming.

The church reminds us of all this by putting this feast, the Immaculate Conception, in the middle of its Advent season. "Prepare your-selves," as Mary was prepared. It is Advent.

For four weeks, while living existentially in this year, in this century, we are projecting ourselves liturgically into those long centuries B.C. The hopes and fears of all those years are telescoped into four quick weeks, and we are asked to purify ourselves by passing through those hopes and fears once more, seeing our personal problems and our world problems as a small part in the history of the race. Seeing the truth of those words of Scripture, "Wisdom reaches from end to end mightily and orders all things sweetly."

Advent, like no other season, confronts us with God's plan working itself out in history, always becoming, always evolving, and using—at this point in history—us.

As Mary was chosen and blessed, we are all of us chosen and blessed in a corresponding, if not quite identical, way. Mary is the sign, the archetype, for the whole church, and for each individual Christian. What she did first, and best, and most beautifully, we all must do. We all must be vessels, receptacles, instruments of God.

For God works through us. He needs us. We are the human means whereby his will in the world is worked.

Mary was filled with God, big with the child that was God. She brought him forth and gave him to the world in a physical but also pre-eminently beautiful and archetypal way. What she did we can all, in our own ways, be about. Giving God to the world.

The philosopher George Santayana once said that Christianity was the most beautiful of myths. He meant that it was the most imaginative way of telling fundamental truths. He didn't subscribe to Christianity's doctrines, but he did sense something of Christianity's fulfillment of the hopes and dreams of the race. "There is no God," he also said. "and Mary is his mother." I think he meant, "I can only believe in God when someone with God in him, or her, shows God to me."

That is what Mary did. That is what we all should be doing. And that is why Mary is important.

The next day, Ellen comes to my office door. She wants a transla-tion of some Greek quoted in a book she is reading for a philosophy course. I invite her to sit down, and I do what I can with the passage, which, lifted as it is from a context I do not know, is tough.

Then she says, politely, "Father, I liked what you said in your ser-mon about seeing our problems as a small part of the whole of human history."

"Thanks, Ellen."

"I hadn't thought that that might be why we have a calendar of feasts."

"It's one reason why we have one. The liturgical calendar is a way of making the past present. In Advent we keep singing about preparing the way of the Lord, as if what happened two thousand years ago will happen all over again this year. And it does happen all over again every year, his coming. If we make our rough ways smooth and crooked ways straight, and speed his way into our hearts."

She pauses. "I hope it does happen, in our hearts. But you also said something about *the world's* problems."

"Well, Ellen, I believe that we're invited in Advent to see the world's problems today as growing out of the past and into the future. What do you think is our biggest problem today."

"Vietnam?"

"Bigger even than that."

"Nuclear war?"

"Almost surely. Whether we will destroy not just civilization but the human race, the earth itself. It's staggering. All other concerns, including the one that so obsesses us—containing Communism—are much smaller concerns than whether we will destroy ourselves and, with ourselves, all future generations."

"You know what some religious people say about that?"

"What?"

"That it may be God's will that the world end in a nuclear war."

I clap my hand to my head. "Is that what we're encouraging people to think? What do you think about that idea?"

"I think it's terrible. It's blasphemous."

"Why so?"

"It's giving God the responsibility for what we've brought on ourselves."

"I agree, Ellen."

"It's also presumptuous, thinking that the problems of our generation are so important that we can end the world in an attempt to solve them."

"To save ourselves, we'll make a wilderness and call it peace."

"That's in Tacitus, isn't it?"

"Yes. That's what he said the Roman armies did. Now our armies are doing it."

"Does Tacitus have any solutions?"

"Not that I know. But the liturgy has. It tells us we can start by seeing our age as one small hour or day or year in the long sweep of human history. That's an Advent vision. It can help us to see our responsibility toward the future. Make us aware of the fact that future generations, birth upon birth upon birth, depend on us."

She waits for me to go on. "Ours may be only one of hundreds of generations, but we are the generation entrusted, for the first time, with that future responsibility—the continuance of the race and the preservation of life on the planet. It's up to us to see that there will be new Homers and Mozarts and Einsteins to tell us who we are and what we can be."

"You're optimistic about the future?"

"I want it to happen. I love the past, Ellen. That must be obvious. But Advent makes me think that the future can be even more wonderful. The birth of Jesus two thousand years ago didn't end everything that I, a teacher of classics, teach. It was a new beginning, not an ending, and it should keep us facing the future."

She moves to the consideration that is, I gather, the main one for her. "And it's in the season of looking forward that we observe the feast of the Immaculate Conception. You made a special point about that."

"Yes, well, what is it that's going to destroy us in the future, if anything does? Not nuclear power alone. That's always been there, waiting to be discovered, in nature. What may destroy us is some flawed human being, pressing the button. The real danger is our own failure as human beings to see beyond our present problems. Human nature is flawed. There's an irrational streak that runs through it like a flaw in metal. Do you know what I mean?"

"I think so. It's what the writers on Shakespeare see in his tragic heroes. The heroes have a tragic flaw that brings them to ruin. They are writ larger than ourselves, but they are ourselves, and they're tragically flawed."

"Yes, that's also what mythologies tell us in their creation myths— that there once was a time when everything existing was one, when our species obeyed natural law instinctively, as other living things did. But when we committed the first sin—when, as Genesis puts it, Adam ate the forbidden fruit—we broke ourselves off from nature and set ourselves on a separate, individualized course. We were driven from the world where nature provided all our needs. We've always thought of that original sin as simple disobedience, or pride. But surely it was something more significant than that. Don't you think?"

She ponders. "Well, the tree in the Genesis story was a special tree. They were told, Adam and Eve, not to eat the fruit of the tree of good and evil."

"Of the *knowledge* of good and evil."

"The first of all sins was seeking knowledge? Can that be?"

"The first of all 'sins' was our coming to know, as the rest of creation has never known, that we humans are capable of both good and evil. Calling it a sin isn't quite right. The story of Adam and Eve, like the 'original sin' myths in other cultures, is a memory of the time when men and women first became *aware* of the difference between good and evil, when we first knew there was a fatal flaw in our human nature—that we could do evil as well as good."

"Why call it a sin, then? It was a step forward."

"Well, we haven't always called it a sin. The church in the Easter liturgy calls it a *felix culpa*, a happy fault. The archaic statues that herald an age of reason in Greece have inscrutable smiles on their lips. There is potential good as well as potential evil in the step the human being took when it became a thinking animal, conscious of itself."

"But we've still called it, for centuries, a sin."

"I think that the human race has always felt guilt about what the creation myths remember. After all, by becoming aware of itself, the human race sundered the instinctive bond with a mothering nature that the animals, in their innocence, still have. Separation from nature there had to be, if humans were to develop their reason. But humans ever after felt guilt about it, about leaving the mother, and they expressed that in myths."

"That's in literature a lot—the longing for lost innocence, that memory of a golden age."

"Right. There has always been something in the human makeup that longs for that original, half-remembered union with nature, that prerational innocence, when humans were like the rest of creation."

"And that is what you said this morning Mary never knew?"

"The doctrine of the Immaculate Conception, that Mary was never touched by original sin, means that, archetypally at least, she never knew that flaw in our nature."

"Doesn't that make her something other than human?"

"No. It makes her an image of what all of us who are human would like to be. Gifted with reason, and so fully human, but still bound to nature, still as intuitive as the rest of creation that we separated ourselves from. Complete and integrated."

"I can believe that Jesus might have been that. He might have inherited our nature without its fault. But, well, my Protestant father would ask, 'Why say that his mother was?'"

"Well, with the idea of God becoming human you reach the profoundest depth of our longing, our yearning, for the union with nature we once had and lost. And nature, in all mythologies, is feminine. God *has* to come to us humans through a woman, a mother."

"So the teaching about the virgin birth—a contradiction in any literal sense—is archetypal."

"I think so. The Assumption, too, is archetypal. Mary is a symbol of all our impossible, mythic hopes about death and rebirth—a real Advent symbol. If one of our race is spared the race's destructive fault, can't that be a sign that the whole race is meant to evolve further still, to a state where consciousness is no longer violent, no longer at odds with nature but at peace with it?"

"I never heard it explained that way before."

"Well, Ellen, we have to keep understanding our traditions in new ways. Besides, it's not new with me."

"But you seem convinced of it."

"Maybe because I'm steeped in Wagner."

"Wagner!"

"Yes. He's one of our great intuiters, you know. When he refashioned a lot of Germanic myths into his *Ring* cycle, he had the 'original sins' committed by male figures, Wotan and Alberich. Both of them do violence to nature, wrest from nature instruments of power which enable them to see into the world and exploit it. But before those original sins, the rivers and trees were presided over by feminine figures who are creatures of intuition, in harmony with nature. The male sinners just about destroy the world. It takes a woman, Brünnhilde, a woman who intuitively sees the deeper meanings of what has happened, to save the world."

"But she's terribly flawed. She's violent."

"Only when she's operating under the curse of male reason. She was born—and she knows it—to defend the father god's intelligence, to work his will. She's a kind of Athena. But then she is reduced from her goddess state to human womanhood, and at the end of the cycle she integrates in herself the two gifts—male reason and female intuition. *Parsifal* tells of the same integration, with a different set of symbols. The spear and the cup."

"It sounds as if Wagner intuited some notion of a feminine element in God."

"There's far more of that in the myths as he gives them to us than in any of his sources."

"So you're saying that it's our masculine reason that has led us, through all our scientific discoveries, to our present dilemma. And it's our feminine intuition that will save us. Is that what you mean to say?"

"Let's say I hope that a true feeling for what nature is, and some insight into how destructive reason can be when isolated from natural feeling—I hope that those things will save us, yes."

"All this in Advent?"

"Yes, in Advent." I smile at her. "That's when we remind ourselves, as we face the future, that our nature is flawed, but that, if one of our race was spared the consequences of the flaw, maybe there is some hope for the rest of us. What Mary is archetypally we all can hope to be."

She is silent for a moment, thinking her way through what we have said before she speaks again.

"I'd like to change the subject, Father. Well, not quite change the subject. I still want to see my small life in what you're saying. You know what I want to be?"

"A writer."

"You knew that?"

"I'm intuitive," I say laughing. "Besides, you're in the poetry seminar."

"What do you think my chances are?"

"Of being a writer? Well, we've been talking about the flaw in human nature. That's something to build on. An insight into what we are."

"Yes, but—how do I start?"

"Start writing, and write, and write some more. You can show me what you're doing piece by piece, if you like, and then we'll see. I'll read anything you bring me. Will it be poetry or prose?"

"Prose. Stories."

"Have you got a lot of ideas?"

"Not big ideas. But I think I see deeper into things than most people do."

"That's a good sign."

"And I'm full of hurt."

A silence, which I have to break. "That's a good sign, too. You can write out of that."

"There are so few people I can talk to."

"That fits a pattern, Ellen. A talent for creative writing is a kind of a curse. The god of creativity, the artist on Olympus, Hephaestus, was lame."

"And ugly."

"And ugly. That's myth's way of saying that, with artistic gifts, nature gives with one hand and takes with the other. Our Beethovens and Michelangelos and Dostoevskys were not handsome or happy or well-adjusted people. They were Hephaestuses. But Hephaestus was married to Aphrodite, who was supremely beautiful."

"And unfaithful to him."

"She loved him, though. Let's say that it was her nature to pass easily from him to Ares—from the god of creativity to the god of destruction."

"Yes, and Hephaestus probably spent the rest of his eternity very sad."

"Oh, I expect he could work his sadness away, making beautiful things at his forge."

She smiles to show she understands. But it is a sad smile. "Do you think anybody else in the seminar has writing talent?"

"It's too early to tell."

"Maybe Janet?"

"Her interests seem to me to be scholarly, not creative."

"Tim Brannigan is very bright."

"I doubt, though, that he feels any need to write. He's just open to ideas and to people. I shouldn't say 'just.' His openness is something I admire very much."

"He does compose songs of his own."

"Yes, that's right. He's Apollo, not Hephaestus."

"I love him, Father."

A pause, which she breaks. "He doesn't know how I feel. And I'm sure I mean nothing to him, but at least he doesn't think I'm odd, like the other students do. He listens to me. Father, he's so handsome and intelligent and sensitive. You don't often get all of those things in one boy."

"So he's your knight in shining armor."

"Well," she blushes intensely, "I want to be with him all the time. I think, though, that I've run out of excuses for talking to him."

"You don't need any excuses with Tim. Just talk about something interesting. Ask him anything about religion. You won't be able to keep him quiet on that subject."

"And how do I hide my feelings?"

"Don't worry too much about that. I think he'll know how to handle that and put you at your ease."

"I know he feels nothing special for me. It hurts me."

"Well, Ellen, all the pain is worth it, just to be in love. Just to be out of yourself. Wouldn't you say that?"

"No. Not the way I feel now." She is dry-eyed.

"Well, you know, Ellen, you're going to fall in love maybe three or four times before you settle down with one man. Tim isn't the only man in the world who respects intelligence and tenderness. There'll be others. Keep looking forward."

"Yes," she says. "It's Advent." She makes a motion to go.

I call her back at the door.

"Remember, start writing. Today. Try writing about what you feel. Without using the first person, if it's easier that way. And you can call the boy in the stories Tom."

16

M ORE WEEKENDS NORTH in friendly German towns enable me to put together the four parts of Wagner's *Ring*: *Rheingold* in Duisburg, *Walküre* in Stuttgart, *Siegfried* in Braunschweig, and *Götterdämmerung* in Saarbrücken. With the rail pass I am like Wagner's hero with his magic helmet, transported at will along rivers and through mountain ranges. The vast work seems disturbingly prophetic: in the manic thunder of the music, our race hurtles toward destruction, while nature waits to purify with fire and regenerate with water.

In Greek tragedy class, we continue to ponder the great questions. What is it that directs human events? God, or fate, or chance? Aeschylus has come down heavily on the side of God. "Zeus, whatever he may be" eventually makes sense of suffering and brings good out of evil.

Sophocles has opted for fate. Everything that happens has been predetermined by some impersonal power. God, or the gods, can do nothing in the face of fate. That is why they warn.

Now Euripides is dismissing both of his predecessors. There is no plan, no meaning in human lives. Everything happens by chance. As for God, Euripides changes his mind with every play: God does not exist. Or, God exists but he, or she, is evil. Or, God is only a projection of the good and evil we have within ourselves.

The first-semester examinations keep the students up for all-night sessions. I am glad to close the account on Horace's *Odes*, on Plato and his dialogues, and on Greek tragedy, and I settle down to reading a stack of essays, followed soon by a stack of examinations. It comes as a surprise that, in all of the courses, God is the students' main concern. It must have been the teacher's main concern, but the teacher seems not to have realized that until now, or to have consciously planned it that way.

A few days before the end of term, the two hundred of us have a Christmas party: cider and wine, pizza and cheese, Italian pastries, a few presentations, carols, and the usual secular paeans to winter, to the snows we aren't going to have in Rome this Christmas. I accompany the singing at the piano. One hour passes.

The songs keep coming, more and more of them out of season. May your days be merry and bright. From the mountains to the prairies. Home again in Indiana. Old times there are not forgotten. His truth is marching on. Cross over into Jordan. Comin' for to carry me home. Me and my true love will never meet again. In the ranks of death you'll find him. Leave a kiss within the cup. Take a sad song and make it better. If it takes forever I will wait for you. There's such a lot of world to see. And there he was, that young boy. I told him I didn't like the way he got things done, sleepin' on the job. Under the shade of a coolibah tree.

A second hour passes. I am still at the piano, pumping away at those Scott Joplin rags from *The Sting*. Then it's If your heart is in your dream, for the four-year-old son of the psychology teacher—and some of it the boy manages by himself as I tell him the words. Solo flights from others, and in other languages: *Torna a Sorriento. Mein Vater war ein Wandersmann. Adios muchachos compañeros de mi vida. Terre de nos aïeux.* Duets: Goldfish in the privacy of bowls, with the wife of the British ambassador, flying too high with some guy in the sky is my idea of nothing to do, the roaring traffic's boom, down by the shore an orchestra's playing. Ensembles: Some things that happen for the first time seem to be happening again. I'm bromidic and bright as a moon-happy night pouring light on the dew. Wild geese that fly with the moon on their wings. Watch a hawk makin' lazy circles in the sky. You fly down the street on a chance that you'll meet. Off you would go in the mist of day. Though your dreams be tossed and blown.

So many songs in my head! Sing, sing a song. There's a place for us. Away above the chimney tops. Is that little brook still leaping there? Sitting absobloomin'lutely still. For one brief shining moment. I remember it well. An' dem dat plants 'em are soon forgotten. An' you'll spread your wings and you'll take the sky. Can you afford to board? The days dwindle down.

I'm at the keyboard for three hours.

The next morning the students scatter for the Christmas holidays. A few—Jennifer, Bergan, and Margaret among them—return home to stay. A few, like Janet, fly home to return, expensively, in January. Most scatter on less costly trips to visit relatives or sightsee in different parts of Europe. One party goes at student rates to Tunisia and Egypt, another to Greece. The planned trip to the Soviet Union is canceled because of political uncertainties.

On Christmas Eve I seek out a priest from the same religious community as my own. He is studying theology a long way across the city. It is warm, for winter. We have supper together and attend Midnight Mass at St. Peter's, celebrated by Paul VI. The pope looks very tired, but we are close enough to him to see his eyes brighten when the diminutive lady behind us, perched on the ledge of a pillar (Bernini or Bramante must have known the need would arise) lifts her tiny voice at a quiet moment to say, "God bless you, Holy Father!" Grace seems to stream through him as he lifts the cup. The press of people is almost intolerable, and tempers are short. There are pickpockets in the crowd. Beneath the great dome, believers eat the bread that is more than bread, drink the wine that is more than wine. The bells toll to inaugurate a Holy Year.

I return to the school to say alone in the early hours my three Christmas Masses—one for the Holy Father's intention; one for my own father, whom I never really came to know, and for others I have known who have gone to their rewards; a third for my mother and my brothers and their families and all the living who are praying for me.

At the third Mass the Gospel is taken from the opening verses of St. John. "In the beginning was the Word . . ." It is a page more powerful even than the first page of Genesis, which says, "In the beginning God created heaven and earth."

That is to say, Theophilus, that once there was a time before creation, before time. No rivers or trees, no men or beasts, no sun or stars, no time or space. Only God. And in that eternal beginning, God spoke a Word, or thought a Thought, or—to put it personally, as Jesus did—fathered a Son.

And the Father and the Son loved each other, so that God was not only one, or two, but somehow three—the Father, the Son, and the Spirit of love between them.

What we Christians know of God—it is only a little, but it is inexhaustible—is that God knows in his Word and loves in his Spirit. God is thought, St. John says in this Christmas Gospel. God is also, John says in his Epistles, love.

And what is it that makes us like God? What is it that makes man the master of the world, the paragon of the animals, the monarch of all he surveys? Godliness. That is to say, his knowing and loving; his intellect and will; his mind that seeks truth and his heart that hungers for love. That, Theophilus, is what the Bible means when it says, on its first page, that man was made in the image of God: he knows and he loves. That is my reason for living as I do.

My holiday takes me with my trusty rail pass north on the Ambrosiano on December 25th. On this day of days, the Trans-Europe Expresses are empty—not just whole compartments but whole cars. I sleep. Doctoring a cold, I board the Gottardo in Milan and am transported drowsily through the St. Gotthard Pass. There is blinding sunshine on the snow the next morning in Switzerland.

It is an operagoer's holiday. On successive days, Freiburg will offer *Elektra*, Düsseldorf *Palestrina*, Hamburg *Moses und Aron*, Cologne *La Clemenza di Tito*. The cold breaks up as I sweat profusely. The anticipation of seeing such an array of operas, some of them for the first time, delivers the coup de grâce to the infection.

And between the operas, as recitative between arias, are the train rides, with animated conversations by day and long, haunted silences by night, with the sight of the engine ahead another reminder of Whitman on his real and imagined journeys:

Thee for my recitative,
Thee in the driving storm even as now, the snow, the winter-day
    declining,
Thee in thy panoply, thy measur'd dual throbbing and thy beat
    convulsive,
Thy black cylindrical body, golden brass and silvery steel . . .
Thy metrical, now swelling pant and roar, now tapering in the distance,
Thy great protruding head-light fix'd in front . . .
Thy train of cars, behind, obedient, merrily following,
Through gale or calm, now swift, now slack, yet steadily careering . . .
With storm and buffeting gusts of wind and falling snow . . .
Law of thyself complete, thine own track firmly holding . . .

The German Intercity trains are carpeted and comfortably heated. They have automatic doors and push-button blinds and indirect lighting. They provide telephones and conference rooms for business-people. They run almost frighteningly on schedule and meet all important connections at adjoining, sheltered platforms. Yet they are mysterious when darkness falls.

A simple *Käsebrot* and yogurt hastily bought in the *Bahnhof* is enough to fortify me during the trips. Almost all the trains are uncrowded and drowsy in first class. In each of the cities there is a budget hotel near the railroad station, a church within a few blocks for saying or hearing Mass, and an opera house with low-priced places in its upper reaches. Some nights I simply sleep on the train.

Vienna has a fresh fall of snow. Some of our students are there, and one of our professors with his family. I don't know where to contact Manfred Schöne, but I see Cardinal König give Benediction in the Dom, which is thickly forested within with Christmas trees. I also allow myself a sentimental time of it attending Mass at the Capuchin church, where the *schöne Musi*, the German chorales devoutly sung by the whole congregation, are as sweet as the incense and the surrounding baroquery.

In a box at Vienna's Staatsoper (I paid a handsome sum for the last-minute ticket), I lean extravagantly far out to watch "The Blue Danube," interpolated as a ballet in the second act of *Die Fledermaus*. I turn to the next box and apologize: "Can you see all right?"

"Of course I can see all right! I'm the American ambassador to Austria, and you can use my box any time you want."

This is New Year's Eve in Vienna, and *Fledermaus* is being done all over town, and the Staatsoper's *Fledermaus* is the one everybody tries to get in to see, as it's the most festive, traditional, and star-studded. By the second act, everyone on both sides of the footlights has had too much champagne. We're all slightly crazy. Even so, I am not prepared for that response from the next box. Either *he* has heard too many Strauss waltzes, I think, or I have. Either *he* has had too many champagne bubbles or I have.

But it *is* the American ambassador. It seems my hastily bought ticket has landed me this time in the UNIDO box, next to his. I talk to him at intermission and sit with him through the third act. On the stage, superannuated Viennese veterans are playing shamelessly to the standee claque, and the favorite actor impersonating Frosch the Jailer is interpolating references to the current state of politics in Austria (bad) and at the Staatsoper (worse). In the box, the ambassador's army assistant tells me the difference between Berlin and Vienna: Berlin, situation serious but not hopeless; Vienna, situation hopeless but not serious. I'm wearing a black turtleneck, not a Roman collar (it never seems right to wear a collar when you have to hustle for a ticket), so I tell the ambassador as I thank him and take my leave, "I'm a Catholic priest."

"I knew *that!*" he replies.

On New Year's Day, eager to be on the go, I take the Prinz Eugen to Würzburg, the Erasmus to Frankfurt, and a local to Darmstadt. En route I see the still lovely spires of the cathedral at Regensburg and the now crumbling stadium built for the Nazi rallies at Nuremberg. Darmstadt offers *Mathis der Maler.* Then, on successive nights, I see *Mitridate* in Duisburg, *Prince Igor* in Kiel, *Fra Diavolo* in Bremerhaven, *Cardillac* in Mannheim, and a new opera on Joan of Arc in Stuttgart, where there is a plaque in the opera house's lobby that identifies this Grosses Haus of the Wittenbergische Staatsoper as the scene of the "laying of the foundation stone for the rebuilding of Germany." On September 6, 1945, American foreign minister James F. Byrne declared that "the American people want to return the government of Germany to the German people," that "the American people want to help the German people win their way back toward an honorable place among the free and peace-loving nations of the world."

From Stuttgart it's Monteverdi's *Poppea* in Strasbourg and Berlioz's *Faust* in Nancy and Offenbach's *Contes d'Hoffmann* at the Opéra in Paris. But the city of light, familiar from past visits, is too expensive to detain me long. I say Mass at Notre-Dame, pray before the statue of St. Joan there, and head back across the Rhine.

I see some of the same people at the opera from night to night—a young man from near London teaching for a year in Aachen; a middle-aged Belgian, father of a large family, who via train transit has seen over a thousand different operas; a charming girl from Vienna who collects *Tristan* performances. None of us has, or spends, very much money. We run into one another at the top of the galleries or in line for standing room or snatching a wurst and beer at some stand-up *Imbiss.* We all consult the international opera schedules published in *Opernwelt* or *Die Welt* or *Die Zeit,* so as to be at the right place at the right time for the rarest operas with the best casts. We have all heard the siren call.

From Paris it is easy to get by train to the Teutoberg Forest, where the Roman armies were decimated by German Arminius, and from there to tiny Bielefeld. You take the Parsifal to Cologne and the Münchener Kindl to the final, snowy destination. I read Gottfried von Strassburg all the way in preparation for the evening's *Tristan*. In Bielefeld I buy a German sailor's hat, an *Elbesegler* with a fancy braid, a real Prinz Heinrich, to remember the trip by. An *Elbesegler!* Politically, the hat will align me with Helmut Schmidt and his liberal policies, as against Franz Josef Strauss and his crazy Bavarian conservatism.

> *D'rum wand'r ich froh so lang ich kann,*
> *Und schwenke meinen Hut.*

On Bielefeld's postage-stamp-sized stage, quite ordinary singers with quite ordinary voices make really extraordinary impressions in *Tristan*, riding the orchestral surges for hours on end with conspicuous ease. *Tristan* is, as always, charged with heavy emotions. Under its influence I think it just may be the greatest opera of all. Certainly it is the most influential work of art of the last hundred years.

And perhaps, as Nietzsche maintained, it is full of pestilential poisons. I need an antidote, and move on to *Nabucco* in Dortmund and *Oberon* in Wiesbaden.

In a low-priced restaurant there I am treated with unusual deference, and wonder why, until the waiter bringing my order says, "Bitte schön, Herr Schiffskapitän." With my black sailor's hat, black turtleneck, and black topcoat, I've given an impression I didn't intend. It's fun pretending to be an old salt only up to a point. I quickly disillusion one and all with a laugh and a burst of American English.

And between the operas, the train rides through the white snow:

That music always round me, unceasing, unbeginning, yet long
    untaught I did not hear,
But now the chorus I hear and am elated,
A tenor, strong, ascending with power and health, with glad notes
    of daybreak I hear,
A soprano at intervals sailing buoyantly over the tops of immense
    waves,
A transparent base shuddering lusciously under and through the
    universe,
The triumphant tutti, the funeral wailings with sweet flutes and violins,
    all these I fill myself with,

I hear not the volumes of sound merely, I am moved by the exquisite
    meanings,
I listen to the different voices winding in and out, striving, contending
    with fiery vehemence to excel each other in emotion;
I do not think the performers know themselves—but now I think I
    begin to know them.

Finally, in Munich to hear Handel's *Alcina* for Johnny Hallagan, I
make another visit to the Glyptothek, this time to seek out which of
the sculptures might have inspired the poem by Rainer Maria Rilke
called *Archaic Torso of Apollo*. Apollo is the god of most of the things
that concern me now, or will concern me soon—music, prophecy, and
healing.

One of the Glyptothek's Apollos matches the details given by Rilke.
The head is gone, and with it the wide staring eyes and the archaic
smile. But somehow, as Rilke says, the eyes and the smile are still
there, dimmed into the torso like the light dimmed down into the
lower globe of a gaslit street lamp when the flame is turned down but
not completely out.

Head, limbs, and genitals are gone, but what remains is full of light.
Now it is the body that stares, the body that smiles. Every broken
edge is radiant as a star. As I look at it, it looks back at me. I have taken
three vows.

Rilke ends his poem with the words the broken Apollo says from
the brightness deep within: "Du musst dein Leben ändern." You must
change your life.

I wonder if this year in Europe, with so much art staring back at me,
smiling and radiant, fragmentary and inscrutable, will bring a transformation in my life.

Part 2

1

Four saints prepare for saints . . .
How many doors how many floors how many windows . . .

T HE SECOND SEMESTER BEGINS. Andrzej and I continue
the year-long seminar on the lyric poem, with Ellen and Tim
and the five others. On my own I plunge into classical epic—
Homer and Virgil—in English translation, with a class of more than
thirty. I also offer Lucretius in Latin and Thucydides in Greek. There
are several Latinists in Lucretius, but Janet is all alone with me reading Thucydides in Greek, and the class becomes a tutorial. We meet
only when she is ready for more, which is very often. She reads the
narrative even more easily than she read Plato last term. But the
speeches in Thucydides challenge her, as I was sure they would.

The students stand in long lines at Maria's office to change Christmas money from America into Italian lire. In Pino's bar I see Ellen and
Tim together sometimes over cappuccinos.

Ellen's stories, which she brings to me faithfully, are unrealistic and
embarrassed. Only one who knows her well can see her experience in
them. They are full of rue but full of promise.

My wanderlust continues to lure me in the winter months to travel
through the Alps. On a wondrously clear January day, I take another
train north, "light-hearted, healthy, free, the world before me."
Europe's trains give me wings again, and the path before me leads, as
Whitman's did, "wherever I choose."

As the train pulls away from Rome, rounding Mount Soracte,
Italy's passing landscape is to me, as America's was to Walt Whitman,
a mirror of my adventure with life itself:

You air that serves me with breath to speak!
You objects that call from diffusion my meanings and give them shape!
You light that wraps me and all things in delicate equable showers!
You paths worn in the irregular hollows by the roadsides!
I believe you are latent with unseen existences, you are so dear to me . . .
You express me better than I can myself . . .

Here are the hill towns of Umbria:

The earth expanding right hand and left hand,
The picture alive, every part in its best light,
The music falling in where it is wanted, and stopping where it is not
    wanted . . .

Here is the approach to Florence:

I think I could stop here myself and do miracles,
I think whatever I shall meet on the road I shall like, and whoever
    beholds me shall like me,
I think whoever I see must be happy.

Here is the stretch between Florence and Bologna:

I inhale great drafts of space,
The east and the west are mine, and the north and the south are mine. . .
I am larger, better than I thought,
I did not know I held so much goodness.

The carriage fills with people, and we talk:

Why are there men and women that while they are nigh me the
    sunlight expands my blood . . .
What is it I interchange so suddenly with strangers . . .
What gives me to be free to a woman's and a man's good-will? what
    gives them to be free to mine?

Here is entering Milan and changing trains and remembering what I
was told to remember:

These are the days that must happen to you:
You shall not heap up what is call'd riches,
You shall scatter with lavish hand all that you earn or achieve,
You but arrive at the city to which you were destin'd, you hardly
    settle yourself to satisfaction before you are call'd by an irresistible
    call to depart.

Here is the entrance to Switzerland, the lakes and the mountains:

Allons! to that which is endless as it was beginningless . . .
To see nothing anywhere but what you may reach it and pass it,
To conceive no time, however distant, but what you may reach it and
    pass it,
To look up or down no road but it stretches and waits for you,
    however long but it stretches and waits for you,
To see no being, not God's or any, but you also go thither,
To see no possession but you may possess it, enjoying all without
    labor or purchase, abstracting the feast yet not abstracting one
    particle of it.

Here, finally, is Germany:

To take your use out of the compact cities as you pass through,
To carry buildings and streets with you afterward wherever you go,
To gather the minds of men out of their brains as you encounter them,
    to gather the love out of their hearts . . .

There is a *Gasthof* in Mannheim, two floors of rooms over an inn, that is clean as a whistle, friendly as a fireplace, and extraordinarily low-priced. It is one of those rare, old-fashioned places that still can be found by the lucky traveler, even in an industrialized push-button Europe. And as it is very cold here north of the Alps, with the familiar outlines of Mannheim made unfamiliar by heaps of snow, I am lucky today to know about it.

Hans the big innkeeper knows me by now. "Oh, hello, Father! *Willkommen!* Come in and get warm. What are they giving at the opera tonight? Would you like the same little room? Mama, call the children."

The kitchen, which fronts directly on the entrance, radiates warmth. Mama, or Anna as I should call her, is bent over a steaming tray she has just drawn from the oven. She lines the children up like organ pipes. The tallest recites his Latin verbs perfectly—well, practically perfectly—smiles, and says, when I ask him what he wants to be, "I want to be an innkeeper like my father." The second tallest, in the lower forms, wants to learn a trade. The two little girls are all happy confusion and shyness. A son older than these is off in America, studying and living with relatives.

"Ridderbusch was here last night for his supper," says the proud father, "and now you're here. So they must be doing Wagner."

"*Die Meistersinger.*"

"Oh, *schön, schön.* It was my mother's *Lieblingsoper.* Have you seen it before?"

"Many times. It's my favorite opera too. I just hope I can get in to see it here tonight, Hans. It starts early, and I haven't got a ticket."

But within an hour, with luck at the ticket office, I find myself transported from snowy twentieth-century Mannheim to summery Reformation Nuremberg. To a dream on midsummer's eve or, as they call it in Nuremberg, *Johannisnacht,* the eve of the feast of John the Baptist. I see once again how Hans Sachs, a shoemaker and poet, instructs his apprentice, David, in the art of making shoes *and* in the art of writing songs: when it comes to craftsmanship, the fine arts aren't all that different from the practical arts. And young David will have to know both if he is somehow to live in Nuremberg, with his sweetheart Magdalena as his wife, for every guild in town has a master of his trade who is also a master of song.

I also see how the richest of the "mastersingers," the goldsmith Pogner, so values art over commerce that he decides to give in marriage his only child, his lovely daughter Eva, to the singer who will sing the most beautiful song the next morning. One of the hopefuls is a young man who knows of song only what he has learned from nature and the poets. Another hopeful is the crotchety town clerk, who knows of song only what he has learned from the guild's book of rules. The contest for Eva's hand will be between Walther, the headstrong romantic, and Beckmesser, the loveless pedant.

The opera is about many more things, things personal to me. The song Walther will sing comes to him in a dream. And Hans Sachs, a master teacher, sees the beauty in it and helps Walther to shape it into verse. He convinces Walther that his new, intuitive vision can be made to conform to the rules sanctioned by the masters of the past. He even devises a way whereby the young man can enter the competition after he has failed to achieve master status. Hans Sachs thereby gives up his own chance of winning Eva, whom he loves, in whom he sees both the young wife and the children he lost in his youth.

Walther and Eva become like a son and daughter to him.

High in the opera house—Mannheim's new, blunt, practical place —the spacious, warm, radiant work wraps me round, embraces, envelops me, speaks to me. Wagner has a way of making his omniscient orchestra say what the characters on stage somehow cannot say, and sometimes do not even know. Hans Sachs has a sorrowful, resigned musical theme that sounds, almost subconsciously, in the midst of his brisk shoemaking. Deep down, he knows that he must give up the hope of marrying, that he must teach the art of song to young Walther and to young David so that they can win the women they love. He faces a future without wife and children of his own.

The resigned theme begins to recur at every moment when that realization hits home. Sometimes it speaks wisely. Sometimes it brings pain. Sometimes it tears through the musical texture with almost tragic savagery.

The theme touches me, as it always has. When the curtains part on the last act of *Die Meistersinger*, Sachs sits bent over a book in his workshop, totally absorbed in wondering about the world, as the morning sunlight on John the Baptist's day streams through his window. There is, he sings, a flaw in human nature, ingrained, a part of us, instinctive, irrational, often destructive. No one can escape it. Nothing in history has happened without it. It is with us so long as we live. He calls it *Wahn*.

More than anything else, this opera is about that flaw in human nature. About what we have in the Christian tradition called our fallen state, the remnant in our consciousness of some original sin. And yet, as Sachs in his wisdom begins to realize, it is out of the same flaw, the same propensity we have for both good and evil, that great works of art come.

A wise man will know this, about human nature and about art, and he will help those who need his insight. All the major characters come that morning, one by one, to see Sachs in his workshop, and all their various problems begin, under the goodly guidance of this master teacher, to solve themselves.

And finally, on the feast of St. John the Baptist, all the townsfolk come together at Nuremberg's riverbank for the singing contest. There, like his namesake the Baptist, Hans Sachs sees to it that everyone is cleansed of the *Wahn* that possessed them the night before. Walther's intuitive song, sprung from the depths of *Wahn* in his own soul, touches all the others in their several ways: Walther wins his Eva, and David his Magdalene. But it was Sachs who first saw what had to be done, who taught Walther to shape his intuition into a thing of beauty, and who at the same time put his own feelings aside to help the younger man.

The conductor reaches the final pages of the massive score. Sachs is standing with his back to the crowd, lost in thought. Eva, after a little conspiratorial conversation with Walther, takes the victor's laurel from Walther's head and crowns Hans Sachs with it. He accepts the laurel with grace but, like any good teacher who has helped his best student, he knows that what he did was only what he should have done.

The inn is only a short walk from the opera house. The children are in bed and Anna is knitting while Hans is having a beer with two of his friends. Anna has some cake and coffee for me, and soon we are talking about the opera. Her eyes shine.

"I used to sing in *Die Meistersinger* before I married Hans. I was in the *Extrachor*. In *Holländer* and *Meistersinger* they need extra choruses."

"It's the best opera in all the world, isn't it?"

"Oh, I think I like *Freischütz* best, or maybe *Tannhäuser*. *Meistersinger* was always such hard work for us, and we had to wait such a long time backstage through the acts."

"But it must be thrilling to have a part in the big chorus in the last scene, when everybody praises Sachs with the chorale he wrote."

"Oh, yes, about the nightingale singing a new song."

"Wagner uses a poem by the historical Hans Sachs there. Did you know?"

"Yes, I remember." She keeps knitting. "It's about Martin Luther."

"But when the chorus all sing it to greet Hans Sachs, the lines seem to me to be not just about Luther but about all the masters of German art—Hans Sachs and Dürer, Goethe and Schiller, Bach and Beethoven—all of them like nightingales singing their songs."

"Oh, yes. The whole opera is about art and music."

"I think I like *Die Meistersinger* best because it's about the wonder of creating works of art. And because Hans Sachs is the good teacher and the good man I would like to be."

Hans the innkeeper has seen his friends to the door. It is close to midnight. He hears us talking and comes over. None of us wants to go to bed just yet. Hans settles down at the table with me. He is suddenly serious, and says in his rough English. "You know, Father, most people in Germany don't go to see *Die Meistersinger* any more. It's too much Hitler."

"Yes, I know that, Hans. Hitler liked it. But he liked vegetables too," I say too quickly. "Are the rest of us supposed to stop eating vegetables for that reason?"

It is a lame response. I try again. "I know that Hitler was moved by Wagner in the theater. But so are the three of us here. So are hundreds of thousands of people. Good people. I don't think that Hitler really understood what he heard in Wagner. I don't think he was moved by Wagner in the ways that we are. He made a public show of liking the music, but in private, in the bunker at the end, he listened to operetta. Léhar, not Wagner."

"Yes, but you know," says Hans with earnestness on his face, "Hitler made his headquarters in Nuremberg in Hans Sachs' house, and built the stadium for his rallies on the river there, just like in *Die Meistersinger.*"

"Don't, Hans," says Anna.

"And before the war we had that last speech of Hans Sachs in the papers and on the streets. The part about keeping German art free from foreigners."

"It was used against the Jews," says Anna quietly.

"I know, I know. Wagner himself was a terrible anti-Semite."

"And he was a bad man. He cheated people and ran off with their wives."

"Don't, Hans."

"He always had to have more and more money, and meddle in politics. You know they ran him out of Munich, and out of Vienna."

"Yes, Hans," I reply. "We know that too, where I come from. It's no secret. But, well, let me say two things. First, in a many-sided genius like Wagner, you get many faults, self-destructive faults, that we ordinary people don't have. That is one reason why the works of art that geniuses produce are so rich. What they can't work out in their lives they are compelled to work out in their art. All the warmth and wisdom in *Die Meistersinger*—that's exactly what was missing in Wagner's personal life. But what he couldn't achieve in his life he did achieve in his art."

"*Aber*, how can that be?" asks Hans.

"Well, your oldest boy, studying now—he may be able to tell you that works of art are often created by very imperfect men, out of a kind of madness that, if wrongly used, can be destructive. That's what Sachs wonders about over his books, and then, as he looks out his window, he resolves to direct that basic drive, that *Wahn*, creatively—in himself and in young Walther and in the city he sees spread out before him, outside his window."

They are listening intently, though Anna doesn't look up from her knitting.

"An artist has to pay for the gift of his genius. Wagner paid. He was defeated, one way or another, all his life. His own self-destructiveness always pursued him—possessed him, even. But what he couldn't do, his characters do. They come to understand themselves and find peace. Especially Hans Sachs."

"He helps all the other people," says Anna.

"He gives up what he knows he cannot have," I say. "And do you remember how he almost despairs over that?"

"Yes," says Anna. "He suffers a lot inside."

"The other thing I wanted to say, Hans, when you brought up Hitler, is that we shouldn't condemn *Die Meistersinger* for the evil use Hitler made of it. The Bible itself has been used, through the ages, to justify oppression and evil. Should we stop reading it because of that? I teach Homer's *Iliad*, a great work of art, but Alexander the Great used it to justify his massacres. And Virgil's *Aeneid*—Virgil, when he died, wanted it burned. I think he was afraid it would be misread. Future generations might think it was a glorification of conquest, not a meditation on conquest that wondered why the innocent had to suffer for any good to be accomplished. Virgil must have known that his *Aeneid* could be used as propaganda, used, against his wishes, to conquer and to oppress.

"Well it's like that, Hans, with *Die Meistersinger*. The opera was misread, by Hitler and the Nazis, made to mean what it doesn't mean. It's not about creating a master race. It's not about the terrible racial laws that were promulgated in Nuremberg a half-century later. It's about facing up to what is destructive in our own human nature and overcoming it. It's about Germany becoming a center of civilization —as Hans Sachs sings at the end—not by going to war but by creating and preserving great works of art. It may be the great German work of art that will enable Germany finally to bury Hitler."

I'd like to think that I'm right, but I'm not really sure they've understood me. And it's now after midnight. I rise from my chair. "Well, it's late."

Hans rises and stretches and puts out the lights. "If it's all right to like Wagner, maybe it's all right to be a German after all." He once fought with Rommel in Africa. "Maybe it's all right to be a German, if what you say is true."

"We're all of us flawed, Hans, and all of us capable of both good and evil. We've got to choose the good."

"And," says Anna, "try to help other people, when we can."

We say good night. They go up the stairs together as they have for years. I follow them and have a dreamless night under their chaste, welcoming roof, in the little room above the children.

2

A MAN IS CHASTE only so that he can love. In the East, in the first days of monasticism, chastity was the only vow. It was considered enough. It meant clinging to God with both hands, embracing him with both arms, and so making it impossible for one to fasten onto anything less than him. Chastity included the other two vows, for if one embraces God wholly it is impossible to grasp at any possessions, and impossible to have any will but his.

In the West, chastity has been thought of in a different metaphor. Seeing. "Blessed are the clean of heart, for they shall see God." Sensuality blinds. The wholly carnal man loses sight of what makes the flesh beautiful. But the chaste are clear-sighted and shining-eyed. How can they not be? They see God.

East or West, Theophilus, the chaste man is chaste only so that he can love. The language of love is the only language appropriate to this vow. The vow of chastity recognizes that love is the law of our life, and it directs all love to Love itself.

To be chaste in this way is to love passionately all the good and beautiful things one sees, and to see them in the one ultimate source of goodness and beauty. It is to find unity, wholeness, and completion, for everything one senses and responds to is seen in the light of one transcendent truth.

Loving and being loved are an absolute necessity for human beings. Affection and delight they must have, if they are to survive. The vow of chastity knows this. A chaste man is not only a lover; he is alive for love. He is given over completely to love. His passions are not dead but quickened, responsive, and ordered. He is in love with Love.

He abstains from sexual pleasure—a crazy thing to do, unless he sees it as making his dedication total. A perilous thing to do, unless he is happy, profoundly happy, about what his chastity does for him. His decision not to give himself to a loving wife and produce children must give him a sense of expansiveness, of self-transcendence; otherwise it is selfish and self-destructive. So he opens his arms completely. He loves everything, everyone. A man in religious life lives with his brothers who have made the same commitment, but he is completely intimate only with his God. He isn't alone, unloved, abandoned, as some people want to think. He senses that God is with him even, perhaps especially, when he suffers. He sees everything that happens to him, even the heartbreaking and terrifying things, as God's return of love. He surrenders.

Once, at a free Bach concert at a university in the southern United States, I turned my eyes from the solo harpsichordist on stage to a woman, about seventy I'd say, and obviously not a woman in possession of conventional wealth, sitting in the front row. She sat perfectly still and small. Her face was blessed with a smile, her eyes closed in quiet rapture. Her arms were open, gently placed on the arm rests of her chair. She was taking the music in as if it were a ray of sunshine. If the soloist on stage was playing the music, then surely the music was playing her, this woman in the audience, and she was saying to it, in her surrender, "Come in. Fill me. Enrich me. Sustain me." I don't know what god she was surrendering to, but my own surrendering made sense to me at that moment.

Sometimes the surrender is one of pain, and God claims his beloved as violently as an invading army storms a city. "Batter my heart, three-person'd God," said John Donne. He hadn't succumbed when God only breathed or shone upon him. He had to be forced. He knew the contradictions involved in submission, knew his own stubbornness, and begged to be thrown down so he could rise and stand. He knew that his reason objected to love's surrender, and he prayed to his God to "bend your force, to break, blow, burn, and make me free," to "take me to you, imprison me." He knew that surrender to God was inviting pain and loss and suffering. But he wanted love in all its fullness:

> For I, except you enthrall me, never shall be free,
> Nor ever chaste, except you ravish me.

Chastity, Theophilus, is openness to God, and complete acceptance of what his love will bring. The new semester, as it turned out, was an occasion for me to learn that that surrender also meant inviting pain and loss.

3

LATE JANUARY BRINGS US RAINS. Some kind of flu hits us hard. Fewer students descend to the city to see its churches and monuments. Money is in shorter supply. Lines are shorter at Maria's window, and weekends are not always the large-scale excursions they were. The boys begin increasingly to desert Pino's cappuccinos for Tonio's place outside the gate, where they can drink beer until late at night. One of the girls returns to her room to find all of her dresser drawers rifled and her toiletries smashed. When this recurs after precautions are taken, Fr. Costello suspects that the culprit is the roommate. None of us can believe this, as the two girls are close friends. But Fr. Costello, wise in these matters, is eventually proved right. It is a case of long-concealed jealousy surfacing. The roommate goes home.

On a long weekend, with the rail pass, I see Gluck's *Iphigeneia at Aulis* in Karlsruhe, Kodály's *Háry János* in Hannover, and Verdi's *Joan of Arc* in Bern. In Hannover, dressed in a black turtleneck, I am eyed favorably by a smiling man in front of the opera house. He glances, grins, and nods several times but says nothing. I'm not sure what to think of these overtures. Finally he approaches and asks, to my relief, "Are you from the Soviet Union?"

It's the *Elbesegler* again. The hat can make me look like a Communist.

In the United States, unemployment reaches a record high as the economy slips. Motor companies offer rebates on auto purchases.

Word comes from my religious community at the University of Toronto that I will be teaching with them next year. My immediate reaction is one of intense disappointment: this year in Europe will be the only such year for me. It's back to bleak Canada.

"But I've heard good things about Toronto," says Johnny Hallagan, reading the *Corriere della Sera* in the faculty room.

"The streets are safe, Johnny, and relatively clean. But it's got a brutish climate. There's no spring to speak of, the summers can be steamy and savagely hot, and the autumn, while it has its colors, brings allergens enough to paralyze a healthy man. Besides that, the postal service has collapsed. It's the worst in the world. And despite a big influx of postwar immigrants—good people who made living better in every way—the newspapers are run and edited by waspish bigots. And there's a lot of rampant, mindless anti-Americanism . . ."

"It has a great university, though. And you'll be there."

"Yes. There is some interest in the good things. But not much in opera. Toronto has no opera house. The best Canadian singers won't sing in Toronto. They don't want to face the insensitive critics—or the audiences that head for the parking lot before the curtain comes down."

"Sounds like you've got your work cut out for you."

He's disappointed that he can't get me to laugh about it. The best I can do is say, "Well, a lot of Italians have settled in Toronto in recent years, and they're changing things for the better."

Tim Brannigan and I get together at Pino's between classes, and he tells me why he has lived in Italy for a year and a half and would like to stay longer: "I hate my father, and I think my father hates me."

I'm sure I look shocked. I say something mildly disapproving. The moment, a sudden shot to the heart, passes. My own disappointment about returning to Canada seems small-minded. He doesn't want me to say anything. He just wants me to hear him say what he thought had to be said.

On another weekend I see Busoni's *Arlecchino* in Florence, Handel's *Semele* in Karlsruhe, and in Munich Verdi's *Simon Boccanegra*, an opera about misunderstanding, long-held hatred, and a father finding his lost daughter. My eyes are shining with the intensity of it all, or so I am told by a man in late middle age who strikes up a conversation with me during intermission in one of the National Theater's spacious lobbies. He introduces me to his friend, a doctor, and when they hear I haven't had anything to eat since breakfast they buy me champagne and sandwiches. The doctor then offers to take my place in standing room while I occupy his seat. Such is the *Kameradschaft* that springs up affectionately and spontaneously between operagoers. I cannot accept the kind offer, especially as the doctor has been in his office from early that morning until just before curtain time. But I do ride afterward with them to the doctor's apartment, in a building where Rilke once lived. The doctor's wife is dead and his children married. Opera fills his life now, and good conversation. He cooks a late meal for the three of us, and we talk about opera, the other arts, and their relevance to a productive life, until almost three in the morning.

Manfred Schöne doesn't keep an office in the school, and he is so involved directing plays and giving lectures across Rome—indeed, across Europe—that to speak with him you have to attend a class and wait your turn afterward with a crowd of admiring students. So when one day I find him alone, short-sleeved in the cold central stairway, I tell him, too profusely, how much his classes on Bramante and Caravaggio have meant to me. He clenches his fists and his tough forearms tighten as he scowls.

"You embarrass me."

But he is, all the same, pleased.

"You are a German," he continues, "and, poor fellow, you have the German's veneration of culture running you a high fever."

"I'm half Irish," I laugh, "and so I may speak occasional blarney."

"An Irishman. A dreamer. That's a bad combination, Irish dreamer and culture-mad German. Will you have some coffee with me?"

We descend to Pino's. No cappuccinos for him. "*Due espressi.*"

"You're German yourself, aren't you, Dr. Schöne? Not Austrian."

"I'm German, yes. The family were Berliners in the last century. We are not Catholics. I'm Protestant, and my wife is part Jewish. Now, I want to tell you, Father, that your absorption in cultural matters can be your undoing. You write books and articles?"

"Yes."

"Many?"

"As many as I can."

"Why?"

"Because scholarly articles are expected of me by my university. But not everything I write is scholarly. I also write things for the popular press." I laugh. "How else do you think I can afford the opera tickets?"

"Don't you really write because you want your work to survive you? So your name will be remembered?"

"You may be right there."

"You like to travel?"

"Yes, I love it. It's my German side. Wanderlust."

"You have vivid dreams at night?"

"Yes, sometimes, but I've never set foot in the house at number 19 Berggasse."

"You are very orderly, in your room, with your books?"

"Yes. Scrupulously. I've got a German sense of order."

"And you always do as you are told."

"No. The Irish in me rebels. You think I'm a German, but I'm not, not all the way."

"Why are you teaching here? Why are you not with your own community of priests, in Canada?"

"That is a long story. You know how complicated university arrangements are. I'll be returning to my community this summer. There is a place for me again at the University of Toronto."

"You are a Faust."

I'm a little startled at that. Then I decide not to take it seriously.

"Oh, come on, Professor Schöne." I laugh, but the familiar and the formal in my response do not sit well together.

"I am not a Professor or a Doctor. Please call me Manfred. And you, Father, you are a Faust, and you should be careful."

"You take me too seriously, Manfred. The *Faust* I know is Gounod's, not Goethe's. And no one, especially no one of us Germans, is supposed to take Gounod seriously any more."

"You'd be better off if you were the sentimental sensualist of that opera. A Frenchman. But you're not. You're a German, a sentimental idealist. You think *Kultur* is some kind of divine force in society. You see it evolving high forms of civilization. Besides that, you have this German soul that never finds rest. Can you be satisfied to see a few churches in Rome, or a few operas in Europe? No. You must see a hundred or more. That is German. *Schrankenlosigkeit*. You see experience as an endless space to be conquered. You are like your Wagner, constantly prolonging his operas by postponing releases for hour on hour, heaping climax on climax. You are like Goethe's Faust, the German Faust, never resting. You are like all the German conquerors who are affronted by boundaries and must cross them."

"I don't see myself that way. But even if I am like that, what of it?"

"Faust is prompted by his own personal demon. The German conquerors were obsessed. Wagner—well, we won't go into that. The German spirit is not just relentless; it is crusading, ambivalent, with a great capacity for evil. It seeks a kind of redemption and always fails to find it. It is self-destructive. And it often destroys others in the course of destroying itself."

"All right, I know about the World Wars. But before Germany it was France, wasn't it? You can't blame Germany for all the woes that have come on Europe."

"Napoleon inherited the old German dream of a Holy Roman Empire."

"Well, granted the attempts at world or European empires were terribly destructive. You still can't make this a completely German thing, not with all the Latin and Slavic and Anglo-Saxon attempts at dominance. And you can't use Faust as a symbol for all the destruction. Especially not since Goethe opted to save his Faust."

"But only when his Faust saw the possibility of rest in one moment's happiness of helping others. And it took Goethe eighty years to make that affirmation. His redeemed Faust is an ideal toward which we Germans can strive. And you see, I said strive. Some Frenchman would have had, for his ideal, something to contemplate and rest in."

I laugh again. "I'm flattered, Manfred, that you see something deeply ambivalent in me. I *am* driven. I may be selfishly concerned about doing what is best, I'm a restless traveler, and I'm crazy about the spiritual content in great works of art. But no one, least of all myself, sees me as profoundly ambivalent."

I think that Schöne himself may be profoundly ambivalent. I haven't seen enough of him to know. He returns to his subject.

"I am telling you because you need to know. You idealize too much. Your vow of chastity—you think of it as a shining ideal. It is a German trick played on young idealists. Charlemagne couldn't contain his nobles, who passed their lands and power on to their sons, so he allied himself with the power of the church and introduced celibacy for the church's elect."

"Oh, I've read the same sort of thing in *Mein Kampf.* You know, Manfred, that the ideal of chastity is older than any German emperor. No one, not even Charlemagne, could have imposed it unless it were already an ideal."

The eyebrows close together on the tough face. "You, typical German, explain away the realities of history with your idealism. You know Schiller's poem about German greatness? Germany is not defeated when it goes down in battle, because Germany is a spiritual reality, more than its kings and rulers. The *Reich* may crumble, again and again, but Germany will survive because it preserves the spiritual and intellectual and moral concepts of all Europe. It's the last thing they sing in your special opera *Die Meistersinger*. It's the ideal of the old Holy Roman Empire, with Germany preserving civilization because only Germany has the greatness of soul to do it. Well, Germany *imposes* culture on others by the sword; it imposes racial purity through extermination camps. The whole dream is as dangerous as it is illusory. And you believe it. Admit it, Father. You're not just obsessed by Europe. You preach it as a Gospel. The next thing you'll want to do is impose it."

I hardly know what to say. "If I feel any of that, I've kept it hidden from myself."

"You do have an idea of education as imposing values and judgments?"

"Not really. I'm only an enthusiast. I may have an unfortunate tendency to think what I think best *is* best, but I'm encouraged in that tendency because the most intelligent students in my classes, the ones who don't have to agree with me, are the ones who almost invariably do. I don't insist that anyone in class subscribe to my views. I think I welcome dissent."

"All the same," he persisted, "your pedagogical method is persuasion."

"So is yours, Manfred. And you're much better at it than I am."

He is taken aback only for a moment. "Well, we both have to be careful. We Germans are philosophers, scientists, poets, and music lovers. And we are the most guilty people in history. The two are connected."

"We may well be the guiltiest people of this century. But the Nazis were thugs, Manfred. You know that better than I. They don't speak for all Germans. You get thugs in any civilization. Even in the great civilizations. In Athens—"

"The intelligences behind Nazism, the real anti-Semites, were not thugs but educated men. Gottfried Benn was a doctor and a poet."

"The Nazis misused him," I counter, surprised at my boldness, "as they did the writings of Nietzsche. And you can find anti-Semitism in England, Spain, almost anywhere in Europe long before the Nazis. There's plenty of it in Catholic history, in Thomas Aquinas—"

"And in Martin Luther. I don't want to waste time apportioning the guilt. I'm saying that there's a connection between intellectual elitism and intolerance, between the worship of culture and a capacity for cruelty, between the compulsion for order and a hatred of the frail and the fallible. And these things are very pronounced among us rest-less Germans. They are ingrained in us. We know it, too, and we can't change, and we can't forgive ourselves for it."

"Then Goethe was wrong when he ended *Faust* with his symbolic man, his German, redeemed and forgiven?"

"I've told you, his *Faust* is a myth of what we want to become. But before Goethe, in the old tradition, Faust the insatiable German was damned."

"Why are you telling me this, Manfred?"

He pauses, shrugs, downs the rest of his coffee, and says, "So you'll stop complimenting me, in public and private, on my lectures."

We both laugh. It is almost a first for him. I hurry to a class, and he to his car.

That weekend, a long one, I make a marathon train trip north. Four operas beyond the wintry Alps:

> Proud music of the storm . . .
> Strong hum of forest tree-tops—wind of the mountains,
> Personified dim shapes—you hidden orchestras,
> You serenades of phantoms with instruments alert . . .
> You chords left as by vast composers—you choruses,
> You formless, free, religious dances . . .
> You undertone of rivers, roar of pouring cataracts . . .
> Entering my lonesome slumber-chamber, why have you seiz'd me?
>
> Come forward O my soul, and let the rest retire,
> Listen, lose not, it is toward thee they tend,
> Parting the midnight, entering my slumber-chamber . . .
>
> The measureless sweet vocalists of ages,
> And for their solvent setting earth's own diapason . . .
>
> Across the stage with pallor on her face, yet lurid passion,
> Stalks Norma brandishing the dagger in her hand.
>
> I see poor crazed Lucia's eyes' unnatural gleam,
> Her hair down her back falls loose and dishevel'd.
>
> I see where Ernani, walking the bridal garden,
> Amid the scent of night roses, radiant, holding his bride by the
>   hand,
> Hears the infernal call, the death-pledge of the horn . . .

Awakening from her woes at last retriev'd Amina sings,
Copious as stars and glad as morning light the torrents of her
    joy . . .

I hear those odes, symphonies, operas,
I hear in the *William Tell* the music of an arous'd and angry
    people,
I hear Meyerbeer's *Huguenots,* the *Prophet,* or *Robert,* Gounod's
    Faust . . .

Give me to hold all sounds, (I madly struggling cry,)
Fill me with all the voices of the universe,
Endow me with their throbbings, Nature's also,
The tempests, waters, winds, operas and chants, marches
    and dances,
Utter, pour in, for I would take them all!

Then I woke softly,
And pausing, questioning awhile the music of my dream,
And questioning all those reminiscences, the tempest in its fury,
And all the songs of sopranos and tenors . . .
I said to my silent curious soul out of the bed of the slumber-
    chamber,
Come, for I have found the clew I sought so long.

But in fact, I had not found the clue I sought so long. And there
was so little time. I would soon be going back to Canada.

4

I T IS FEBRUARY. Rome has sunshine, and Mount Soracte, clearly visible from the roof, has snow.

In Italy, strikes continue and inflation is rampant. American students who are watching their lire carefully wonder how Italians can dress so extravagantly. Right-wing extremists bomb our gate house. I have a couple of articles published back in the States, and a couple turned down. Ellen brings me more stories about Tom. The faculty have taken to dining more often in warm Trastevere restaurants. We welcome a series of visiting lecturers and host a concert by two Italian singers who specialize in Neapolitan songs.

Maria Parenti is next to me at the concert. I tell her about the trip I made to Naples, with Tim, to the Virgil places. She tells me her husband was from Posillipo, which is near Cumae. They fell in love over a Neapolitan song popular at the time: a fisherman rowing on the sea at Posillipo sings to his "Maria who is far away from me." Her husband was killed in the war. She is not sentimental about any of her memories.

I have only a short time left on my rail pass. The sense of limitless freedom, of being able to wing across Europe at will, will be gone in a few weeks. Soon after that I will be back in Toronto, held in tighter reign by a superior perhaps younger and almost certainly wiser than I, with the usual round of committee meetings, administrative duties, and assignments to complicate my teaching, instead of all these opportunities to lighten and enrich it. That is the way my return begins to look to me.

Obedience is, in the end, the hardest of the three vows. The collar chafes—the yoke is not always sweet and light. Poverty might separate me from possessions, and chastity eliminate any possibility of wife and family, but obedience—the longer I live with it, the more it takes from me what I will. If I stay with it, will it bend me to *its* will? Will it rob me of myself?

I didn't vow obedience to the printed rule or to any individual superior. I vowed it to God. It should make my life simpler and more beautiful, if I can surrender to it. But, practically speaking, God speaks through the rule I have accepted and the superior I have a voice in electing. It's never easy. And if God were to speak in some other way, would I know his voice?

Tim is a good companion as we continue to explore Rome's churches. One day we visit all four major basilicas and say the prescribed prayers to gain the Holy Year blessing.

The thought won't leave me that I might have had a son like him. I'm grateful for his companionship, for our friendship, which is rich and full despite the difference in our ages. But I am rueful about not ever being able to have a son like him for my own.

When he and I return to the school after the day's pilgrimage, I say Mass and he serves. He reads the Epistle, I the Gospel:

> But looking up Jesus saw the rich who were putting their gifts into the treasury. And he saw also a certain poor widow putting in two mites. And he said, "Truly I say unto you, this poor widow has put in more than any of them. For they out of their abundance have made their gifts to God: but she out of her want has put in all that she had to live on."

That cuts close to the bone, I think to myself. If I'd been there when Jesus said that, I might have interrupted: "Yes, what you say is true. But isn't it comparatively easy for the widow to put in all she has and trust the rest to God, if all she has is two small coins. What about the rest of us who have many mites and many talents? It's actually harder for us, isn't it? If we put in all that we've got—not just coins but, as you clearly mean to imply, all our lives—then we're making a bigger sacrifice than she is. *Are* we supposed to give up everything for you?"

And Jesus, if he is consistent at all, would answer me, "Of course. Give up everything. That's what I'm saying. That's what your religious life is all about."

Well, it's hard. There's a big chance that, when I hear those words, I might go away sad, like the rich young man in the Gospel who did just that. I'm a poor, middle-aged man, but I just might go away anyway, clutching the few things I've still got left.

What does he want, anyway? Give up everything! I've already given up having a family, which was only a little hard to do when I was nineteen and wasn't ready for the responsibility. Now that I'm over forty I can see what the real sacrifice was. I haven't got a son. "And do you mean, Lord, that this young man whose interest in art, music, and literature I've shared and nurtured this year, and who is more like me now than I was myself when I was his age, who is in every way except the biological a son to me—do you mean I have to give him up?"

"Of course. That's what I'm saying. He's not yours."

And when I was nineteen, I gave up making money, which wasn't so hard to do then because nobody I knew seemed to have very much of it. But now that I'm over forty, and most of them have made a pretty comfortable pile, I've got nothing to pass on to the son I haven't got. "And do I still have to give up what little I have?"

"Of course. That's what I'm saying. Give it away. Like the widow."

And when I was nineteen I gave up the right to make my own decisions about my life, which wasn't very hard to do at all, because I certainly didn't know what I should do with my life then and I thought maybe somebody else did. Now that I'm over forty, I realize what that youthful sacrifice meant. I've spent years working at what someone else told me to work at. That has meant a contribution to and perhaps even some prestige for the work of the Church. But, well, "Jesus, what I want to say now is, I'm as good as that widow. I'm a widower of sorts. I've put in as much of my substance as she ever did. And now I want to know, not what do I finally get out of it, but why, why did you ask it? And are you going to keep on asking it?"

The thoughts continue through the consecration of the Mass, when Jesus says through me, "This is my Body. This is my Blood." My hands tremble as I lift the chalice.

Tim can tell that something is getting to me. He embraces me at the kiss of peace. It is not just the usual handclasp. He receives communion under both forms, kneels for the blessing, thanks me, and leaves quietly.

Johnny Hallagan is in his room, bundled up against the chill and reading Dickens, as if it were Christmas in London.

"Can I come in, Johnny?"

"Any time."

It takes a while to come to the point: "It's not poverty that's the problem now. It's all three."

More spills out of me than I ever expected. Not just the widow's mite, but Aeneas and Faust and Hans Sachs.

"You've got as many characters in your head as Dickens ever put in a book like this one," he says. "Probably any one of those ideals of yours could give you an answer to your problems. But Jesus is the one who started all this, tonight and years ago when you were—how old?"

"Nineteen."

"Well, Jesus is the son of the God you made your promises to. So suppose you actually said those reproachful things to him when the widow dropped her two coins into the treasury. What Jesus always did on such embarrassing occasions was to answer in parables. A few shocking little stories to shatter the questioners and complainers into a sense of what sense their lives had. Well, Luke, what parable would he give you? The man who hid his talent in the ground? That doesn't apply to you. The laborers in the vineyard who complained that the latecomers who worked less got paid as much as they did themselves? I hardly think that applies either. No, Luke, He'd give you this parable, I think . . ."

For a moment I'm more humiliated than humbled. He's going to preach to me! Then I think, if Johnny can't help me, no one can. I'd better listen.

"You remember the man who had two sons. The older was serious, a good worker, with duty in his blood. Maybe too much duty and too little love. He certainly didn't love his father as much as his father loved him. And he resented his younger brother because the father seemed to have a weakness, as so many fathers seem to have, for the younger.

"And the younger boy took his share of the inheritance and spent it all in the wide world until it all was gone, and he was caught in a famine, and swallowed his pride, and went back home. And his father forgave him."

I chafe. "I don't see how this applies to me now."

"Well, Luke, that's not the end of the story. When the father kissed his prodigal son, and put a new robe on him, and killed the fatted calf for a feast for him, what happened then? The older son came back from the fields, heard the servants singing, and asked them. 'Why all this music?'

"'Your brother has come home.'

"'Then tell my father I will not come in.'"

It is the usually disregarded part of the story. Johnny isn't afraid to dramatize a little: "All the music stopped inside, and the father came out. And the son said, in anger, 'Sir, all these years I have served you faithfully and never broken one of your commandments. And you never even gave me a kid so I could make merry with my friends. But when this other son of yours comes home, this sinner who has spent his inheritance on harlots, you kill for him the fatted calf.'

"Now, Luke, what did the father say?"

I didn't want to hear this in the first place, and I don't want to answer now. But I do.

"He said, 'Can't I do what I want to?'"

"Come on, Luke! The father said, and he's saying it to you now, 'My son, you are with me always, and all I have is yours. But please understand, I *had* to do this for your brother. He was lost and now is found again.' And then what happened?"

"Nothing. That's the end."

"That's as far as Jesus could go, because the story still hasn't ended. It's still going on."

I don't say anything.

"So what are you going to say, you dutiful son? 'It's late, but I want my share of the inheritance before it's *too* late'? 'I'm going to leave now after all my years of good service'? 'I'm the innocent one here, the one that's done his duty, and I demand my full share'? Will you say that?"

"Not fair, mummy."

"What's that?"

"Not fair, mummy. It's what Deborah Kerr used to say when she was disappointed. And her mother told her, 'There is no such thing as not fair. Life isn't fair.'"

"It doesn't look fair. But maybe it *is* fair. Jesus seems to think it is. He's saying everything is fair, despite all appearances. Our Father, who appears to be partial, and to all appearances loves unequally, actually loves with an infinite love. There is no unequal and no unfair about infinity. Our Father says, even to sons like you, 'You are with me always, and all I have is yours.'"

"Yes, but all those years the elder son never knew that. His father never told him."

"There are a lot of things about our Father we are never told. We're supposed to surrender to him."

That is what I didn't want to hear.

"Yes, Luke, we do what we can, you and I, to make this world as good a place as we can. We work hard at that. And if things don't always seem right, we have to trust him."

"Trust him. You said that before."

"Yes, trust him even though your life doesn't seem fair. Even though the whole world seems wrong. My God, Luke, when I look around and see all the ugliness and cruelty and inequality! The world, reality, whatever you want to call it, is to all appearances a terrible place." He talks for a minute about what he knows, what he most cares about. "To all appearances a terrible place. Junkies in our cities stealing and even killing for a fix, comfortable suburbanites living off poor prostitutes who sell themselves to keep their kids in clothes, whole communities starving in Africa, political prisoners in whole archipelagoes of death camps, and nuclear weapons ready to incinerate the great cities of Europe. Is that what the world really is, always was since life evolved, and will be until we blow ourselves up? Or is there any truth in the parables of Jesus? In what your music says, Luke, and your Greek and Latin? Are those testaments just illusions, or is there something in your music and your poetry that keeps telling you, 'Love me, trust me, surrender to me, you are always with me, all I have is yours'?"

I wait a while before I answer.

"I think that both God and the evils of the world exist. You make it sound as if the reality of the world is either one or the other."

"The one is the hope for the other. Evil isn't the only reality. We've chosen to affirm the good and to work for it."

"And give ourselves to it."

"Yes. You've already given yourself to it."

"That goes way beyond the parable."

"Jesus might have said all that if he'd finished the parable. But he didn't, just as his Father didn't finish this imperfect world. He left us something to respond to and work for. I'd say the meaning of what Jesus has told us is simply, 'Love, because God loves you. Give yourself away completely because that's what God does. And forget about the rest.' Can you subscribe to that?"

"I wish I could. I think I did once."

"Some people have subscribed to it completely. They believed that, despite all appearances, the world made sense. That God was in love with them personally. That he was gracious and forgiving to a fault. They were the Albert Schweitzers and Mother Teresas of the world. They dropped everything into the treasury."

"I don't suppose they could have done anything less," I say, "if they believed in what Jesus said."

"What Jesus said may be the only thing that will save us."

A long pause.

"Feel better about all this now, Luke?" Of course, Philadelphian that he is, he has said, "Feel better about awl this now, Luke?"

I have to laugh. "I should, John. It's my Gospel, not yours, that has the story of the Prodigal Son in it."

That weekend I board the Settebello, the seven-times-beautiful train, for points north and two of our greatest operatic testaments.

Actually the Settebello, after years of good service, is now more elegantly dowdy than beautiful, and its bored clientele draw enfolding blue curtains across the windows and glass doors so as not to be distracted by the da Vinci landscapes that nature has bounteously laid out for them from Rome to Florence to Bologna to Milan.

In Florence, a well-dressed American girl, pretty if not quite beautiful, shares the compartment with me. We pull the blue curtains back and let the landscape in and laugh. She has just moved to Milan with, apparently, a lot of money to set up a shop. Women's wear. But, strangely enough, she knows no Italian.

We talk in English about what she has seen in Florence. For someone who has chosen to live in Italy, she knows surprisingly little about the Renaissance. Of the famous people who lived in Florence in its shining moment she has heard of Dante and Beatrice, of Michelangelo, Raphael, Galileo, and the Medici. But she does not know the scores of other great Florentines who gave the world the Italian language, some of its finest literature, experimental science, modern political theory, possibly its greatest painting and sculpture and, finally, the first operas.

I tell her what to look for the next time she goes to Florence. We talk about the Piazza della Signoria, and its male chauvinist pieces—Cellini's Perseus holding aloft the severed head of the monstrous Medusa, Giambologna's massive Roman men carrying off distressed Sabine women, Ammanante's heroic Neptune, Bandinelli's vulgar Hercules, and Michelangelo's defiant David—all of them huge embodiments of Florence's aggressively naked, masculine, humanistic spirit. And I mention, finally, Donatello restoring the balance in the square with a small and quietly discreet statue of Judith, fully clothed, holding the severed head of Holofernes.

"Women know how to manage these things," I say. "Clothes are very important."

Her eyes widen. "You are not like most Americans."

"Oh, there are plenty of Americans like me in Europe. You'll find us at the schools and art galleries and opera houses—and at the low-cost restaurants and hotels."

"Stay with me in Milan."

I realize with a start that my enthusiasm has carried me too far. "Oh, no. Thank you. You are very kind."

The moment passes. The conversation continues, but with somewhat less zest.

We pass through Bologna, and we talk about the United States. She is very lonely. She feels now that she may have missed some of "the best things to be had" back there. I assure her that there is a lot to be had wherever she may find herself.

We claim our baggage from the baggage car in Milan. Our breath streams before us in the cold. The porter, a young fellow with a trim mustache, smiles at me knowingly. "Together?"

"No. Just friends. We separate here."

I'm alone much of the time in the compartment from Milan to Zurich. The usually spectacular ride is obscured by mist and rain. They press against the window. As the train mounts higher, snow dashes and swirls and shifts against the panes, like the last sands in an hour glass.

Train travel has become something more now than merely having wings. These last weeks, for the long, solitary hours when the world's richest civilization is passing by beyond the windows, I feel something around me and within, gently and silently possessing my senses. It presses softly, Theophilus. But I am afraid of it. I do not want to hear what it says.

High in the mountain passes, time acquires a dimension of its own. Horace, who wrote many poems on the passing of time, wrote one to a young man, not much more than a boy, that begins:

> *Vides ut alta stet nive candidum*
> *Soracte . . .*

You see how Soracte stands shimmering in deep snow.
How the straining woods no longer support their burden.
How the rivers are halted by the sharp ice.

Bent trees and frozen rivers—Horace's images of life made images of death! He asks the boy to contemplate death:

Leave the rest to the gods, for once they have stilled
The winds that clash over the seething deep,
There is only stillness in the cypresses and old ash trees.

Contemplate death, and live in the present. In ode after ode, Horace sings that we should grasp the present moment. *Carpe diem*. Grasp and hold it. But increasingly I find that I cannot grasp or hold. Each irreversible moment is gone in the instant of becoming. Horace, a good Epicurean, knew that too. *Dum loquimur*—even as we talk, time has already fled.

As the train moves through the Alps and the blown snow presses against the window pane, I sleep fitfully and dream.

The mountain is shimmering in snow, saw-toothed, steep, and glistening. The trees beneath me bend under their weight of whiteness, their straining tips pointed to the ground. The rivers are halted. The sky above is radiantly clear, and I can see, it seems, infinitely far in all directions. Somewhere, in one direction, I should see Rome, its churches and monuments, and my hill, my window, my bed. But I cannot find them. Then I remark how strangely flat and dimensionless Italy has become. There is nothing on the horizon. The trees and rivers beneath me fade and disappear. This is not Italy or Canada or any landscape I have ever seen. Everything is white. Someone is calling my name. White! No. That's Leukos. Leukos is white. But my name, Loukos, does not mean white. Luke was the evangelist healer, the doctor with healing hands.

In the dream I tell the boy who is suddenly there beside me, looking at the mountain, to think about dying. Leave the rest to God. God hasn't finished the story yet.

The rest of the dream is gone.

In the morning sun, snowy Zurich is, from the wet windows of a clanging tram, a mass of colors. Busy shoppers crowd the tree-lined avenues. Store windows immodestly display chocolates by the hundreds. Prosperity preaches from every warm scarf and ruddy face. The river, broad and dull beneath its bridges, provides some relief from the relentless technicolor. The boy Ganymede, elegantly sculpted, with snow on his head and shoulders, keeps watch over the lake.

At the opera they are giving *Der Rosenkavalier*. On the stage is a superb actress with a silvery voice. She sings the role which is the finest creation of Richard Strauss and his librettist Hugo von Hofmannsthal —the Marschallin, the field marshall's wife. Forced into marriage at a tender age to an army officer much older than she, she has played the part expected of her with dignity and kindness for many years. She has also consoled herself with aristocratic lovers, and the one she is with now is younger than she.

Then she is alone in her silver-white boudoir. Her mind runs back to the time when she was young and innocent. Where, she wonders as she looks into her mirror, is that little girl now? Where are the snows of yesteryear? Surely this is one of the mysteries of life. One feels oneself always the same person, yet one knows that he or she is constantly changing. The mirror shows that the face changes. Innocence, purity, sweetness all fade. Compromises are invariably made, with life, with principles, with promises—and yet somehow one remains the same. How can God let this happen? And if it must happen, why has he given *her* an understanding of it? Could he not have hidden it from her? Or could she not simply disregard it, as others do? It is too much to bear.

Now she is confiding to the young man she has loved. It is time to let him go. "Time," she sings, "is a strange thing. When you live for the moment, it means nothing at all. Then, of a sudden, there seems to be nothing else."

He doesn't understand.

"Time is all around us," she says. "It is inside us. It shifts in our faces. It swirls in the mirror. It flows in my temples. It flows between you and me. Silent, like the sands in an hourglass. Oh, often I hear it flowing, irrevocably. Often I get up in the middle of the night, and make all, all the clocks, stand still . . ."

He doesn't understand.

She tries to explain. It is time for her to let him go. One must take what one takes lightly, with light heart and light hands. "Hold and take, hold and let go." All things are passing. Both life and God will have it so.

He understands a little, and leaves.

All of a sudden, she realizes she has seen him for the last time on intimate terms, and calls him back—too late. He has slipped from her, like any lightly held object caught in the flux of time.

She sits again at her dressing table and slowly lifts the mirror to her face. The music is radiant. With infinite sadness, she lowers the hand that holds the mirror.

Hurtling back through an Alpine storm, I sleep dreamlessly through Switzerland. Each moment passes by, and the present becomes, irrevocably, the past. The train moves forward, braving its way into the swirling snow.

In Milan, the new production of Verdi's *Otello* is *esaurito*. In most cities the "sold out" sign doesn't stop a seasoned operagoer, but in Milan, one of the three or four great opera centers in the world, even veteran ticket hustlers quail when they see the notice. "Sold out" at La Scala really means you don't get in.

I cross the street, make my way through the Galleria, and emerge from its far end to fill my eyes with one of Europe's greatest cathedrals, its massive doors sculpted with archetypal scenes, its delicate Gothic spires a lacework against a slate-gray sky. I have a toast and a caffe latte at a small bar that is welcomely warm, and return to La Scala to wait in line for standing room. The atmosphere is very like that among standees at the Met or in Munich or Vienna. Standees everywhere are knowledgeable, opinionated, ruthless, and wary of any unfamiliar face. No one is accepted until he is tested on operatic lore, much of it local, much of it trivial, some of it significant. I pass the test.

We standees are treated by the ticket sellers with less condescension than are the harried Japanese and American tourists who hope to get seats that night. The contempt displayed by the box office for those unfortunates is a wonder to behold.

Finally the ushers open the doors and, elderly veterans as they are, carefully stand back as we who have paid about eighty cents each clatter up a side staircase pell-mell to fill the standing places with the best views. I am not sufficiently nimble of foot or knowledgeable of doorways to secure a central location.

The sound is slightly disappointing from my upper-side vantage point, but the atmosphere in the vast auditorium is wonderfully tense and the performance is fiery enough to warm my chilled bones and make me forget the hard discomfort of standing at an angle: I've grasped a support to get a full view of the stage and I stay suspended in body and spirit through the four acts. This is Italian opera at the shrine of Italian opera.

Verdi sends a great, dissonant chord crashing through the vast theater at the very start of *Otello*, and at that chord the curtain rises, almost as in fear, on a storm. Winds clash over the seething deep. Huddled and fearful Cypriots are looking out from shore. Through flashes of lightning we see Otello's ships braving the elements. The people on shore sing that some savage, blind, inscrutable power is moving in the storm. They pray that it may spare them. I've always thought of that power in the storm as the God that Verdi said, all his life, we could never know.

Verdi's telling of the tale is more savage, more terrifying than Shakespeare's. It isn't just that his music, the music of a powerful old man, batters its way through the story as even Shakespeare's words do not. It's that Verdi has turned the story into an agnostic's question. Is the God who hurls the forked lightning and whirls the exterminating sea a force of good or of evil? Is his human agent the chilling Iago who sings "I believe in one God, a cruel God, who made me in his own image"? Or does he work instead through the gentle Desdemona? It hardly seems that that can be true. Her very name seems to indicate that she is helpless in the hands of a malignant power. She dies at Otello's hands. Iago escapes.

The world, reality, whatever you want to call it, is a terrible place. It always was, since we evolved from the "primeval slime" Iago sings of. And it always will be until, like Iago, we go to our graves and find that after death there is nothing.

At least, that is the way *Otello* speaks to me this night. Even the infinitely compassionate music Verdi gives his heartbroken, dark-skinned soldier-hero at the close does not seem, tonight, to soften the terrifying message.

God may be good. But so far as Verdi can see, God is not good.

Next morning from the window of a noisy Italian train, I watch the morning break along the Apennines, then drop off to sleep again. Back in sunny Rome, I find my room just as I left it, and I climb to the roof to see Mount Soracte, peacefully shimmering in snow.

5

LENT IS ALMOST UPON US, and on the last long weekend before Ash Wednesday, I take my last long train ride before the rail pass expires. It will take me briefly behind the Iron Curtain.

More and more, the train rides have been opportunities for solitude. I have awaited them eagerly. At the end of each trip is some great work of art through which I can meet and commune with someone, a painter or architect or dramatist or composer, greater than I, more sensitive and more intimately acquainted with the feelings I am now more and more confronted with.

But on these winter days, equally rewarding as the experience at the final destination have been the long solitudes on the way there and back, gently imposed by the onward movement of the train.

Even when the compartment is full of people, Italians sharing with me their bread and wine or arguing politics heatedly with each other, or even when I have been alone with some man or woman who tells me his or her heartrending story—even then I can feel something of a presence that, when I am left alone, begins to wrap me round. I feel it strongly and surely when, at the entrance to the mountains, I am alone in a compartment speeding past the familiar villages.

O beata solitudo—O blessed solitude—was the legend over the entrance to the cloistered convent where once, in the early years of my priesthood, I served as chaplain. The place was so silent I used to say that the silence spoke. God sometimes needs silence to make himself heard. When Jesus wanted to meet his Father, he found a place of solitude. And there his Father wrapped him round.

These long train rides, more than any monastic discipline I have known, have taught me the blessedness of solitude. The world speeding by without, I within caught by the strange, still feeling that seems always hovering around me, trying to possess me. On the early trips I was conscious mainly of my own eagerness to see and hear, to identify the lakes and hill towns. Orvieto, where Fra Angelico, blessed in his poverty, began painting his Apocalypse in a great marble cathedral set on a rock fastness. Trasimene, where Hannibal outmaneuvered the Roman armies. Garda, where the poet Catullus returned from his travels to his almost-island home. Vicenza, where Palladio created his chaste architectural wonders.

But on subsequent trips, the pleasures of discovery have given way to deeper feelings. I have become aware of my own restlessness and compulsiveness, driven always to fill the available time with the most experience. I have begun to realize that the real encounter, the real experience, is within me. I travel as often and as quickly as before, but now with the anticipation of surrendering to the stillness that will surround me once the train speeds on its way. In the lakes of Italy's north, in the mountains of Switzerland, in the forests and along the rivers of Germany, I hear the stillness which is the speaking of God. I discover that as the only place where I can discover myself.

"You ought always to pray," St. Paul told his churches.

Sister Teresina, the little nun who taught us in first grade, insisted, "You ought always to pray." And she told this story: "An Indian chief once asked a missionary what he should do to be with God. The missionary said he ought always to pray. The Indian started off on a long journey to the mountains. When he returned the missionary asked him, 'How often did you pray?' The Indian answered, 'Only once. But that was all the way.'"

The train reaches the mountains. Thunder and lightning crack and roar. The car shudders to a halt, then starts up through pelting rain. I sleep:

> And the angel of the Lord said to Elijah, "Thou hast a long way to go." And he walked forty days and forty nights unto Horeb, the mountain of God. And when he came there, he went into a cave and spent the night in it. Then the word of the Lord came to him. "Go out and stand on the mountain before the Lord."
>
> And the Lord himself went by. There came a mighty wind, so strong it shook the mountains and shattered the rocks before the Lord. But the Lord was not in the wind.
>
> After the wind came an earthquake. But the Lord was not in the earthquake.
>
> After the earthquake came a fire. But the Lord was not in the fire.
>
> After the fire there came the sound of a gentle breeze. And when

Elijah heard this, he covered his face with his cloak and stood at the entrance of the cave.

I awake and turn my face, trembling for what I might hear. I hear nothing. Sharp pains are jabbing at my ears. For a moment there is no sound in them. Then the pain passes.

"Do you now believe?" Jesus said. "I am not alone, because my Father is with me. These things I have spoken to you that in me you may have peace."

The train moves upward into the night. It is easy to pray:

> O Lord, you have probed me and you know me.
> You know when I sit and when I stand.
> You understand my thoughts from afar.
>
> Even before a word is on my tongue,
> Behold, O Lord, you know the whole of it.
>
> Behind me and before, you hem me in
> And rest your hand upon me.
>
> Such knowledge is too wonderful for me,
> Too lofty for me to attain.
>
> Where can I go from your spirit?
> From your presence where can I flee?
>
> If I go up to the heavens, you are there.
> If I sink to the nether world, you are present there.
>
> If I take the wings of the dawn,
> If I settle at the farthest limits of the sea,
>
> Even there your hand shall guide me,
> And your right hand hold me fast.
>
> If I say, "Surely the darkness shall hide me,
> And night shall be my light,"
>
> For you darkness itself is not dark,
> And night shines as the day.
>
> Truly you have formed my inmost being.
> You knit me in my mother's womb.
>
> I give you thanks that I am fearfully, wonderfully made.
> Wonderful are your works.

My soul also you knew full well, nor was my frame unknown
    to you,
When I was made in secret, when I was fashioned in the depths
    of the earth.

Your eyes have seen my actions. In your book they are all written.
My days were limited before one of them existed.

How weighty are your designs, O God,
How vast the sum of them!

Were I to recount them they would outnumber the sands.
Did I reach the end of them, I should still be with you.

Rain is still dashing against the window. I want to pray more, but I
drop off to sleep.

Lucerne is not, this day, the idyllic place where Wagner wrote his
Meistersinger in a poplar-lined villa beneath Mount Pilatus. It is blustery and businesslike. In the trim little opera house not far from the
lake where, on a clear day, you can easily feel you are on top of the
world, Mozart's Idomeneo steers his ship out of a storm after praying
to his god that, if he be saved, he will sacrifice the first living creature
that he shall find on shore. The first living thing he finds on shore is
his own son. And the god expects to be paid.

A raw wind sweeps through Vienna as the train pulls in. The palaces
inside the Ring seem more forlorn, the shopkeepers surlier, the coffeehouses shabbier, than I remembered. St. Stephen's, the center of
the city, looks forbidding.

Mozart died here, in a little house, now demolished, a few blocks
from St. Stephen's. He was only thirty-five, but his strength was
utterly spent. He had been made to pass his early years in the cruel and
exhausting business of being exhibited publicly, before kings and
queens, as a phenomenon of nature—for he was composing at the age
of four and playing at the keyboard before that. He wrote sonatas
when he was six, symphonies when he was eight, operas when he was
twelve. Even as a boy, he could improvise any kind of music on
request, in any key. He could carry hours of music in his head. His
own music—fully composed but not yet committed to paper—or
someone else's, like the papal *Miserere* of Allegri that no one, under
pain of excommunication, could copy. The boy Mozart heard it, and

wrote it out note for note. The pope, utterly astonished, made him a knight.

But the great world was more interested in him when he was a boy to marvel at than when he was a man and able to work real miracles with his music. He wrote so many compositions that it would take an average man thirty-five years just to get the notes down on paper— more than six hundred works, in every field of musical composition. There were concertos and quintets so delicately nuanced that at moments it seemed a breath might blow them away; yet they were structurally as strong and solid as any conservatory fugue. There were songs, too, and Masses and chamber works and symphonies and sonatas and serenades. Above all, there were operas—prismatic dramas in which past conventions were swept aside, characters were vividly realized, and the tragic was boldly interlaid with the comic.

His music was neither tragic nor comic but a marvelous fusion of both. It wasn't Italian or German or French but was all of those traditions blended in a new style. It was all-encompassing music that looked back upon baroque and rococo and forward to Romanticism. Today it seems surprisingly modern.

But it wasn't music to meet his expenses or pay his debts. In those days, a Mozart quartet with enough inspiration in it to last most composers a lifetime could be commissioned for a pittance, performed once before an indifferent audience, and then discarded. To live, a composer needed a position, and Mozart had few friends, and many enemies, at the imperial courts and salons. He had to write quickly, often for popular tastes, to make the money that was never enough, somehow, to pay the bills. And as he lay dying, he wrote, "I have come to an end before I have realized the fullness of my talent." It is one of the glories of mankind that he lived at all, and one of the tragedies that he lived so briefly. He died still trying, in his delirium, to complete the Requiem Mass he had come to feel he was composing for his own death. Meanwhile a new opera, perhaps the greatest of his works, *The Magic Flute*, was playing in a people's theater across the city.

And it is *The Magic Flute* that I see in Vienna that night, for a little outlay of money, in the Volksoper, a popular counterpart to the great Staatsoper. It is carnival time, and the house is full of children, whose mothers and fathers have brought them to see Papageno the bird-man make music with his magic glockenspiel and leap into a nest with his Papagena to beget a family of little bird-people.

But the children in the theater are interested in the main characters as well—the childlike prince and princess who travel from the world of the mother, the Queen of the Night, to the world of the father, the mysterious Sarastro.

The fairy-tale opera is full of folk tunes, Masonic symbols, intimations of older Italian operas, and anticipations of forthcoming German operas. It is fearfully, wonderfully made. It is, like so much of Mozart, a miraculous fusion of tragic and comic elements. The symbolic story has echoes of Virgil and anticipations of Goethe.

And there is a crazy insouciance in the scenic motifs demanded by the text—palm trees, pyramids, floating aircraft, bells, mystic temples, animals both wild and charmingly tamed. Most of all, there are the symbols of rebirth—the prince and princess together pass through the masculine element, fire, and the feminine, water. At the end, Sarastro's sun rises and lights up the whole theater. While the music is still playing, lights go on all over the house, and it is as if we in the audience are part of the performance, kin with the prancing animals and with the happy couples united after all their trials.

If Mozart could compose such a wonder at thirty-five, what might he have done in his mature years? Operas on the *Odyssey*, *The Tempest*, *Faust*. Never to be written.

There is a quotation from Mozart in the program. Something he wrote his father to silence that insistent man's moral strictures. "Do not be worried. I have God always before my eyes. I recognize his power. I feel his anger. But I also know his compassion and his charity toward his creatures. He will not abandon his servant. What happens according to his will happens also according to mine."

Surrender. I have heard that strain at the profoundest moments in his music. He was God's instrument, sent to bear witness in his music to the wonder of flesh and blood, of heart and of mind, and to the existence of a truth and beauty beyond these. God let his instrument play only long enough to convince us of those important things. Then he silenced him.

The Iron Curtain has been partially lifted. In Dresden, which is again accessible to American travelers—diplomatic relations having been established only this year between the United States and East Germany—I am given a brochure at the train station: "Welcome to Dresden. Today we would like to invite you to our socialist city."

That greeting matches the first impression of the famous old Saxon capital as seen from the train. What must once have been the most beautiful baroque city in Europe, more beautiful even than Salzburg, Würzburg, or Prague, is, a quarter-century after the bombing, still something of a wasteland. A mile of cheapjack pseudo-modern buildings and vast empty stretches of bleak pavement lead the eye to a few, pathetically few, eighteenth-century domes on a misty skyline. The city that once looked to Paris for its spirit and was often called Florence on the Elbe now draws its life from the Soviet East. Signs read Leninplatz, Café Leningrad, and "Socialism conquers." As the brochure puts it, "The city of Dresden is friendly tied with many towns in the world. The ties are especially close with the city of Leningrad which has a lot in common with the city of Dresden, and also with Wroclaw, Ostrava, and Skopje."

It is "Springtime in Cuba" the radio plays as I plump my suitcase down in my cheerless prepaid room. The brochure reminds me, "For centuries the brilliant and pompous royal court of Saxon Sovereigns swallowed vast fortunes which had to be earned by the people. Glory was placed upon Pöppelmann, Permoser, and Chiaveri who were the creators of the world-renowned baroque buildings, yet unnamed remained the numerous constructors whose craftsmanship contributed much toward Dresden's worldwide fame."

I head toward the Elbe. The brochure continues. "Capitalism developed quickly in the nineteenth century. . . . A new stage of exploiting the people was born. . . . it was always the working class which fought against reaction and terror."

Near the Elbe the Zwinger stands proudly, restored to some of its "brilliant and pompous" state, with Raphael's Sistine Madonna in the place of honor. The spiel of a tour guide takes over from the brochure. "In the centuries of superstition in Europe, artists were forced to paint religious subjects." True up to a point, I grant, as passing through the gallery I see an Angelico *Annunciation* and a Correggio *Nativity* and two of the most famous faces of Christ—Veronese's *Wedding at Cana* and Titian's *Paying the Tribute*. Forced to paint religious subjects? All of the pictures seem to me to have about as much real devotion in them as have the depictions of St. George and St. Cecilia, familiar from childhood prayer books, that hang in their company.

The collection is a great one—Velázquez, Tintoretto, Rembrandt, El Greco. Some of the paintings are scenes from antiquity, not without traces of humor—Rubens's *Judgment of Paris,* with its three oversized goddesses, Reni's *Bacchus* performing a natural function, and Jordaens's *Hercules Drunk.*

Many of the tourists are Russian, soldiers and peasants and poor folk, staring uncomprehendingly at what they see. Two Soviet soldiers, boys perhaps not yet out of their teens, dutifully inspect the paintings and respond, not with middle-class wisecracks and put-downs, as American soldiers might, but with modest, quiet, puzzled expressions. I offer to explain, in German, who Hercules was and how he came to drink so much. I tell them a little bit, too, about Virgil's sixth eclogue, which contributed something to the picture. They listen attentively and understand the German, but not the explanation. They see nothing humorous about the pictures, though they smile politely and thank me. I ask where they are from. One is from a farm, the other from Kiev. Where am I from? The United States. The smiles fade, and they exchange worried glances. Though they are soldiers, they look nervously about to see who has seen us talking together. Nothing I say after that gets any response. Shy before, they are defensive now. They quickly move away from me.

Why shouldn't they? In the world war that destroyed Dresden, fifty-six million people perished. Of those, twenty million were their people. Twenty million! Now I represent the country that is, to those young men, another threat—worse, perhaps, than the Germans had been.

I stroll the upper and lower levels of the smoke-blackened but still beautiful rococo complex, see its Nymphenbad grotto and its famous porcelain collection. The complex and delicate figurines can almost be set in motion by walking around them. They have, a plaque proclaims, been rescued by the Soviet government from the fascists of the West and are now restored to their rightful owners, the people of the German Democratic Republic, by their Soviet brothers. But if I remember rightly, it was the Germans who hid the treasures of the Zwinger underground before the air raids began, and the Soviets who claimed them and carried them off after the war, and the Germans again who insisted on their being restored to Dresden.

But Dresden is not a place to sort out the guilt and try to scale down the blame on this side or that. I am humbled, not offended, when a young girl in the post office refuses to answer my queries about mailing to the United States, refuses in fact to speak to me about anything. As the brochure reminds me almost impassively, "Dresden was buried under debris shortly before the end of the Second World War, although the defeat of the Hitler Germany was inevitable. In the night from 13 to 14 February, 1945, Anglo-American bombers discharged their deadly load upon the city. Almost half a million incendiary and high-explosive bombs fell in the city, killing 35,000 men, women and children. 75,000 homes, mainly in the working-class quarters, were completely destroyed, and further 100,000 damaged." The statistics go on, speaking for themselves.

They almost surely understate. Probably more people were trapped and killed here than in either Hiroshima or Nagasaki, perhaps more than in the two atom-bombed cities combined.

Dresden was fire-bombed. Back at the school, I had read the terrible story as David Irving told it. The war in Europe had less than three months to go, and Dresden had been spared, save for one raid, which the local inhabitants wrote off as an Allied mistake, and another air attack confined to the rail yards. The Dresdeners thought that their inner city would be spared because it was so beautiful. They thought that there was some agreement that the English would spare Dresden if the Germans spared Oxford. Their economy, after all, rested chiefly on their city's art and music, and on only a few small industries. And they were fond of the British. When a British private, a prisoner of war in the city, was killed in the second Allied raid, the Dresdeners respected the Geneva Convention and buried him with full military honors.

Their feeling of security increased as their city was called on to house more and more civilian and military hospital facilities. It also contained thousands of POWs, many of them British and American, and for four months it had been taking in Silesian and other refugees fleeing, in midwinter, the advance of the Soviet armies from the East. That exodus eventually numbered some five million. Hundreds of thousands of those streamed into Dresden. They were mostly women and children. The city swelled to more than twice its peacetime population. Irving says, "It was as though fate were conspiring to ensure that by the time that the middle days of February arrived, the maximum number of refugees would be sheltering in the capital city of Saxony."

Then at ten o'clock on the eve of Ash Wednesday, some of the people must have noticed flares dropping over parts of the city, and still more must have heard the oncoming roar of the first attack of the mightiest armada ever sent into the skies. That night and the following morning the British launched fourteen hundred planes in two separate waves. Bombs began raining down on Dresden's inner city, and never anywhere had they rained so heavily. The British, famous for precision bombing, proved themselves equally adept at what came to be called saturation bombing. They systematically distributed to each square yard of the inner city an equal weight of explosives. They found their task amazingly easy, as Dresden was virtually undefended. The British flew across the rooftops at low altitudes with no antiaircraft to oppose them. Their weapons were, as the phrase goes, conventional.

The high-explosive bombs, lit by flares, crashed through the inner city's domed churches, gilded palaces, rococo buildings, and thousand-year-old half-timbered houses lined along cobbled streets. That first wave of aircraft left the city a flaming beacon in the night to guide a second airborne attack three hours later—mighty Lancasters with their load of a half-million incendiary bombs. These were dropped according to calculations designed to start a firestorm. The great vortices of wind and fire that had unexpectedly formed in previous air raids on Hamburg, Kassel, Darmstadt, and Braunschweig were deliberately planned this time for Dresden. These were the first man-made tornadoes, whirling tornadoes of fire, unprecedented in their destructive power.

The whirlwind of fire in Dresden was far more devastating than any previous firestorm. It covered virtually the whole of the old city, eleven square miles. The flaming buildings heated the air overhead to such intensity that winds were sucked in from all sides of the bombed area with hurricane force. Great sheets of flame fifty feet long went shooting through the streets from all directions, to converge in a single mass of fire. People fleeing the flames were lifted up and hurled screaming into the inferno. What could a child do if even a great tree could be sucked up from its roots by the stupendous force of the firestorm winds and swept away to extinction?

People in the bomb shelters were no more fortunate, for the intense heat of the firestorm turned the shelters into crematoria. The shelterers were incinerated.

People in the neighboring villages heard the sounds of the bombs exploding, and then they heard a sound new to human ears—the steady roar of the man-made whirlwind howling in the streets of Dresden.

> Quis cladem illius noctis, quis funera fando
> explicet aut possit lacrimis aequare labores?
> Urbs antiqua ruit multos dominata per annos.

So the prophetic Virgil wondered, looking back on the fall of Troy and, perhaps, forward to this devastation: "Who could tell the destruction of that night? Who could count the number of the dead, or match their suffering with his tears? A city that had surpassed all others in beauty through many years was falling in ruin."

As Ash Wednesday dawned, a cloud of yellow smoke three miles high hung over Dresden. Fragments of baroque buildings and pieces of human bodies were still being caught up by the firestorm, to be rained down days later many miles away.

At noon American forces took over from the British with more than a thousand additional planes—Flying Fortresses with maximum bomb-carrying capacity, and Mustangs to fly low over the fringes of the old city and strafe anything that still moved. They did not attack the German airfields, and they did minimal damage to the rail yards. The intent was to destroy the city and its people. They opened fire on the choirboys from the Frauenkirche fleeing along the Tiergarten-strasse, on the homeless groups huddled by the banks of the Elbe, and even on animals in the zoo.

Later on Ash Wednesday, the British launched another expedition to nearby Chemnitz with orders "to fire on any refugees who may have escaped from Dresden." The legitimate targets in Chemnitz, its tank works and its rail yards, were not destroyed.

The next day another American force, finding visibility poor over Ruhland, dropped their load on Dresden instead. But by that time a few more hundred tons of bombs hardly mattered. Dresden was by then a flaming corpse: *Tum vero omne mihi visum considere in ignis Ilium.*

The city burned for five, six, seven days. When the churches and hospitals, houses and palaces were smoldering heaps of rubble, the survivors from the edges of the old city had little time to feel sorry for themselves. The danger of a typhus epidemic threatened, and the Soviet army was only seventy miles away. They began the terrible work of cleaning up, though parts of the city were too hot even to enter for several weeks. When the inner shelters were finally opened, everything left inside them instantly burst into flames.

In the homes that had lain within the whirlwind, they found, as people had found in Kassel after the firestorm there, bodies turned brilliant colors by asphyxiation. In the streets they found, as people had found in Darmstadt, charred logs three feet long that once had been men and women. In the shelters, it was worse. One cellar was inundated with a foot-deep pool of human blood, flesh, and bone, all that remained of some two or three hundred people. Hardened soldiers refused orders to go on with the cleaning up and were summarily executed. *Plurima perque vias*: "The dead lay everywhere—they lay in the streets, they lay in the houses, they lay on the steps of the places where they had worshiped . . . " But Virgil had not foreseen the worst.

Near the railroad station, for reasons no one knew, there were piles of dead children. Parts of bodies littered the streets, heads and arms torn away. Eventually attempts to identify corpses had to be halted and what were once human beings were bulldozed into mass graves. In the center of the city the dead were stacked in piles of five hundred on quickly improvised grids and set afire. Some still had bits of festive clothing on. The eve of Ash Wednesday had been carnival time.

Meanwhile, even as the dead were being burned and buried, five hundred more American aircraft attacked other parts of the city.

A month and a half later, hundreds of basements had still not been cleared, and the rats started taking over what was left from the worst destruction in the history of warfare.

There are still some people who say that the Dresdeners and the refugees they sheltered were guilty and deserved their fate, that they were only being paid back for what was done in the concentration camps.

Almost thirty years after the destruction of Dresden, I walk the partially rebuilt streets with emotions as strong as any I have ever felt. Occasionally, at the ruins of the Frauenkirche or the Semper Opera House, I can see something of the beauty that once was. In front of the house where nine of Richard Strauss's operas received their first performances, I say to an old woman with a shopping bag, hardly knowing how I intend my words to sound, "It's still very beautiful."

She will not look at me. "It was more beautiful before," she says laconically, and walks on.

It is late Saturday afternoon, and I hear Mass at the Katholisches Hofkirche, partially restored. The Gospel is about Jesus rebuking Thomas for his little faith. At the Prayer of the Faithful, the congregation prays for forgiveness for its lack of faith. I am abashed and full of wonder as I see that most of the people are my age and older. Surely their terrible experience was the greatest possible test of faith, in God and in the men he made.

At the opera that night, in a theater that will serve till the Semper is rebuilt, I am seated on the main floor next to a man in his sixties who wears a heavy black glove on an artificial hand and breathes with great effort from a mutilated face. He does not apologize to me for the constant noise he so painfully produces. He doesn't look at me at all, or at anyone else. He keeps his head fixed rigidly forward, his face intent on the stage action. A soldier still. His wife sits at his side, simply but elegantly dressed. She knows when to help him and when to leave him to himself. She rests her arm on his through the performance. Her face, lined and thin and circled by abundant silvery hair, is quietly beautiful. I am reminded of the faithful wife by her suffering husband's side in Beethoven's *Fidelio*, but the opera that night is Verdi's *Nabucco*, a work increasingly popular in postwar Germany. The Jewish exiles on stage, paraphrasing Psalm 137, sing "Go, thought, on golden wings and light on the hills where the winds of our native land blow soft. O my country so lovely and so lost! May the Lord give us the strength to endure our suffering." It is as if whole peoples, on both sides of the worst war mankind has known, are lifting their voices.

On another misty, wet morning, I resolve to see Dresden from the vantage point of the famous 1945 photograph, from the top of the *Rathausturm*—an angel bending consolingly over a city devastated as far as the eye can see. I take the elevator to the top of the Rathaus and stand alone where the photographer stood that morning, near the consoling angel—actually, I now see, a personified virtue. The city lies far below, the outlines of its streets clear in the dampness, but not so clear as they were that midnight when Ash Wednesday began. When the second wave of British bombers flew over the city that night, they saw Dresden in flames from one end to the other. One of the navigators recorded that his pilot called him from his position to "come and have a look." He saw a city etched in fire. The river itself seemed to be on fire, as in Virgil the straits of Sigaeum reflected the flames of falling Troy. The heat over Dresden was so intense that, at twenty thousand feet, the airmen could feel it inside their planes. The midnight sky was white, streaked with red. As they flew off, they could see the flames from two hundred miles away.

How many died here? German, British, American, and Soviet estimates range from 35,000 to 150,000 and more. No one can tell. Thousands of homeless refugees were never found after the war, and it is presumed that many of them perished in the wind-driven firestorm at Dresden.

We still do not know why Dresden, a virtually defenseless city, was singled out to be the victim of the largest air attack in history. The English master bomber who had what he was told was the honor of dropping the first bomb on a virgin target thought the purpose of his mission was to destroy rail connections—but in fact the railway lines lay completely out of the sector designated for saturation bombing, and Dresden's trains were running again within three days. British, Canadian, and Australian bomber crews were informed that the city was a German army headquarters, that it housed arms and supply dumps, that it was the center of a munitions industry, that it contained a poison gas plant, that it was a Gestapo headquarters—but little if any of this was true. For the British chief of staff a prime motive for the attack on the German city was to drive its thousands of refugees out onto the roads and so impede the progress of the German armies—but in fact most of the refugees were trapped in the inferno and never escaped from the city to clog the roads. It was said afterward that the destruction was done in retaliation for the German bombing of Coventry—but if so, it was horrendous overkill, as the carnage in Dresden was a hundred times that in Coventry, and the damage to the city was incalculably greater.

It was said afterward that Dresden was bombed in payment for what the Germans had done to Rotterdam (and indeed the whole madness of civilian bombing can be said to have started there, by the order of the crazed German High Command), but for every death in Rotterdam, after the issue of an ultimatum, fifty died in Dresden, without advance warning.

The only convincing reason for the attack, and a terrible reason it is, is that the Allies wanted, after the Yalta conference, to demonstrate to the Soviets the sheer destructive power of their air forces. The American State Department, eight years later, announced that the bombing was undertaken "in response to Soviet requests for increased aerial support, and was cleared in advance with the Soviet authorities." If that was so, the gesture failed utterly in its aims. The Soviets said nothing and did not advance. They entered the city only when the war was won. Thereafter they used the destruction of Dresden as a typical example of capitalist savagery.

I stand looking over a Communist Dresden. In 1945, the poet Gerhardt Hauptmann looked on it from a hillside as it burned day after day. He saw the beautiful old city die. He was eighty-three, and his heart almost gave way. He sent a message to the world, pleading with all of us to learn again to weep. He knew there were good people in England and America. With all his heart he asked God to show us, on both sides of the fighting, his love. He begged God to help us purify ourselves.

As little as possible was said about Dresden in England and America. In his six-volume account of the war, Winston Churchill gave the bombing of Dresden one noncommittal sentence.

The elevator man at the *Rathausturm,* old enough to be my father, does not, I think, see my wet face as he opens his gate to take me down, his only customer that morning. He seems to have his gaze permanently directed downward. But when I turn away from him, I think he sees my shoulders shake with sobs.

It is Sunday. The churches, Lutheran and Catholic, are packed, the boy choirs equally good in the Kreuzkirche and the Hofkirche, where the Silberman organ has been restored and the "Amens" roll like thunder from the pews. It is both humbling and heartening to see and hear this affirmation—heartening, for the vast new government Culture Palace has also opened early this Sunday, with competitive attractions like low-priced movies. There Lenin's picture, in large and small reproductions, faces the worshiper at every turn. But there are no crowds.

How can anyone feel bitterness toward these survivors? The suffering Jews who survived the death camps refounded their homeland and saw it flourish. The suffering survivors of Hiroshima and Nagasaki were able to rebuild their cities, and their country thrived. The Dresdeners who survived found that their city, when it was rebuilt, was not their city any more. It was a Russian outpost.

Who can apportion the guilt for these terrible happenings? After we in the West destroyed the body of this city, the Communist East began destroying its soul. If I had been born in Dresden between the wars, had survived that horrendous February, and then seen my city, famous for its art and music, rise from its ashes a jerry-built socialist showcase, I think I would have despaired.

On the short train ride to Leipzig I talk with two teenage boys, one homely and studious, wearing thick glasses, the other handsome and self-assured under his little red cap. They have never spoken with an American before, but they are quick to make jokes, which I am expected to find amusing, about American slums and shooting in the streets. "From Detroit!" they exclaim. "Where is your gun?" they ask. "How many blacks have you killed?"

I try to win them over with quiet responses, accepting some of their accusations as true, refuting others without passion or rue. I ask them about their city, Leipzig, and they tell me, with no special pride, that it has the largest railroad station in Europe. I ask about the Thomaskirche, where Bach labored for many years, and for which he wrote his *Saint Matthew Passion.*

"God is dead," says the handsome one.

"With us he is not," I say quickly, in German too simple, I think, to be effective. And yet that registers. The boy has not expected quiet admissions of failure and a firm belief in God from an American. (I do not wear my collar. Travelling in Eastern Europe is too complicated for that kind of affirmation.)

I tell them of the feelings I had in Dresden, and I cannot help betraying some emotion. This, again, is not how Americans are supposed to feel. But, like Tim, the boys are not interested in talking about past wars, which are not their wars. The studious one asks about Henry and William James, about Thoreau and Melville. I ask him about Goethe, Lessing, and Schiller. (They don't seem to know our twentieth-century writers and I don't want to take a chance on their reaction to my knowing theirs.) They ask what I do for a living.

"I teach Latin and Greek."

They look stunned.

"Yes, we are interested in such things in the United States."

We have almost reached Leipzig when I feel that I am getting through to them. The thought occurs here, as it had in Rome with Tim, that these could be my sons, had I been born in East Germany, and married.

The handsome one, slower of the two to come round, asks suddenly, "What year were you born?"

I tell him.

"You are so old as my father."

The look I give him—Virgilian *pietas?*—is too much for him. He turns away quickly.

At one of the many gates in the truly immense train station, I say good-bye to the two boys, so friendly now that they point my direction to the proper tram line for my prepaid hotel, and insist on putting the fare in my hand.

The bombing here was not so heavy, and Leipzig is, happily, still recognizable as a German city. Though the central squares are bedecked with red placards and filled, again, with Russian soldiers, though the new opera house is festooned with banners announcing *Springtime in Ukraine* as the current attraction, some of the homes and narrow streets look almost as they might have when Wagner was a boy here.

It is evening, and snow is falling. I watch the brass-buttoned, bemedaled Russian officers and their expensively dressed wives entering the opera house, which for sheer massiveness holds its own with the railway station and dwarfs my hotel, also full of Soviets. I stroll to Auerbach's Cellar, where Goethe's Faust once drank with the devil and astonished the university students. The cellar now is touristy—Faust and Mephistopheles are sculpted on the staircase—and very popular with the locals. I have a beer there with three workers in their late twenties.

"*Amerikaner?*" They can't believe it. Americans don't come to Leipzig, or if they do they don't descend to Auerbach's Cellar alone and drink with the natives.

The three are outspoken and friendly, as all Germans are over their beer. They want to know what I am doing in Europe.

"Teaching for a year, in Rome."

One of the three had gone to university as long as he could afford it. "Rome. *Gott*, how I would like to see Rome," he says—too loudly, I think. He asks about the city, and I start in, perhaps too volubly, about the Vatican, the Pantheon . . .

His eyes widen, then narrow.

"I want to go to Rome."

"Quiet, Helmut!"

"Rome!" Louder this time. "I don't want a week in Skopje. I want to see Rome!"

They clutch at his coat as he gets up on his chair.

"To hell with Kiev! To hell with Ostrava and Sofia!" He's up on the table, with his beer mug held high. "Paris! Venice! Rome! I want to see Rome!"

They pull him down and quiet him and tell me I'd better leave.

I do.

Outside, the snow is falling heavily. The old city looks like a Christmas card, with its sixteenth-century Alt Rathaus, its delicately rococo

Börse and its monuments to Goethe and Luther and Bach all edged in white.

Behind Bach is the church for which he wrote music for more than twenty years, the Thomaskirche. I am lucky they are not singing a real opera at the opera house this evening, for I might have gone there and missed the concert in the Thomaskirche—one of its bimonthly Sunday night organ recitals. I find a seat on the upper level and sit in meditation through six of the master's pieces played with affectionate care. The other quiet listeners are almost all young people, university students, bound as if by a spell. Everyone senses the sincerity and faith of the man who wrote a thousand works so important for his successors that he is called the "father of music." (And he once said, half meaning it, I think, "Any devout man could do as much as I have, if he worked as hard.")

My gaze lingers on the pulpit where Luther preached, and on the baptismal font where Wagner was christened. From Luther's hymns to Bach's choral preludes to the great opening and closing choruses of that baptismal opera *Die Meistersinger*, Germany's art and faith were once rock fast, the soundest cultural foundation in Europe. Then came the terrible events of our century, visited by and on a Germany gone mad. Will this be a warning for us in the future? Will this unfortunate part of Germany ever reclaim its rightful heritage, or will it, within a generation, turn its face completely to the Soviet East?

The snow is still falling after the concert. The monuments of the famous Germans are thickly white, now rendered faceless and shapeless. The red placards, too, and the banners and pictures of Lenin are silent under nature's quiet covering.

All is calm.

In the morning I leap to the window. The snow has stopped, and the early sun on it makes the whole blanketed city sparkle. On the main floor of the hotel is a grand piano, and as this is the city of cities for keyboards, I presume to play on it. For an hour and a half. The hotel personnel presume that I have the necessary permission. I haven't, but before long the manager and his employees enter and listen and smile and ask me no questions. I don't attempt to play Bach, a presumption that wouldn't keep me at the keyboard for long. I play songs from *The Merry Widow* and *The White Horse Inn*, and then from *My Fair Lady* and *Fiddler on the Roof*. The Germans recognize the American tunes as well as the Continental favorites, and some of them sing along. The Russian tourists listen solemnly, not knowing that they aren't expected to take this music as seriously as the art they saw in the museums yesterday afternoon. They have been allowed to come to Germany to see and to learn, and they approach every experience with the same sense of duty.

A cheerful old man behind the desk calls me over when I play my last thirty-two bars. He tells me that he recognized every piece I played, and thanks me profusely. He remembers when the Viennese operettas were new. He is eighty years old, a veteran of World War I.

"So you remember when Leipzig was a happier place?"

"I've known four Leipzigs. And I knew them all in this hotel. This Leipzig is better than the two previous. It is not so bad as you think. Anyone here your age or younger will not remember happier days than these we have now. Most people are happy now because they have never known anything better. But the first Leipzig I remember, when we first heard the melodies from *The Merry Widow* and went crazy over them, ah, those were the happiest days anyone ever had anywhere. Then life was beautiful! Yes, I tell you, beautiful!"

The train back to the West passes Weimar, but not much of that center of high culture—and nothing at all of nearby Buchenwald, the scene of unspeakable Nazi horrors—is visible from the train window. We pass through Erfurt, then through the forested hills of Thuringia, with walled castles perched on steeps that slope into snowy valleys. Each successive castle seems a perfect setting for *Tannhäuser*. Then we reach the actual setting for *Tannhäuser*, the great Wartburg, high above the medieval city of Eisenach. I cannot visit any of these places, as I have not cleared a stop in advance with the East German authorities. Insultingly superior border police board the train. I spend the last of my East German marks on *Apfelsaft* for the six of us in the compartment and, during the inspection, we boldly toast the day when the two Germanies will be united again. The train, before it finally enters the West, passes out of the East twice. The old tracks cut back and forth across the present border, oblivious to the barbed wire and the watchtowers.

It isn't until I'm back in West Germany, alone in a compartment on a fast Intercity train and speeding south to the Alps and Italy again that I feel the gentle pressures once more, drop off to sleep, and awake with the pain in my ears.

6

O N ASH WEDNESDAY we resume classes and, in the plain white chapel, concelebrate Mass. Fr. Costello blesses the ashes and signs me with a black cross on my brow, saying, "Remember, man, that thou art dust, and unto dust thou shalt return." Johnny and Andrzej and I sign one another and the staff and students in attendance. We carry on our foreheads the reminder that someday we shall die.

We are vested in penitential purple, ready to spend forty days in prayer and fasting, ready to live again this year with Jesus the forty days he spent in the desert preparing himself for his mission. His life will be ours as we look forward to the spring.

The liturgy of the church enables us, each year, to relive his life, to pass through his birth, his suffering, his death, and his rising from death. In the cycle of his feasts his life becomes our year. We merge our lives in the life he once lived, and set them together in the cycle of the seasons. All three—his life, our lives, and the seasons—turn as one. As spring struggles for release from nature's winter, we struggle with our natures for the death of what in us is destructive, and we move daily toward the release and rebirth that is Easter.

Jesus is not just a model for us. In the liturgy we are born with him and suffer, and die, and are reborn with him as the seasons move in succession.

Poets before Jesus sang that nature's annual cycle is an image of human life. In the procession of spring, summer, autumn, and winter the poets of ancient Rome saw the youth, maturity, aging, and death of a human life. The wind and rain, the sun and moon, the rivers and trees, the storms at sea and the calms—all of these, the poets said, tell us about ourselves. They image our hopes, struggles, sufferings, successes, and failures. But there is an important difference, they say, between nature's phenomena and human living. Nature's cycle goes on, constantly renewing itself. A man lives only once. There is no second spring, not for him.

With Horace, the cycle is shorter than with the other poets. His image is not the year, but the month: "The moon loses her light and wins it back, but we, once we die, we are dust and dreams."

With Catullus, who died young, the cycle is shorter still—not the month but the day: "The sun can set and rise again, but with us, when once our brief day has set, there is only everlasting night to be slept through."

It is perhaps the most beautiful thought antiquity ever pondered.

Jesus changed all that. We do not altogether die nature's death. He called himself the vine with clustering branches bearing fruit that would *remain*. He called his kingdom a harvest that would be *gathered in*. He saw human life and death in nature, but he saw them fulfilled on a final day when good would be rewarded and evil punished. Though human beings ripen, age, and die, there is more than nature's cycle in their lives. There is ultimate meaning.

Jesus himself set the pattern for this—living, suffering, dying *and then* coming back to life.

There is no sadness in the celebration of his feasts, from Advent to Christmas through Lent to Holy Week and Easter to Ascension and Pentecost. There is no melancholy thought that in our lives the cycle runs but once. We put his life in nature's cycle and renew it every year. And we add our lives to his, Theophilus. We shall renew ourselves as nature does. We shall not forever die, for he did not.

I shall turn to dust and ashes. I shall also live forever.

That afternoon, I tell Jack Costello my reactions to Dresden, destroyed on an Ash Wednesday more than a quarter century earlier. He has read Irving's book. He mistrusts it because of Irving's largely discredited later work. But with his wartime experience he is still impressed with the known facts: "Saturation bombing with conventional weapons to create a firestorm," he says. "More devastation than at Hiroshima, where one nuclear explosion also created a firestorm.

"Now, Luke, can you imagine what can happen today? We're capable of saturation bombing *with nuclear weapons*. We can have Dresden multiplied thousands of times over. A cloud over every Dresden in Europe. A firestorm in every American city. We have the power to do it, and others to do it to us. It would mean the end of all that

Dresden was all over the world, the end of all of our art and music and literature. The annihilation of all the people of all the Dresdens. If it happens there may be no survivors. A series of suns more powerful than the sun we know would burst over the planet and destroy our atmosphere. It would be the death of the earth."

He says all of this calmly enough, but his eyes are intense. Maria Parenti almost interrupts us with some business, but thinks better of it and leaves us to ourselves. It now seems that this is what the president has always wanted to say to me, and he says it person to person.

"If we've got a mission in the world today, Luke, it's to stop that from happening. Anyone with any moral authority is duty-bound to speak out about it. We have to, the church has to. Jesus didn't send us just to preach to individuals on matters of private morality. We have a mandate to speak to the nations. Those were his last words to us, and the church may be the only institution on earth capable of beginning such a mission."

He relaxes a little. "What you saw in Dresden and what I saw in Dachau—after the event, in each case—is a reminder of the capacity for evil inherent in us all. They're like early questions in a test we're taking. So far, we've failed."

I can't say anything for a minute.

"What do you mean, a test we're taking?"

"I mean, Luke, that God let us evolve beyond all the other species on his earth. He allowed us to learn and to grow until, finally, we discovered the secret of the physical energy that binds the world together. That discovery may be the most important step we've taken since our emergence into consciousness. The year 1945 may be the most important date in recorded history. We can't pretend now that we didn't make the discovery. It's done. We've reached a level of awareness that makes it impossible to return to our previous ways, when we, the human race, failed at Dachau and Dresden. We've made the discovery. The test now is how we're going to use it—to end hunger and want and all the problems that have led to wars, or to destroy ourselves in the last and final war. I don't think we're passing the test so far."

"You think that the discovery of nuclear power was providential?"

"Yes, I do. It can be the beginning of a new evolutionary stage for us. Or the end of the evolution of everything on earth."

"But we haven't got any way of dealing with the problem. We don't know how to disarm."

"So far we don't. But we can learn. We can face the future in a new way. We can think not just of ourselves who would be destroyed in a nuclear war, but of all those millions upon millions of people who, if we make the planet uninhabitable, if we extinguish the human race entirely, will never live, never do the good things that humans have the potential to do in this world."

"You believe in a kind of evolution?"

"Oh, yes. A Teilhardian kind, perhaps. It seems to me obvious that humanity has a lot of unfulfilled potential—in energy, brain cells, moral impulses, even physical strength—that we haven't even begun to develop or use. They, the generations of the future—I think they have a task, a providential task, an evolutionary task, set out for them. If *we* don't forestall the whole thing first."

"I've found myself thinking much the same thing, Jack, and I've spoken to some of my students about it. But I've kept it out of my sermons."

"Why?"

"I guess because I didn't know what to say. Our moral systems and our theologies haven't, so far, addressed the problem except in very conventional terms."

"Well, Luke, our theologians should reread the Bible, which is a much more future-oriented testament than they make it now. They—maybe *we*, you and I—have got to rethink and reforge our morality. Yes, I really do think we're faced with a kind of test. Will we use our new discovery to advance the cause of civilization, or will we destroy ourselves?"

"Andrzej would say we won't pass the test. The worse alternative is the one we'll choose."

"Not if we are led into an awareness of our changed situation in the world."

"Who is going to do that for us?"

"God has sent us heroes in the past."

"He sent his son."

"He sent his son, yes."

He looks away for some time. Then he fixes his eyes on me. "Luke, you know the prophetic artists of the past. What do they predict for us?"

"I think some would say we're going to fail the test, but nobly. Others, if artists are prophetic, see us as capable of healing ourselves. If we lose our reason, intuition may come to save us."

"Do your artists imply that the greatest healing power is love?"

"Yes. In one word, love."

"That's something we've always had. It's high time we learned to use it. By making war obsolete."

7

W AR IS WHAT MY COURSE in literature in translation is concerned with this semester—*arma virumque*, war and man. We'll be reading Homer's *Iliad* and *Odyssey* and Virgil's *Aeneid*. I find epic more congenial than Greek drama, and so, I soon discover, do the thirty students. Last semester's agonies of Orestes and Oedipus and Pentheus seem stagebound and stylized, whatever the richness of imagery or weight of ideas or psychological perceptions the three authors give them, compared to what one finds, much more simply and poignantly, in Homer.

Aeschylus called his plays "crumbs from Homer's table." Keats felt that first sighting Homer's expanse was like sighting a new planet or an undiscovered ocean, and Shelley thought that the *Iliad* surpassed any other single product of the human mind. Helen Keller, sightless and deaf, found her paradise in the same vivid poem, for its hundreds of similes taught her, from the senses she had, about the senses she did not have.

No one in the class fails to respond to the scene in the sixth book of the *Iliad* which moved me long ago, where Hector, knowing that he will die, and knowing that soon after that his city will be completely destroyed, says good-bye at the gate of Troy—the West or Scaean Gate—to his wife, and takes off his flashing helmet to kiss his infant son. Like most of us who teach classics and love Homer, I do not trust my emotions sufficiently to read the scene aloud. I call on a lovely Jewish girl and a thick-necked Protestant boy and let *them* break down as they read it. They almost do.

> Hector headed down the well-built streets, and when he had crossed the great city and come to the Scaean Gate, he was just on the point of passing on to the battlefield again when his bounteous wife came running to meet him—Andromache, daughter of great-hearted Eëtion, who dwelt under wooded Placus, in Thebe-under-Placus, ruling over

Cilician men. It was Eëtion's daughter that bronze-clad Hector had to wife.

She found him there at the gate, and her maidservant came with her, carrying the child at her breast—a merry-hearted boy, just a baby, Hector's darling son, like to a beautiful star. Hector called him Scamandrius, but everyone else called him Astyanax, that is, Prince of the City —because Hector alone was Troy's defense.

Hector smiled as he looked silently on his son.

But Andromache came alongside him, and let a tear fall, and put her hand to him and spoke out and named him true: "My ill-starred husband! Your courage is going to destroy you. You show no pity for your infant son and for me, the unhappy woman who will soon be your widow. The Greeks will kill you, all of them setting on you at once, and for me it will be better, when I lose you, to pass beneath the earth. For there will be no comfort for me when you have met your fate, but only sorrows.

"I have no father, no lady mother. Bright Achilles slew my father when he sacked the well-peopled city of the Cilicians, Thebe of the high gates. He slew Eëtion, but he did not despoil him, for he knew in his heart that that would be wrong. He burned my father's body, still clad in its richly wrought armor, and heaped a tomb over it. And the mountain nymphs, the daughters of aegis-bearing Zeus, planted elm trees all around.

"I had seven brothers in the halls, and all of them on a single day passed within the house of Hades. Bright, fleet-footed Achilles slew them all, amid their rolling herds of oxen and their silver-white sheep.

"And my mother, who was queen under wooded Placus—Achilles brought her here to the Greek camp with the rest of his spoils, but then he took a great ransom and let her go, and she died in her ancestral home of the heart-pangs Artemis sends with her bow.

"Now, Hector, *you* are my father and lady mother. You are my brother. You are my blossoming husband. Take pity on me now. Stay here at the wall. Do not make your child an orphan and your wife a widow. Station your army by the fig tree there, where the city is especially vulnerable, where the wall needs defending . . ."

Andromache knows that, if Hector goes down to the plain, Achilles will kill him as he has killed all her family, and that he may not treat his corpse as chivalrously as he treated her father's. He may not give Hector the hero's burial that is his due, or ransom the body if the Trojans ask for it.

And Hector has a presentiment that she may be right, but he has to be gently firm with her. He uses the word Jesus used to his mother:

"Woman, all these concerns I have at heart. But how shamed I would be before the Trojans and the Trojan women with their trailing garments if, like a coward, I hid myself from war. My heart does not tell me to act so. The lesson I have learned is to be a good soldier and to fight out in front alongside the other Trojans, and win great glory for my father and myself.

"I know full well in my heart and soul that a day will come when sacred Troy will be destroyed, and my father Priam, and all the people of Priam of the good ashen spear. But my heart aches not so much for the future fate of the Trojans, or even of my mother Hecabe, or my father king Priam, or my brothers who will fall, many and good, in the dust at the foeman's hands—my heart aches not so much for what will happen to them as for what will happen to you, when some one of the bronze-clad Greeks will lead you away in tears, to a life of slavery. And in Argos, perhaps, you will carry water from Messeis or Hypereia, all against your will, for harsh necessity will press upon you. And someday someone will say, when he sees you weeping, 'That is Hector's wife. He was the best of all the horse-taming Trojans, the best at fighting when they fought around Troy.' Someday someone will say that. And the sorrow will break out again, at the thought that you had no such man as I to defend you on the day slavery came. Oh, may the heaped-up earth cover me before I hear your cries as they drag you away."

He has tried to remind her of his responsibilities, and he has been carried away. He has tried to tell her that, as he must take the place of her father and mother and brother, so too she is all of those to him. But he has said too much. What can he do now to undo what he has said and still somehow say it? How can he remind her more gently about the realities of war?

Glorious Hector reached for his child. But the child shrank back into the bosom of his well-girt nurse, wailing, terrified at the sight of his own father, frightened at the bronze and the horse-hair crest, when he saw it waving fearsomely from the helmet's top. His father and lady mother laughed aloud at that, and straightaway glorious Hector took the helmet from his head and placed it on the ground, all gleaming. Then he kissed his son and rocked him in his arms, and spoke in prayer to Zeus and the other gods:

"Zeus and ye other gods, grant that this boy of mine will be, even as I, preeminent among the Trojans. May he be as strong and brave as I, and may he rule Troy valiantly. And may someone say someday, as he comes back from battle, 'He is much better than his father.' May he slay his enemy and wear his bloody spoils, and may his mother be glad at the sight."

It is a terrible consolation, this prayer addressed to Zeus, which is really a reminder to his wife, this grim hope for the future when Hector knows that his city will soon be utterly destroyed. He has said too much again. But what can he do, realist and fatalist at once?

> Hector placed his son in the arms of his dear wife, and she took the child to her fragrant bosom, smiling through her tears. Her husband saw she was weeping and was sorry for her, and put his hand to her, and spoke out and named her true: "My ill-starred wife! Do not keep so much sorrow in your heart. No one will send me to my death before the time comes, and no one, brave or base, has ever—I know it well—escaped his fate, when once for all it has been decreed. So go home now, and attend to your work, the loom and the spindle, and see that the maidservants get on with their work, too. I shall attend to *my* work—war. That is my special concern, and the concern of all men born in Troy."
>
> With these words glorious Hector took up his helmet with its horsehair crest. And his wife started home. But she turned around from time to time, and let fall a blossoming tear. And as soon as she came to the well-peopled house of Hector slayer of men, and found her many handmaids within, she stirred them all to lamentation. They sang a lament for Hector in his house while he was still alive, for they no longer thought that he would come back from battle. They knew that he would not now escape the might and the hands of the Greeks.

Most of the class feels, from this early page on, that Hector is the hero of the poem. But different ages expect different things of their heroes, and the *Iliad* is some thirty centuries old. Probably their judgment, which is also mine, is wrong. Almost surely it is not Hector but the terrible, passionate Achilles who is the poem's real hero, as the Greeks of the classical age, several centuries after Homer, thought he was.

What is a hero? We have to come to grips with the question.

The class, sure of their feelings and anxious to get on with the story now that they are hooked on Hector, almost resents the question. But one of them, who had been in the Greek drama class, volunteers an answer in the form of a tentative question: "Isn't a hero supposed to be a character larger than life, who falls from greatness because of some tragic flaw?"

"Yes. That's a good Aristotelian answer. A tragic hero, on the stage, is a figure greater in almost every way than we are, so great in fact that he, or she, absorbs all of us into him. Or into her—for of course many of the tragic figures in Greek drama are women. But Antigone or Oedipus has some tragic flaw in her or his makeup that, ironically, none of us ordinary people would have. And when she or he is brought low, the kingdom, or the royal house, or the *polis* is destroyed as well. That's what we, for centuries, have made of a few remarks on tragedy in Aristotle.

"The problem is, all of that applies more to Shakespeare and to later drama than it does to the Greek plays. The Greek dramatists wrote earlier than Aristotle. They hadn't read him or even heard of him. I don't recall making much of that Aristotelian definition of a hero last semester, and I don't think we want it here. The Homeric hero antedates tragedy by several centuries."

I've snowed them under. It takes some time to get other definitions after that. But eventually several more are volunteered: a hero is a man admired for his superior qualities, or a conqueror whose fame grows with succeeding ages, or a man who seems almost a god to his contemporaries and becomes one after his death.

Many of the students have had courses in mythology, and some venture answers from Lord Raglan ("I can't list all the features, but there are twenty-two points to the whole hero pattern, and some heroes like Oedipus are twenty-two pointers, while others only get fifteen points or so"), or from Joseph Campbell ("A hero goes on a journey that symbolizes how a young man passes from adolescence to manhood").

"Those are good suggestions," I reply, "and I hope some of you follow them up in your essays. I'd also like to get essays about what a hero is from a sociological point of view, if you're reading Lévi-Strauss in some other course, or from an anthropological point of view, if you're reading Mircea Eliade. But just now I want to take yet another view, from George Frideric Handel, who says in his *Philosophy of History* . . ."

This is greeted with some alert looks of astonishment, though many in the class dutifully take it down.

"Did I say Handel? Sorry. It's February. I meant Hegel. Georg Wilhelm Friedrich Hegel." They take that down. "In the nineteenth century, when the idea of evolution was beginning to excite intellectuals, Hegel talked about heroes from a new perspective. In his lectures on the philosophy of history he said . . ."

There is a pedagogical pause as the pens are poised over the notebooks.

". . . that the role of heroes in history was to bring a new world into being. That the great heroes of history and legend are those who lead the human race into a whole new area of awareness."

All that goes down on paper. Not all of them will think it through. A few will think to challenge it.

"Heroes, for Hegel, do not do this of themselves. They are the instruments of a higher power. They are the means whereby a superior force realizes its evolutionary ends. Hegel called it the *Weltgeist*. We might think of it here, in Homer, as the father god, Zeus.

"So, as we read our way the next few weeks through the *Iliad*, let's ask which of our characters, Hector or Achilles, meets that definition of a hero. Which of the two is a figurehead for the race as it evolves? Which leads us to a new level of awareness? Which is an Abraham, a Buddha, a Jesus, a Lincoln? Which is history's agent, the instrument of Zeus, under whom a new world arises, under whom, as symbol, the Bronze Age warrior, or the classic Greek, or in a larger view all of humankind moves into a new sensibility?"

Some look uninterested in such concerns. Some fairly obviously think them concerns unrelated to epics thousands of years old. I have to say, almost apologetically, "That's not a random question. Remember that Homer says, at the beginning of his epic, 'And the plan of Zeus was fulfilled.' This is the way we're going to view our three epics here. What we say about Homer's two poems will be equally true of Virgil's. A real hero leads his Greeks, his Romans, his Jews, his Asians, his Americans to a new awareness, a new world."

They are writing frantically, so I pause for a few seconds before I add, again, "As the instrument of a higher power."

8

L ENT IS AN AUSTERE, businesslike time of year. You eat less, pray more, and work harder. The students soon get the feel of it. Everything picks up. Lent is an old Germanic word for spring. Already in Rome, we can sense that spring is coming.

The news is full of Henry Kissinger's shuttle diplomacy, of Israel and Egypt, of Phnom Penh and the Mekong Delta. In Italy there are several alarming kidnappings.

Students at the school plan "last splurge" trips for the Easter holiday. Pino's local buddies, *giovanotti* who call him Pinuccio or simply Pinooch, haunt our downstairs canteen and make unsubtle passes at the American girls. The Hector and Andromache from my epic-in-translation class are quietly seeing a lot of each other.

We come to the twenty-fourth and last book of the *Iliad*. Hector has killed Achilles' close friend, Patroclus, in battle. Achilles has in turn killed Hector and, filled with a madness, a terrible wrath he can neither understand nor control, has dragged the corpse in the dust behind his chariot wheels. We return to the question we asked weeks before. Who is the hero of this oldest of epics in the Western world? They've done some thinking about it. (The question is, of course, a natural for inclusion on the final exam.)

"If you go way back to the first page and take that as your basis," Joe begins—surprisingly, for he has been slow to speak in the poetry seminar—"then Achilles has got to be the hero. He's mentioned in the first line. The first word in the poem is 'wrath'—his wrath. The wrath of Achilles. The whole first book is about him—"

"I'm sure you're right, Joe. Achilles is the hero . . ."

The class isn't happy about that at all.

". . . if we accept Hegel's view that a hero is one who brings a new world into being, a figurehead for humanity as it moves into a whole new consciousness. And that starts happening where we are now, at the last book . . ."

But Joe isn't ready to say more, and the rest aren't at all convinced of the choice we've made. I've got to go it alone.

"I know that at this point in the poem Achilles appears to be nothing better than a savage. To avenge his friend he's killed Hector, and nowhere in the poem does his wrath flare up so savagely as when he degrades Hector's body, mutilating it and dragging it behind his chariot. Andromache knew that her Hector would be killed, but she hoped she would not see the desecration of his body. Achilles had killed all her family, but he had also shown them in death a Bronze Age hero's chivalry. She hoped that, when the inevitable time came for Hector to die at the same hands, the same humane treatment would be given him. But she had not foreseen the savage wrath which, by now, is tearing Achilles apart—wrath so furiously directed against Hector's body that Achilles' comrades are concerned for his sanity and, here at the start of the last book, the gods themselves are shocked and moved to intervene. They, or some providence, or Hegel's *Weltgeist*, is about to lead the Greek hero to a new world, a new sensibility.

"What have we read for today' s class? Zeus sends his rainbow goddess to Hector's old father, King Priam. The patriarch is discovered in his courtyard, surrounded by his few surviving sons. He had had fifty sons, but most of them have been slain in the fighting, most of them have been killed by Achilles—and now the finest of them, Hector, is gone. But Zeus's messenger tells Priam to heap a wagon with treasure and take a herald with him and travel by night behind the enemy lines to Achilles' tent. There he will ransom the body of his dearest son.

"Priam obeys instantly. No one can dissuade him from the dangerous mission. How could they? Higher powers are at work, and a great, providential moment is at hand."

The class is almost preternaturally quiet.

"Priam leaves the city and crosses the plain and comes to the river, and there in the mist he sees an apparition. It is a young man, smiling, come to help. It is the father god's own son, Hermes, disguised as a young warrior on the Greek side. Gently, Hermes takes old Priam by the hand and gives him, in a single word, the solution the whole epic has, all along, been moving toward. 'Father,' he says. Did you notice how 'father' and 'son' run like motifs in the conversation between the young god and the old king in the mist at the river-crossing?"

"Father, aren't you afraid to be here in the middle of the night so near the Greek camp? Well, I will not harm you. I'll protect you, because you remind me of my father."

"The gods are kind, dear boy, sending me a wayfarer like you, so handsome and so good! Blessed be the father who begot you."

"Are you fleeing from Troy now because your son, who always protected you, is now dead?"

"How do you know about my son? Who are you?"

"Oh, I've seen your Hector a lot, in the fighting. I'm from Achilles' camp, a Myrmidon. My father is Polyctor. I'm the youngest of his seven sons."

"Then tell me about my son's body. Has Achilles cast it to the dogs to be devoured?"

"Not at all! You'd be astonished to see how dewy-fresh it is. The gods are blessing your son because they love him."

"Ah, yes. My Hector always honored the gods. Here, my boy, take this goblet as a gift, and guide me to Achilles."

"Oh, I couldn't take a bribe! Not behind Achilles' back!"

So it is that, guided by the guileful Hermes, protected from all danger, the old king moves through the night straight into the Greek camp, past the guards dropped off to sleep, through the doors miraculously unbolted. Hermes brings him before Achilles, then disappears."

They sit like little children enraptured by the story, though they have read it already in anticipation of the class.

"The old king says nothing at first. He kneels and kisses the hands of Achilles. He kisses 'the terrible man-slaying hands that had killed so many of his sons.' And then, remembering the word Hermes had put in his head, Priam says to the savage Achilles, 'Remember your father.'

"And that is when Achilles at last finds release from the wrath that had possessed him all through the poem. He weeps. His terrible, uncontrollable passion ebbs away in tears for his father, old and alone back in Greece. And in tears too for the friend he killed Hector to avenge—Patroclus, whose name, I think it is time now to remark, means 'the glory of the father.'

"So Achilles gives Hector's body back to the old king. He has it washed and clothed. He lifts it with his own hands onto the litter, and then, with his own men, onto Priam's wagon. He and Priam exchange lingering glances, as if now for the first time each sees the other for what he is. It is a moment familiar from many later stories of war: when enemies really see each others' faces—really see each other as human beings—they cannot hate each other.

"So, under the providential action of the father god, Achilles has found release from his terrible wrath. He has come to a sense of fatherhood in himself, to a realization that the glory of a relentless warrior is not so wonderful as 'the glory of the father.' And why do I say he is the hero of the poem? Where does Hegel's idea of a hero come into all this?

"I think we can say that Achilles in the *Iliad* is the figurehead for a spiritual movement among Greek peoples, a forward movement from the older values of the Bronze Age warrior, so prevalent all through the first twenty-three books of the poem, to the newer values that will animate the *Odyssey* and eventually build classical Greece. Most of the *Iliad* reflects the values of an age where men prove their manhood by fighting. But by the end, the *Iliad* has become something of a new testament of spiritual growth and awareness. When Achilles forsakes his wrath to honor the father of his enemy, a new sensibility comes into being in Greece. A new world."

A hand goes up at last, pen poised in the other to take down the answer. "What, precisely, is the new sensibility?"

"Well, first, please don't think that this is the only, or even the ordinary interpretation of the *Iliad*. Or that you must give it back to me on an exam. It's only my view. I'm saying that Achilles passes to an awareness that human relationships are more important than the old Bronze Age warrior's code of *kudos*, of fighting for glory. Peace is worth more than war. Tenderness is better than wrath. I'm not sure it's a lesson Greece took completely to heart, any more than we have learned the lessons of our own New Testament. But I do think it became an ideal for them, a new idea for a new age in Greece."

"So Achilles is really the hero of the poem?"

"Yes, I'd say so. The Hegelian hero."

"What is it again that Achilles becomes aware of?" Another student with pen poised wants more precision. But I can't or won't reduce the end of the *Iliad* to a single statement.

"Hating is self-destructive. Enemies cannot remain enemies if they see each another in their humanity, face to face. A man becomes a man not from winning glory in the eyes of his peers on the battlefield but in becoming, in a spiritual sense, a father. Any or all of those things Achilles now sees."

"Well, then," says the thick-necked boy who several classes before had read aloud the words of Hector saying good-bye to Andromache, "Hector is the real hero in the *Iliad*. He is, right from the start, the man Achilles only begins to be at the close. He's a good father and a good son, and he's fighting not for glory but to defend his city."

"He's the best man on either side in the war," says another voice, and I can see that many more would like to say the same.

"He's a 'verray parfit gentil knight,'" I remark.

"He's not perfect, though." It is the shy Jewish girl who earlier spoke the words of Hector's wife. "He is a bully with his younger brother Paris, and with his allies."

"He hectors them," I add. "And he's not a good tactician. He won't do the prudent thing and admit his mistakes, for fear of what the Trojans, especially the Trojan women, might say."

"And," comes another voice, "when he finally comes face to face with Achilles, he runs away."

"But those are human faults," objects the thick-necked Hector in the class, his eyes flashing. "Achilles' faults are much greater and more destructive."

"I think," says one girl, "that Hector is just as appealing when he runs away as he is when he says good-bye to his wife and baby. The most moving part of the whole poem for me is when he runs, and Achilles catches up with him, and he finally stands and faces his death."

"And he's thinking about his wife at the time," I remind them. "In the long soliloquy, when he sees Achilles coming like a destructive star across the plain, Hector is trying to think about anything except Andromache. He's afraid the thought of her might make him lose his nerve. He doesn't want to remember how they said good-bye before he left for battle. But he has a little jingle in his head at that moment, about a girl and a boy 'tarrying,' as he and his young wife 'tarried' at the Scaean Gate. And when Achilles takes his life, those are his last words: 'the Scaean Gate.' These are small touches, but they tell us that Andromache is hovering just below Hector's consciousness in his last moments, even though he dare not think of her."

"Hector gets more of those subtle touches than Achilles does," observes the girl.

"Well, Homer is subtle with both his heroes. He never describes them completely, the way he does with lesser characters. We only get an accumulation of small details. Achilles has an angry glance, a shaggy chest, a stout hand at his heavy sword hilt. Hector has a spear sixteen feet long and a big body shield, and he has a reputation for taming horses. About one hundred times Achilles is called 'fleet-footed,' and about as many times Hector is called 'Hector of the flashing helmet.' And those epithets eventually come alive in the story—fleet-footed Achilles pursues Hector in a race for his life in book 22, and Hector doffs his flashing helmet when it frightens his infant son in book 6. What was that quotation you had?" I ask our own Hector in the class. "The quote from that Toronto author about Hector taking off his helmet so his child won't be frightened of him?"

"Hector the *warrior* the baby has never seen, but Hector the *father* he knows very well."

"There! That's Homer at his subtlest and most delicate. Unhelmeted, Hector already is what Achilles has to become. So how can Hector be the hero of the poem in our definition—in Hegel's sense? He's not an instrument through which some higher power, some *Weltgeist*, some Zeus, achieves its ends. He doesn't move, as an epic hero must, to a new sensibility. I don't think Hegel would call him a hero—not in his sense of what a hero must be. Hector doesn't bring a whole world into being. In fact, his world, his Troy, is doomed and he knows it."

"Maybe Hegel's isn't the best definition of a hero," suggests our class Hector, ruefully.

"Oh, but Hector *can* be the hero of the poem," exclaims our shy Andromache. "In death. It's his body, his dead body that effects the whole transition in Achilles. Hector's body suffers every indignity Achilles can visit on it, and still the gods preserve it, and Achilles gives it back when Hector's father comes to ask for it. That," she continues with increasing conviction, "is how Achilles makes his epic passage into a new world of feeling. Giving Hector's body back to his father. Nothing would have come of all the suffering in the *Iliad* if it weren't for Hector's death and Hector's body."

The class is sure she is right. The class Hector speaks for them all, and firmly: "So it *is* possible that Hector is the hero, even in Hegel's sense."

"It is, indeed." I hope I have by indirection steered them in the right direction. "Can I read you something from Hector's most eloquent English defender? It's an unlikely source, G. K. Chesterton:

The poet has so conceived the poem that his sympathies apparently, and those of the reader certainly, are on the side of the vanquished rather than of the victor. And this is a sentiment which increases in the poetical tradition. . . . Achilles has some status as a sort of demigod in pagan times, but he disappears altogether in later times, while Hector grows greater as the ages pass. It is Hector's name that is the name of a Knight of the Round Table, and his sword that legend puts into the hand of Roland, laying about him with the weapon of the defeated Hector in the last ruin and splendour of his own defeat. The name Hector anticipates all the defeats through which our race and religion were to pass. . . . Troy standing was a small thing that may have stood nameless for ages. But Troy falling has been caught up in a flame and suspended in an immortal instant. . . . And as with the city so with the hero; traced in archaic lines in that primeval twilight is . . . the first figure of the knight . . . in the long, leaping word with which the *Iliad* ends.

"The long leaping word," I explain as I write it in Greek on the board, "is *hippodamoio*. The last words of the *Iliad*, after Hecuba and Helen and Andromache have wept over Hector's body, are *Hectoros hippodamoio*. Hector the tamer of horses. Hector the knight. Perhaps under Achilles Greece moved to a new sensibility, but, in the centuries that followed, it can be said that under Hector all Europe, all Christendom, the whole Western tradition moved forward.

"It seems almost impossible that it could have happened, for medieval Europe couldn't read Greek. The link, as in so many things between Greece and later Western civilization, is Virgil, whose Roman epic we'll soon be reading. Virgil traced the foundations of his Rome back not to victorious Greece but to defeated Troy. Virgil's hero, Aeneas, is Hector's cousin. He is the Trojan who soldiers on when Hector dies. He gets his mission—to take the Trojan survivors to Italy —he gets that when Hector comes to him in a dream. And you'll read in another few weeks the passage near the end of the *Aeneid* where Aeneas makes Hector the ideal for his own son. The boy isn't so young as Hector's baby was. He's eleven or twelve, and he knows what war is like. So Aeneas doesn't have to take his helmet off to kiss his son as he hurries off for battle. He kisses his son *through the visor* of his helmet. Virgil, you'll find, is always resonant at such moments.

"So we'd better say that Hector did become a hero, for more people and across vaster stretches of time and space, than ever did Achilles. It's a measure of the greatness of the *Iliad* that it has *two* such Hegelian heroes."

"Achilles in the first line," says our class Andromache quietly, "and Hector in the last."

"Yes," I say, closing the book. "And what a stroke of genius it is for Homer to end not with the newly aware hero his Greeks were to identify with but with the defeated enemy whose head, without its flashing helmet but miraculously preserved from all defilement, is held by Andromache in her defeat. Hector too, Hector the chivalrous, was a hero through whom a new world was to arise."

9

HOLY WEEK NEARS. Manfred Schöne leaves for Vienna to assist one of Europe's leading directors in a new production of Goethe's *Iphigeneia*. The school's artist-in-residence has a successful showing of his vivid, almost three-dimensional pictures. Our maestro-in-residence is off to Milan to conduct Puccini and Smetana operas for RAI. I leap at the opportunity to teach some of the maestro's classes—on how to listen to, not make, music.

In the small Latin seminar, the students are dazed by the Epicurean poet Lucretius. Through thousands of Latin hexameter verses of great idiosyncrasy and often striking beauty, he tells us insistently that religion is the source of most of the evil in the world, tormenting humanity as it does with the fear of God and with needless apprehensions about dying. A good Epicurean knows that the gods, whatever concept of them we may have, care nothing about us, that death is not to be feared, for when we die we will lose all consciousness of who or what we were. What we are until then are chance formations of atoms in a void. Annihilation awaits us all. Yet, after twenty centuries, we are still reading Lucretius's poem, whose very permanence has in effect refuted, if not quite defeated, its poet.

In March, with the rail pass now expired, I make only short, second-class trips. In arcaded Bologna I see Gounod's *Faust*, a melodious affirmation of bourgeois belief in God and in good and evil. No German profundities. No Lucretian questions.

In the street after the performance I am pointed out by a tough young Italian who nods to his three tough-looking companions. They advance on me quickly, and the first fellow reaches to his hip pocket. I quail. He speaks, excitedly.

"Where did you get that hat?"

"In Bielefeld," I confess, surprised, having forgotten entirely about the *Elbesegler* on my head.

"O-o-o-oh! In Bielefeld," he whistles, suitably impressed. It doesn't sound as if he knows where Bielefeld is, but I suspect that he thinks it is somewhere in the Soviet Union. Bologna, more efficient than most Italian cities, is run by Italian communists.

"Will you sell it to me?" The hand at his hip pulls out his wallet. I'm not altogether reassured as the others crowd around admiringly.

"Oh, not until I show it to my mama back in the United States," I counter, with nervous cheerfulness, moving away. In Italy a reference to one's mama seems always to defeat even the most formidable ruffian. This one knits his heavy brows for a moment, then smiles. The four of them tip their hats politely, and go their way.

In Parma to see *Tristan und Isolde*, I have the uncomfortable feeling that the hotel I'm staying in is something more, or perhaps less, than a hotel. Keys are passed about mysteriously at the desk, and when I reach for the one I suppose is mine, the proprietress panics. "Oh, no, *signore*, not *that* key!"

In the gallery of Parma's Teatro Reggio, the toughest theater in the world, with an audience that can reduce to tears any singer it finds worthy of disapproval, I make a scene. It seems, at this theater, the proper thing for me to do. The audience is not so knowledgeable as reputation has it, and when it realizes after about twenty minutes that Wagner's music is not going to change to a more congenial idiom, talking breaks out, with communal groans at what is considered inaccurate singing. My problem is that it isn't inaccurate at all. It's the Parma audience that can't tell good from bad Wagnerian singing. I move through the benches to find the man who seems the chief offender, show my fist, and say menacingly, "*Du—kannst du nicht schweigen?*"

His eyes widen at my German, and again the *Elbesegler* does the appropriate trick as I pull it dangerously low over my brow. His friends pull him back to prevent the expected retaliation, whispering, "Careful! The *signore* is German!" I am held in some awe because I may actually understand the words that Wagner's tormented characters are singing. The gallery is quiet for the rest of the evening, though many of the Parmesani leave, disenchanted with Wagner and his incomprehensible music. German profundities! *Questi tedeschi!*

Riding back to Rome, I'm in the compartment with two young men, clearly Americans, with expensive luggage. One of them is something of a roughneck, sporting boots with massive, elaborate heels.

"You're a Catholic priest?"

"Yes."

"An American?"

"Yes."

"Then what are you doing here, in Italy, in March? It's not vacation time."

The tone is superior. I bristle. "I'm teaching Latin and Greek. What are you doing here?"

He looks at his companion. "We take our vacations when we want to. In the off-seasons."

There is a short silence. Then, "Why is your Church so hard on us?"

"On who?"

"I don't have to tell you. Gay guys."

The word is new to me, but the meaning is clear. "I'm not so sure that the church is hard on homosexuals. I don't think that *I* am."

"Come on! You say we're living in sin. Which is no surprise, because your church has always had a big hang-up about sex and sin. You father confessors and mother superiors."

"I'm not going to argue with you. I'll discuss the matter if it's a discussion you want."

The other young man, gentler and possibly older, says, by way of mediating, "Yes. It *is* a discussion we want. We really do want to know, and we want you to listen, too."

"I'll listen."

But they don't speak. They expect me to start. I start badly.

"Now don't think that I'm going to quote the passages in St. Paul and in the Old Testament that are taken to be explicit condemnations of homosexuality. We're not so sure, today, that they *are* condemnations of homosexuality. And I'm not going to try to defend everything that was said in the early church—by Tertullian or by John Damascene. What they said about sex, mainly about women, can hardly be understood in the context of their own day, let alone now. They were right about some matters, but no one is right about everything, all the time."

The surly one is not patient with all this clearing the air.

"That was then."

"Yes, that was then. But today's attitudes in the Church were shaped a long time back, by other writers, very respected ones."

"You mean, I suppose, Thomas Aquinas and St. Augustine," the gentler one says, while the less gentle fellow simply looks exasperated.

They are the gentler and the less gentle. The older and the younger. We exchange no names in this encounter.

"Yes," I say. "Have you read them?"

"A lot of Augustine and a little Aquinas. I once minored in philosophy."

"Well, you're ahead of me there," I confess, laughing a little. "Most of the philosophy I studied is pre-Christian. The Greeks. Anyway, if you've studied philosophy you know that no thinker has a corner on all the truth."

"You'd say that, about Thomas Aquinas?"

"I don't think we can say that either St. Thomas or St. Augustine was correct in all his views about human nature. But they do give us —with the Bible too, of course—a foundation, an orientation."

They're still listening, so I start again, at the point where I should have started in the first place.

"Sex has got to be a good thing, because God endowed us with it. It's part of his creation, and its clear purpose is the transmission of life. And new life has to be carefully tended. So the church has for centuries accepted Augustine's teaching that sex is only permissible within marriage. And Thomas, with the old concept of natural law, taught that any forms of sexual expression that defeated its clear purpose were unnatural."

"There, that's what I mean," says the younger. "Unnatural." He turns to stare out the window.

"Couldn't they say anything about love being a good thing?" asks his friend.

"Both of them wrote very movingly about love. Real Catholic teaching says that sex has two legitimate ends, procreation *and* mutual affection. Both are essential. The giving of love for love is a legitimate end of sex. That's pretty well where we are today."

"Is it?" asks the younger, turning back to me. "In New York, where we live, we've had to fight discrimination in housing and employment and, well, yes, we did get support from some priests, but we got only hell and damnation from your authorities, your archdiocese. They were afraid that, if they gave us legal support, people would think they were saying the way we live was OK for everyone."

Not much of this has been in Europe's papers. I say nothing. The other asks, with hurt in his eyes, "What are we doing that is so terrible? We're no menace to family life. We just want justice, and an end to hate, and to be left alone."

Then, pleadingly, "We didn't choose to be the way we are."

I am reminded of the moving little book we were given to read, in moral theology class, before we were ordained. Written by an invert, as the author called himself. Advising priests what to say when they counsel men like himself: Don't be discouraged. You can practice virtue just as much as any other man. You even have some advantages over others—your special sensitivity in some matters, your relative freedom from responsibilities. He offered a verse from the Bible to anyone like himself who might be bitter with God, or to any of us who might be inclined to judge: Shall the vessel say to the maker, "Why hast thou made me thus?"

The memory of that softens me.

"I agree that our thinking in the church has been legalistic and our practice often unworthy of Christ. In the United States, more I think than in Europe, we've somehow got the idea that sexual sins are more reprehensible than sins against justice and charity. And that's not what Jesus taught."

"Why call it sin at all?" the one with the boots hurries in. "Why is sex a sin? You priests! You don't know anything about sex because you never have any. At least I'm told you don't have any, and it sure sounds like you don't know from experience. You don't know that sex can be good for the soul, and fun."

"I know that it can be funny," I say, in another attempt to clear the air. "I teach Aristophanes. I know that this human condition we're in, with the ever-insistent itch toward sexual activity, is funny when looked at dispassionately. It's the subject of most farces. But sex is serious too. It isn't just fun, it's a powerful force in human nature, and if you give it full rein, it can take over. It can be destructive."

"It needn't be destructive," says the gentler one, embarrassed for his friend. "And in our case it isn't."

"You can't tell me," says the other angrily, "that homosexuality is any more destructive than heterosexuality."

"I didn't say that it was," I counter, too defensively, and reach for something I know and feel. "The eroticism in Walt Whitman is clearly homoerotic, and it fills his whole world with energy. It's teeming and exuberant. *And* it's outer-directed. That's what makes it so wonderful there."

They look a little surprised. "What's wonderful where?"

"The eroticism in Whitman's poetry, inspired by and directed at the whole world. There's no question that sex is an important part of anyone's psychological makeup. But it's not all there is to life. And it's got to be put at the service of something bigger than itself."

They are still for a moment.

"What I don't like," the younger starts up, "is the idea that sex between him and me will send us to hell, while sex between two married people is always all right. Think of all the marriages your church has blessed where people start to hate each another and produce children who have miserable lives. At least we're not hurting anyone."

"Yes, but consequences aren't the only consideration in human acts—"

"We love each another," says the older, quietly. "It's natural for us to make love. You're going to say it's unnatural, and you shouldn't tell us that. You shouldn't tell us to stay celibate. *You* have taken a vow. We haven't. *You* are being given the grace to keep it. We don't have that grace. But we are not promiscuous. We are faithful to each other. Besides that, we work hard. We keep the law. We would like to be able to go to church. We need the help you can give us."

"All right," I say, for his reference to grace has touched a nerve. "It seems to me what I must say is this. And I'll say it to myself as much as to you. Love is the most important thing in life. Respect your sexuality because it is one of the ways you show your love. But remember it is not the only way you can show your love. There's much else that you can do, especially for people who need you."

The quieter one says, "That's what we've always thought, too."

The one less quiet asks, more with concern than with impatience, "You talk like you're issuing commandments. Why does your church think it has to make laws about sex?"

"Because sex is such a powerful force in human lives, and the church has a teaching mission. Every society has tried to contain and domesticate the sexual instinct. I think that the Church, with its teaching mission, has really tried, through the centuries, to understand the force of sexuality in human lives. It found its teaching mainly in the Book it preserved for the world. In that Book, the most important passages for understanding sexuality are—I think I can say this— two. In the Old Testament, 'God said, let us make man in our own image and likeness, male and female.' And then, more simply, in the New Testament, 'God is love.' The love of human beings for each other is the image of God. *Is* God."

"We don't buy that male and female any more," says the one with the boots.

The other, speaking perhaps for both, says "We believe that God is love, and that is enough for us."

"Well, you know, the story goes that St. John said 'God is love' so often that people asked him if he didn't have anything else to preach. And he said, 'There's nothing else to say. That's all you need to know.'"

"Is that Catholic theology?"

"I'm no expert in theology. I teach Greek and Latin, and mainly poetry at that. And after thousands of years of poetry telling us what love is, we are still a long way from really understanding it."

"And after almost as many years of the Church teaching us what love is, we are still a long way from understanding it, too." There is no malice in his quiet response.

"Maybe," he continues, "lovers can help *the church* understand what love is."

"Maybe. The church has always depended on its witnesses to help it arrive at the truth."

"Can we quote you on that?" asks the younger fellow.

"You," I respond to him alone, and trying not to point, "can say that I was touched by what he, your friend, said—'We didn't choose to be the way we are.' You can quote this Catholic priest as saying that sex is an important part of life, but not *everything* in life. *Love* is everything of importance in life."

The gentler asks the perhaps inevitable question, so pleadingly that it must be answered. "Haven't you ever had homosexual feelings yourself?"

"Most men do at some times, don't they? When we are struggling to find out who we are. You are not so alone as you may think. Each of you is as lovable to God as any other human being. And the important thing, in all of this, is trying to be as good a human being as you can possibly be."

The train, I note with some relief, is pulling in to Rome.

"I thought," says the older fellow, "you'd be more convinced by what your church teaches."

"I'm dedicated to the church and I try to understand what it teaches. But, you know, real conviction isn't convinced that what it says is the whole truth. That's absolutism. No priest I know is an absolutist in these matters. You can't spend much time in the confessional without knowing that the church's teaching must be applied with care and compassion in every individual case. But you also discover, very soon, that people need guidelines in their lives, that there must be moral precepts."

"We'll never get you to say that the way we live is a good way to live."

"I don't think I can say what you want me to say."

They are silent. I am sorry that I cannot help them more. For a moment I can't help wondering what kind of fathering they had, but dismiss the thought. We know so little, and if my experience as a teacher and a priest has taught me anything, it's that each one of us has his or her own individual problems. In some ways, every man is an island.

The corridors outside are filling with people hurrying to disembark. Because this is Italy, they are mostly family groups, boisterous and happy.

"We're alike in one way," I remark quietly in the face of all the noise in the corridor. "We're not any of us going to have children. So we can't afford to have loveless lives."

They reach for their coats.

I push the compartment door open and turn to face them.

"I hope you'll both take heart that the church is coming to understand your problems. It knows that God can reveal his truth in many kinds of human experience. Say a prayer for me, here in Rome."

I need the prayer. I see a doctor about the pain in my ears. He can't quite account for it. There has been some permanent hearing loss. Distant sounds are now louder than those close up, which tend to blur.

Reading Homer's *Odyssey* with the large class that knows only English, I come to the series of recognition scenes.

No one in Ithaca recognizes Odysseus when he returns home poor and wrinkled and dressed in rags, so he is able to observe his nineteen-year-old son Telemachus quietly and from a distance and see what kind of son he has become in all the years without fathering. He soon sees that Telemachus is as good a son as one could hope for—courteous toward strangers, generous and intelligent, and above all eager to find his father. In epic writings the quest for one's father is very much the quest for oneself. In this epic, both father and son have journeyed over the sea in their quests for each other.

The goddess of wisdom, unseen by the boy, touches the withered, ragged Odysseus with her golden wand and transforms him back to his vigorous self and clothes him in a splendid mantle and tunic. Telemachus stares in amazement at his father, not knowing what he sees *is* his father . . .

"You are one of the gods! Have pity on me!"

"I am no god. I am your father, in whose absence you suffered so much." Odysseus kisses his son, and a tear falls from his cheek to the ground.

"You are not my father. You cannot be."

"Believe me, I am your father. I have come back after nineteen years of suffering and wandering on the sea. Athena has done this for me."

Telemachus throws his arms around his father, and they weep, father and son, like sea birds who have lost their unfledged young. Homer in his knowing way introduces the note of loss at the moment of finding, at the moment when the hero is fulfilled as a father and the son discovers himself and comes of age. Why, at such a moment, weep for what is *lost*, Theophilus?

Surely, for the lost years of separation. For all the moments they might have shared, when Telemachus was two and seven and twelve and seventeen.

I feel something of that loss.

In Thucydides class, Janet, the only student, turns out to be quite a strategist and isn't satisfied until she has mapped out the battles at Plataea and Pylos.

Ellen brings me another story, this one without a trace of Tim in it, wry and perceptive and full of patterned imagery. She is clearly learning from Fr. Zielinski in the poetry seminar, even though Fr. Zielinski seldom takes any notice of her.

For a few weeks there isn't much time to get to the opera, and opera goes out of my head until, one day, Tim comes to my office door. "Can I ask a theological question that has no answer?"

"Sure, so long as you don't expect any breakthrough from me. Sit down."

He does, and wastes no time getting to the question. "Can a prayer said here in Rome actually affect someone back in Chicago?"

"Yes. Why shouldn't it?"

"Well, I can see that a prayer might have some effect on the one who prays. It puts him in a proper disposition to receive what God is trying to give him. But that my prayer for, say, my brother Kenny back home—that my prayer here will actually affect him there—well, do you believe it can?"

"There are some theologians today who might answer, more or less flatly, no, it cannot."

"But you say it can?"

"I say it can. I'm old-fashioned enough still to believe quite literally in what we call, in the Creed, the Communion of Saints."

"You mean that we can pray for those who have died, and help them."

"Yes, and also that we can pray for the living, and help *them.*"

"Even if they don't know we're praying for them? I mean, Father, I can see someone being helped by the knowledge that there is a good person praying for him. If he knows that, and believes strongly enough, some inner strength—call it psychic energy or whatever—may activate him. That's what happens at faith healings, isn't it? A person sick in mind or body believes so strongly that—"

"That he comes out of himself, yes, and masters his own problem, at least for a while."

"That's a release of psychic energy."

"I think you could call it that."

"But what if my brother Kenny doesn't know I'm praying for him? Or doesn't believe in the power of prayer? I'm not so sure Kenny does. Can my asking God to help him really help him?"

"Well, first, I don't think we can say that God is changed in any way by our prayers. I don't think we can say, even on the strength of some Old Testament narratives like Jonah, that we can placate God, or appease His wrath, or change His mind, or force his hand. Those Bible stories aren't about God changing his mind, but about men coming to a new sense of God and their dependence on him. They say, in their mythic ways, that prayer affects the one who prays, and I think that pretty well sums up the contemporary position on the subject."

"But *you* were going to say . . ."

"I was going to say that, though God cannot be changed by our prayers, He is most certainly active in the world. His power is everywhere. It sustains us and constantly invites us to come out of ourselves in response to joy, sorrow, wonder, delight, work, responsibility—all the various calls to self-transcendence. Love is the greatest of those, of course. No experience pulls us out of ourselves so forcefully. I also think that we're full of unrealized potential, we poor humans. Fr. Costello says that we're still evolving, that we've got powers that are still undeveloped. We've been given not just psychic but physical and moral energy that we haven't begun to use. Prayer activates that."

"You mean, it activates that in the one who prays. But what about the one prayed for?"

"He has the assurance that someone who loves him is concentrating his heart and mind on him in a most powerful way, in touch with the very power that penetrates and sustains him."

"But he has to know, then, that he is being prayed for."

"He has at least to be open to the power that prayer activates. I think that's all I can say."

A long pause. Then Tim asks, very like the serious young man on the train, "Is this in Christian theology?"

"It's been part of the Creed since the fifth century—in the teaching of the Communion of Saints. And the notion of it goes back earlier than that in the Christian East. I, with my special interests, like to think it's as old as Homer. In the *Odyssey*, a message passes between Odysseus and his young son, when they are miles apart, separated by Homer's 'sounding sea.' The father and son are searching for each other, and there is a shadowy figure—Theoclymenus, 'he who is listened to by God'—through whom the message between them seems to pass. Communications also pass between Odysseus and his wife, Penelope, when he returns home but is still disguised and separated from her. Most of the communications pass when the characters are semiconscious, and so open to other than rational influences. The strength of one soul passes to the other."

"I never heard that about Homer."

"Well," I laugh, "you're hearing it now. I'll admit I'm no orthodox Homerist, but those special, personal communications are there. Everything I know is in Homer somewhere. And if you're not convinced by the *Odyssey*, I can tell you about a work of our own century that answers your question, very affirmatively. It's an opera, of course. *Dialogues of the Carmelites*. Do you know it?"

"No."

"Music by Poulenc, text by Georges Bernanos. It's based on an incident from the French Revolution, during the reign of terror, under the guillotine. A young girl, an aristocrat, enters a Carmelite convent because she is afraid to die and believes that she will be safe from the Revolution there. The old prioress receives her serenely and kindly and then very soon dies in fear and terror, with a vision of what is soon to happen. The old prioress almost curses God as she dies.

"Then the Revolution comes to the convent doors. The sisters take a vow to meet death bravely together. The timid young sister runs away, but she can't stay away from the place of execution when the day comes for her fellow religious to die. She is in the crowd, at the guillotine. And when the last sister, her own age, turns and looks at her as she mounts the scaffold and goes to her death, the timid sister comes out of the crowd and mounts the scaffold too—calmly and fearlessly. Why she does this is worked out in the music. That's what we expect of a good opera. But why do *you* suppose the timid sister has the strength, finally, to go to her death with the others?"

"Because the others were praying for her?"

"More than that. Because the old prioress had already died the timid sister's death for her. *There was an exchange of deaths.* The young sister received the peaceful, fearless death of the old prioress, who had already died her fearful, terrible death for her."

His eyes flash.

"That may seem an extreme statement of the notion of the Communion of Saints," I say. "But it's something that has happened, over and over again, at moments of heroism. It's the sudden action of what you have called psychic power and what Christians have called grace. Grace passing from soul to soul."

"Exchanges of grace," he says. "Is that why the opera is called *Dialogues?*" He is brighter than I. I hadn't thought that that was what Bernanos meant by his title.

"You know about Fr. Maximilian Kolbe at Auschwitz?"

"Yes," he answers. "He took another man's place there, and died for him."

"The other man was sentenced to execution and cried out that he had a wife and children. Kolbe had none. He volunteered to die for the other man. That's the ultimate prayer, and the greatest love."

"And it's at the heart of Christianity, right? Christ died all our deaths for us. So now we don't have to fear."

I let him have the last word on the subject.

As Lent enters its last week, knowing that I will soon be teaching Virgil, I ask at the Vatican Library for permission to see the famous

Codex Palatinus, the majestic fourth-century manuscript that preserves almost all of the hexameters of the greatest of all Latin writers.

The old priest at the desk is a Gurnemanz, kindly but firm. He asks my name and my university affiliation. He sizes me up quickly. I am only a Parsifal. I look a little foolish but I am, from all appearances, guileless. Certainly not a scholar.

I ought to have put my glasses on. They might have made the right impression. But they're snug in my breast pocket.

My Italian is halting. He answers in English.

"And why do you want to see the Virgil? It is one of our most priceless manuscripts."

I do not want to tell him that I am seeking an aesthetic experience, not a scholarly one. At least I can say, "I've taught Virgil on the graduate level in Chicago, and I hope one day to write a book on him."

"A new edition? A paleographical work?"

"No. An appreciation. A literary analysis."

"Then why must you see the Codex Palatinus?"

I have to drop the scholarly pretense.

"Because, Father, I am in Rome, and the *Aeneid* is the epic of Rome, and the epic of all epics on fathers and sons, which is what I want to write about."

It is not a response calculated to convince him. Yet, with an amiable stare over his glasses, he quietly makes out a pass for me, and says a "*figlio*" in Italian that sounds like the "*Du siehst, mein Sohn*" that Gurnemanz said to Parsifal.

Awed, I ascend to the reading room. The mighty volume is brought to my assigned desk and carefully placed on the lectern in front of me. I am told to turn the pages slowly, not to touch them any more than is necessary, to signal if I need any assistance. No wonder my hands tremble. The great lines look out at me across sixteen centuries.

First, Virgil's *Eclogues*. Ten little pastoral poems. Shepherds and poets and gods in dialogue, all of it metaphor on the brink of metamorphosis. Everything means something else. Forty years before the birth of Christ, the world has reached a moment of crisis. A century of civil war that became a world war is drawing to a close. Will the world move forward to a golden age or revert to its self-destructive past and gradually disintegrate? The young Virgil holds out hopes for the former but fears, even believes, that the latter will be the case. One of the poems seems to predict the birth of Jesus and the coming of peace. Another tells us that human nature is flawed, that it may not be possible to mend it. Virgil is an arcadian, not a utopian. The Latin hexameters are full of unanswered questions.

I turn the old pages carefully, and my eyes mist.

Here are Virgil's *Georgics*. He has been too pessimistic in the *Eclogues*. There is hope for the future. Civilization can rise from the ashes of defeat. Now, thirty years before the birth of Jesus, world peace has been won. But there is much still to be done. The *Georgics* are four books on reworking the earth, on caring for crops, vines, farm animals, bees. Here, as nowhere else in poetry, is love of the land. Here too, beneath the finished poetic surfaces, is a moral creed, a belief in a providential power at work in the world, which needs humanity to work its purposes. An admission that suffering and evil exist, but an affirmation that advances against them can, even in this flawed world, be made, and are in fact already under way. But the final pages that tell of this are, I see, missing from the codex, lost across the centuries.

Gone, too, are the opening pages of the great *Aeneid*. But soon the story is unfolding—how Aeneas led his Trojans out of fallen Troy to found a new city, Rome. The story holds the hope that in Virgil's day Augustus will lead that same city, Rome, out of its century of war. And yet Aeneas and Augustus are, like any of us, fallible. Will there be more wars, or peace? The great tome on the desk before me ends with the hero who brought a civilization back to life caught agonizingly in the act of killing so that that civilization can survive. Virgil asks, on the last page as on virtually every page, "Why, in order that good be done, must the innocent suffer and die? And what is God, who wills that such things must happen?"

Sixteen centuries after the manuscript was copied, and twenty after the poem was composed, we still do not have the answers. Virgil, in his metaphors, implies that there are no answers.

During the three days of Holy Week we have the traditional ceremonies in the chapel.

On Holy Thursday, Johnny Hallagan is the celebrant. Like Jesus on the night before he died, he washes the feet of twelve of his students, then speaks words of love, then changes bread and wine into the body and blood of Christ. Andrzej and I are concelebrants. We all partake of the sacrament and, filled with his grace, carry the consecrated bread in procession to an altar where we can kneel in adoration before it through the night. We sing Thomas Aquinas's *Pange Lingua* amid clouds of incense.

On Good Friday, three students read the Passion according to St. John, dividing the parts among them. They have been trained by Manfred Schöne, and the reading is so dramatic that it all but bursts the formal bonds of the ceremony. Fr. Costello leads the long intercessory prayers for all the world and preaches powerfully for peace. We trust that our prayers said in Rome can reach and touch the rest of the world. We all receive the sacrament. Then the chapel is stripped bare of its ornaments, the tabernacle left empty, its door open.

On Holy Saturday, close to midnight, in near darkness, we light the Easter fire. I stand before the Easter candle and sing the *Exultet*, the most beautiful of all the songs in the church's liturgy, adapting the old chant to the new English translation, but leaving the central part, which calls the flaw in our nature a *felix culpa*, a happy fault, in its centuries-old Latin. All of us light our candles from the new fire and, holding the new brightness in our hands, bless the Easter water. Three times I dip the lighted candle into the filled basin. The fire illumines the water like male impregnating female, like reason immersed in intuition. Out of such elements comes new birth.

Midnight passes. It is Easter morning, and the ceremony continues. At the *Gloria* of the Mass, we sound our small bell as mightier bells ring out all over the city below us. Andrzej, in a quavery baritone, sings the triple Alleluia which signals the rebirth of the church, passed now through the darkness by purifying rites of fire and water. The altar is decked with lilies, and the four of us priests concelebrate. We extend our hands and say the words of consecration. Jesus is no longer dead, but with us again, under the forms of bread and wine. We embrace each other with a kiss of peace. We have only white beams for a dome over our heads, and twanging student folk songs instead of "Dresden Amens." But as we eat the bread and drink the wine, the sacramental grace is real, and the power of God moves among us.

Perhaps even a prayer said elsewhere in Rome—I think for a moment of the two young men on the train—perhaps that prayer is strengthening me as I enter the last part of this year of learning.

10

A PRIL. Italy's strikes proliferate. The postal system, like Canada's, is on the brink of collapse. Prices rise. Student attention, which picked up in March, wavers noticeably after Easter. The tough American Hector and his Jewish Andromache are clearly affected by the Roman spring, as is Joe, the quiet boy in the poetry seminar, now lovesick for a slim girl from Tennessee. In Chicago, Mayor Daley is reelected. In Hollywood, *The Godfather II* and Fellini's *Amarcord* are named the year's best movies. We Americans who have lived in Italy feel specially qualified to endorse the Academy's judgments, even though we haven't yet seen the pictures.

One suddenly warm night I sleep fitfully and awake to open the shutters and gaze out into the night, over the treetops. When I sleep again, I dream.

I am within a wire enclosure. There are strange, dim shapes drying in the sun. A doctor in a white coat demands to know my name.

"Theophilus."

"What kind of a name is that?"

"A Greek name."

"It is a Jewish name."

"It is Greek. It means 'he who is loved by God.'"

"You must say after me, 'I am not the son of my father.'"

"I am not the son of my father."

"You must say after me, 'I shall never beget a son.'"

"I shall never beget a son."

I am on my back. I hear him say to his attendants, "He will not have to die. There will be an exchange of deaths."

Someone beyond the enclosure is praying for me, and I am not harmed.

In the year-long poetry seminar, Andrzej and I have read with the students, among other authors, Propertius, Villon, Petrarch, Hölderlin, Ungaretti, Mallarmé, Lorca, Li Po, and Andrzej himself. Before the students submit their own poems, we come, in the penultimate session, to Rainer Maria Rilke. Andrzej is on the *qui vive*, as it is my turn, not his, to conduct the class of seven budding poets.

"In the last year of the nineteenth century, when he was about your age, Rilke wrote his *Stundenbuch*, his *Book of Hours*. He speaks in these poems like a monk in a monastery speaking to his God. These are poems that have appealed to the devout and the skeptical reader alike. Rilke wrote the *Book of Hours* here in Italy, rapidly, after his first trip to Russia. Mother Russia, as he called her, made an overwhelming impression on him. He traveled widely there, met Tolstoy and other writers and intellectuals, and found in the common people a strength and spirituality he had not known in Western Europe. He described his experience in his letters. There's one quotation that, perhaps, should guide us here. 'Russia,' he said, was 'the land where the people are solitary people, each with a world in himself.'

"And Rilke found among those people a different God than he had known—'a never-defined, ever-changing, growing God.'"

I pass copies of the poem around, the German and a close English translation. We take turns reading it aloud in German to let the sounds, the stresses, the rhythms, and the calculated pauses make their effects alone, apart from the sense. The German is conversational and simple, however, and a lot of the meaning registers even without our translating:

> Was wirst du tun, Gott, wenn ich sterbe?
> Ich bin dein Krug (wenn ich zerschwerbe?)
> Ich bin dein Trank (wenn ich verderbe?)
> Bin dein Gewand und dein Gewerbe,
> mit mir verlierst du deinen Sinn.
>
> Nach mir hast du kein Haus, darin
> dich Worte, nah und warm, begrüßen.
> Es fällt von deinen müden Füßen
> die Samtsandale, die ich bin.
> Dein großer Mantel lässt dich los.
> Dein Blick, den ich mit meiner Wange
> warm, wie mit einem Pfühl, empfange,
> wird kommen, wird mich suchen, lange—

und legt beim Sonnenuntergange
sich fremdem Steinen in den Schooß.

Was wirst du tun, Gott? ich bin bange.

Then we translate, making sure we know what each individual word means and how the words fit together:

What will you do, God, when I die?
I am your jug. What if I am smashed?
I am your drink. What if I spoil?
I am your garment and your trade.
If you lose me, you lose your meaning.

After I die, you have no house in which
words, close and warm, may greet you.
There falls, from your tired feet,
the comfortable slipper that I am.
Your great mantle lets you go.
Your gaze, which I receive with my cheek
warmly, as with a pillow,
will come, will search for me, far—
and lie down at sunset
in the lap of unfriendly rocks.

What will you do, God? I am afraid.

As the thought of the poem is end-stopped, or opens out easily into couplets, we adopt the procedure of each person, around the table, taking a line or couplet and giving a two- or three-minute impression. I begin.

I: "'*What will you do, God when I die?*' Rilke quietly sends a shock through the reader. The monk, or the poet, asks a simple question that instantly reverses our traditional theological alignments. Christians have always believed that God loved them, personally and individually. The threat of death is not so frightening when one thinks that after death he will be received personally into that infinite love which God is. God, in the traditional view, is all. And man is nothing, or next to nothing, his days on earth just a passing shadow, as the Psalmist said. God, and only God, gives a man value, gives his life meaning. Or so we may think. But here, Rilke implies that the reverse is true. Man is the important figure. He gives God meaning. When man dies, God will somehow be diminished. God will not know what to do. It's an utterly simple, powerful opening. A devout blasphemy."

Andrzej: "*I am your jug. What if I am smashed?*' In the New Testament, God says of St Paul, 'This man is a chosen vessel unto me.' Rilke takes that for his first metaphor. Man is a vessel. What are the implications? A vessel is meant only to contain, and to pour out its contents when tipped. It is of no importance in itself and yet, when it is filled, it is all-important to the contained fluid. Smash the wine jug and the wine spills. So, in a traditional theological perspective like St. Paul's, we, as vessels, are of no importance and also of great importance. Of ourselves we are nothing, but when we are filled with the grace of God, which we can offer to others, we are almost everything.

"A nice thought. But of course Rilke, or Rilke's monk, sees it differently. Man is not a vessel full of God. He is a vessel full of a drink *for* God. God needs him. Dag Hammerskjöld took that idea up when he wrote, 'I am the vessel . . . the draught is God's . . . and God is the thirsty one.'

"So what will God do if his cup is smashed? The usual theological position would say something like 'God will get another cup off the shelf. He has a lot of cups. And he can always make more.' But this monk has a very personal theology. He is the only cup. He and God are the only ones in his private world. And God needs him. If he is destroyed, God will be thirsty. I don't like this poem."

Joe: "*I am your drink. What if I spoil?*' I guess that takes the same thought a little further. Even if the cup isn't smashed, the drink inside might go sour. God won't be able to drink it and will still be thirsty. That's all."

Tim: "*I am your garment and your trade.*' Go on? Couplet? OK. *'If you lose me you lose your meaning.*'Well, I guess that means that, just like a man, God needs clothes and something to work at—at least in Rilke's view he does. Without them, God is naked and has no purpose. What gives God substance and purpose is man. It's pretty blasphemous, on any surface level. Every line seems to be a twist on some passage in the Bible. The last one took off from 'You are the salt of the earth, and if the salt lose its savor . . .' And this one calls to mind, 'I was naked and you clothed me.' But Jesus was talking, in that passage, about loving God in your fellow man. He said that God is every man we meet. Every man in trouble. Rilke means something quite different here. God himself is in need. He is someone who needs man to

give his existence meaning. It's a complete reversal of Christian theology."

Janet: "*'After I die, you have no house in which words, close and
warm, greet you.'* I don't know of any scriptural passage that might
derive from. I think, because at this point we pass to a new stanza and
a new rhyme scheme, Rilke has shifted ground, away from the bibli-
cal. In any case, he is a poet, and his stock-in-trade is words, and he
builds a poem, as a craftsman builds a house, out of those words.
When he dies, there will be no words for God to house himself in.

"Well, no—it can't be quite that. A poem lives on after the poet
who wrote it dies. Rilke must be thinking more existentially: each new
poem, while it is being spoken, when the words are still warm—greeting God and hugging him close—is like a house, a shelter. But God
needs poem after poem to sustain him and, when the poet dies, God
won't have that hospitality any more."

Kim: "*'There falls, from your tired feet, the comfortable slipper that I
am.'* I think in this part of the poem it becomes clearer that the poet
really loves God and wants to shelter and speak to and embrace him,
and comfort him when he is weary. A man, or a woman, is the slipper
God wears when he, or she, comes home at night. And when, some
night, that slipper—that is to say, me—falls to the floor, then God will
go barefoot, and comfortless, and cold. I like the way 'I am' comes at
the end, not the beginning of the line. It's touching. 'Your slipper
falls. That slipper I am.'"

Tim interrupts: "Hey, the word for God in Hebrew, Yahweh,
means 'I am'! Is Rilke's monk, with all these 'I am's,' reversing
Hebrew thought and making the monk who speaks the poem God?"

We keep to the ground rules. No one answers him, and I nod to
Jerry to go next.

Jerry: "*'Your great mantle lets you go.'* He doesn't say, this time, '*I
am your mantle.*' Just that God's great mantle slips off, like the slipper did. But I think the thought is the same as before. Rilke means to
say: when I die, it will be like your big coat falling off you, leaving you
cold and helpless.

"No, wait! There *is* something new here. Before this line, man was a small thing, and God was like some sort of giant. Man was the giant's jug, his drink, his clothes, his slipper. Even the house seemed like a little house for a big God. Up until now, God was big. He only needed a few things. Now, God seems small, and man is the big one, protecting God because God is frail. Man loves God and holds on to him and wraps around him to keep him warm. So when man dies, like a big coat that slips off and falls to the ground, what will God do?"

Ellen: "I guess I've got the long sentence. '*Your gaze, which I usually receive with my cheek warmly, as if my cheek were a pillow, will come looking for me far and wide, and I won't be there to receive it, and it will lie down at sunset in the lap of hard and unfamiliar rocks.*' That's over-translating, I know, but these lines are harder than the rest. I think they mean that now, while I'm alive, God looks at me and I return his look, and my look receives him lovingly, the way a pillow receives a tired head. But when I die, my look won't be there any more. It will be as if the sun had gone under the earth. That German word for sunset, *Sonnenuntergang*, is especially descriptive—the going-under-of-the-sun. When I die, the light of the world goes out for God. Evening comes, and God wants to sleep, and there is no glance to greet him, and no pillow for his head. He has to put his head down on the only thing he finds left when I am gone—rocky ground. That's the only lap he can find. This is the first time Rilke has indicated what would be left when the jug and the clothes and the house are gone. We might suppose there'd be nothing left on God's landscape. But no, there are these strange rocks. Strange because they don't return God's loving glance. They don't recognize him. They don't respond. Man is the only thing in God's creation that can love him in return. When man dies, God still has the other things in creation—but the other things in creation can't respond as man can, with warmth and affection. We human beings are the only ones on earth who can give God a lap for him to lay his head on. I've gone on too long."

Tina: "'*What will you do, God? I am afraid.*' Of course this last line looks back to the first, which is a device a lot of poets use. Everything between the first line and this one is an elaboration. But we are gradually set up for the last line by the rhyme scheme. We've passed from the first line's *sterbe* through *zerschwerbe, verderbe, Gewerbe* to a series of intermediate rhymes until we pick up the final sequence of *Wange, empfange, lange, Sonnenuntergange* and, after a pause, '*ich bin bange* . . . I am afraid.' That last line shocks us as much as the first one does because, while we expect a rhyme, we don't expect the *word* that rhymes, *bange*. We don't expect the monk to say, at the end, 'I am uneasy. I am afraid. I am anxious about you.' Afraid of what will happen to God. People are afraid of death because they're afraid of what will happen to *themselves*. I guess Rilke wants to challenge that kind of thinking."

I thank them for their remarks, not saying that I have the feeling that they do not seem to like the poem as much as I do. Andrzej is the first to comment.

"Nobody has made, so far, what seems to me should be an obvious comment. The monk talking to his God is also the poet talking to what it is that inspires him. 'God' here is what the Muse is in more conventional poetry. Inspiration. And inspiration can huff and puff as much as it likes, but if it hasn't got a poet to breathe into any more, Rilke says, there is no future for it any more."

Silence. So he goes on.

"I say, 'huff and puff' because 'breathing into' is what inspiration means. Rilke fancies it up by trotting in his own metaphors, that's all. He represents the thing that inspires him as a big male Muse, who needs a poet to be his drink and his cup and so on. The big male Muse consumes the poet, puts him on and wears him, lives in him, looks around for him, lies down on him. He finds the poet very convenient. So the poet, who is the only one who does anything of interest in this relationship, says, 'When I'm gone you'll be sorry. You won't find anybody else like me.' It's the same sentimental thing you find the boy saying to the girl in a thousand popular songs. 'By the time I get to Phoenix . . . .' It's terrible, terrible."

He's baiting us, of course. It will take studious Ellen to put him in his place. She does, without even looking up.

"Isn't that what we did say? Rilke's God and his Muse are the same. If what you've always insisted upon is true, Father, and everything in poetry means something else, then we shouldn't have to limit the poem to the relationship between the poet and his God."

"And we don't," I add, "have to make the poem look ridiculous by concentrating only on one metaphorical level."

"I apologize," says Andrzej, a prosecutor who has made his point, though the objection against him is sustained. "Actually, I like this poem."

"I *did* say something about words, and I *did* imply that the poem was about poetry, not religion," says Janet indignantly.

It's my duty to clear the air. "Well, yes, we said at the start that the poems in the *Book of Hours* speak both to the believer and the skeptic, each of whom reads them his own way. It becomes fairly clear halfway through that the monk in this poem is also the poet writing it."

"But he's more poet than a monk," says Andrzej. "His inspiration is more the Muse I know than the God I know."

"But the God here is the God Rilke found in Russia," Ellen insists. "A special kind of God, new to Rilke, and one he found he could relate to. What was the description you read, Father?" She turns to me, careful as always to call both Andrzej and me Father.

I read: "'A never-defined, ever-changing, growing God.' Yes, that seems to me pretty much the God in the poem. And if the monk speaks as if he and this evolving God were the only ones in the world, that too, Rilke said, he found in Russia—'the land where each person is a world in himself.' Rilke didn't respond to the Christianity he found in the West. He had problems about many things in German-speaking Europe. Then, as a young man about the age of most of you here, he found this much more congenial Russian Orthodox God and, in a few weeks, wrote a whole series of poems to him. It was as if the former years of repressed religious feeling suddenly found an outlet."

"You mean he found himself as a poet when he found that God," argues Andrzej. "He made quite a few false starts before the *Book of Hours*. But he found his muse when he found this Russian God. So we're right in seeing his God and his poetic inspiration as one."

I turn to Tim. "Is the poem as blasphemous as you thought?"

"Well, actually, it might have been written to defeat the old blasphemies," he answers "If Rilke didn't respond to the God he found in German churches—"

"Or Austrian, or Czech," I add.

"—it was probably because they worshiped God and preached him exclusively in old formulas. Most of the theological notions of God— the Trinity, Father and Son and Spirit, even 'first mover' and '*ipsum esse subsistens*,' are beautiful notions, and they can lead to beautiful insights. But they can be deadening, too, especially to a young person when they are presented as dogmas. Rilke was probably turned off. Then he found this different kind of God in Russia. One he could really respond to."

Andrzej finds that too much by half. "The theological teachings of the West were hammered out over the centuries, with great intellectual effort and great faith. Rilke is scrapping all that for the religion of a Russian peasant. It may be more appealing to him, and to you, than dogmatic definitions are. But it's pretty close to sentimental. Russian peasants aren't sentimental, but Rilke turns their feeling into something that can easily turn sentimental and get out of hand and obscure the truth. He himself is artist and intellectual enough to discipline his feelings—he was never satisfied with these early poems, you know. But we, in our sentimental age, may find ourselves uncritically rejecting a very important part of our intellectual heritage if we read the *Stundenbuch* uncritically."

"Right, Father," says Tim. "Now say the rest." He knew that Andrzej was, as always, playing devil's advocate. "What the church has formulated on these matters is, after all, only what human minds—guided by the Spirit, true, but human for all that—are capable of conceiving. Even the formulas of saints and theologians and church councils can't contain all that God is. And the saints, like Thomas Aquinas, are the first to agree."

"I agree, too," says Andrzej. "I admit that Rilke's Russian-peasant way of thinking about and speaking to God can have its uses. It helped him, and it might help some of us, come closer to a notion of what God is. But we can't make Rilke's God into a formula, either. To think that God depends on us for his meaning, needs us, and can't survive without us can result in a formula too, just as easily as the traditional way of thinking of God as omnipotent, omniscient, and the rest. It can be just as deadening, and much more limiting."

"It's good for a start, though," says Tim, "to think of God as close to you, part of you. Nothing in the old piety makes me want to love him so much as thinking that, maybe, he needs me."

"It's a better kind of love," says Tina, "to give to one who needs you than to take from someone who is self-sufficient."

"Very good, Tina. And . . ." I add, "Rilke's idea of God isn't as foreign to the West as he thought. Meister Eckhart said something like it in Germany centuries before: 'I never give God thanks for loving me, because he can't help it.'"

"'It is his nature, whether he wants to or not,'" says Andrzej, completing the quotation and showing he knows the passage too.

"I *like* that idea of God," says Joe, the quiet one.

"I like the idea of God as helplessly in love with each individual man and woman," says Tina, who knows theology as well as German. "But I can't accept that notion of a changing God. It seems to me that all the foundations of what we're supposed to believe in can be shaken if God can change."

"Yes," I say. "One of the attributes of God in our theology *is* that he is immutable. But if, as is surely the case, we are unable to capture all of God in a concept, or even in many concepts, perhaps *our* conception of him should keep changing. Perhaps our theology should keep evolving and developing. Rilke has another poem, also in the *Stundenbuch*, on that. Listen.

> Workers are we—apprentices, journeymen, masters—
> And we are building you, you great midship . . .
>
> We climb up on the cradling scaffolding,
> and the hammers hang heavy in our hands,
> till there comes an hour that kisses our foreheads
> radiantly, as if it knew all these things.
> It comes from you, like a wind from the sea.
>
> Then there is a clang from the many hammers,
> and through the mountains the sound goes, stroke on stroke.
> Only when it grows dark do we let you go,
> and then your emerging contours glow with light.
>
> God, you are vast.

"God is growing. Man is building him, as carpenters build a ship or, as I think is the case here, the nave of a great cathedral. Man finds his labor wearisome, but when the hour for returning to work arrives, the structure itself—radiant, all-knowing, loving—stirs him to action again. When evening comes, and the day's work ends, and man pauses to look at his work, he sees how stupendous God is.

"Now, does this make God blasphemously dependent on man? Or is it saying that man fashions an image of God, a concept, an intellectual notion—which is all he *can* do—and thereby captures something of God's ineffable qualities? In the evening—the evening of life, perhaps—man sees that his work, his intellectual labor, is massive, but unfinished. We never contain God, not in a formula, not in a vast cathedral."

"You left something out!" Andrzej hurries in to say, "Something important. Rilke also says that occasionally someone comes along to help the workmen with their work. An Augustine or a Thomas Aquinas comes along."

He quotes :

> And sometimes there comes to us an earnest traveller,
> who passes like a brightness through our hundred minds
> and shows us, trembling, a new concept.

"I left that out so you could supply it," I say laughing.

"Well, it shouldn't be left out, because it makes my point about our needing other theological perspectives, from great thinkers!"

"So Rilke sees all our theologizing as gradually rising, concept on concept, with the help of great thinkers, toward a complete notion of God?" asks Tim.

"With the occasional help of great thinkers—yes, I believe so," I answer. "And what Fr. Zielinski translated as 'concept' is, in German, *Griff*. That's a handhold or a foothold in mountain climbing. The thinkers who come along show us new ways of mounting the scaffolding so as to build our understanding of him higher and higher. Each new grip, each new concept sends a thrill through us who watch, and the thinker or saint or prophet or scientist who tries it trembles at his daring, reaching out with his hand to grasp some new part of the structure at a stratospheric height. And God himself keeps kissing our foreheads, encouraging us and urging us on to climb higher and higher with our building, to know more and more. A lifetime isn't enough to complete our awareness of him, but as we grow old, in the evening of life, we catch some glimmer of his vastness, and are lost in wonder."

"We need new thoughts about God like that," says Joe.

"It's an impressive poem," says Tim, "but man's image of God isn't God. No human concept of God is God."

"Well, Rilke doesn't imply that the cathedral structure will ever be completed, does he? He knows that our concepts are never enough, and that they can get in the way of our understanding and our love of God. Let's look at another poem in the *Book of Hours*, a famous one. Rilke is again the monk, and God is the monk in the next cell:

> You, neighbor God, if several times
> in the long night I disturb you with loud knocking
> it's because I seldom hear you breathing,

and I know that you are alone in your cell.
And if you should need anything, there's no one there
to lift a drink to your grasp.
I'm always listening. Give me a little sign.
I am very near.

Only a thin wall is between us,
by accident. So it could happen –
one call from your mouth or from mine
and the wall would tumble
completely, without disturbance, without a wound.

The wall is built out of your images.

And your images stand before you like names.
And when sometimes the light blazes within me,
the light whereby my depths know you,
the brightness is wasted on their frames.

And my senses, which are quickly spent,
have no homeland, separated from you.

Love for God may blaze up in us, and then some man-made concept of God will defeat it. We oughtn't to let *anything* stand between us and God. Not even the images we have of him, not even the dogmas we have fashioned, out of Scripture. We have fashioned the beautiful concept of God being three—the Father and the Son and the Love that passes between them, or the Knower and the One Known and the Love that passes between them. And we ourselves are the only creatures on the earth that can know and love. We are like God, knowing and loving, made in that image of him. But even that, beautiful as it is and close to us as it is, is inadequate. No concept completely conveys the notion of God, and we can't let any concepts stand as a wall between us and God when it comes to loving him."

"These poems are important," says quiet Joe. "They tell us that God exists and, though we can never know him completely, we miss everything in life if we don't know him at least a little."

"So we should let ourselves," says Tim, "be his drink and his clothes and his shelter."

"And," adds the gentle Kim, remembering her part of the poem, "his comfortable old slipper."

It's not a bad place to stop. "When we meet next week, bring your own poems."

11

THE WAR IN VIETNAM ENDS, an unconditional surrender only hours after the emergency evacuation via helicopters by order of President Ford. In Cambodia, thousands of refugees are forcibly evicted under Communist orders. Some students can't believe that the United States has actually lost a war, has given up. Most know that the war's end, whatever suffering it may still bring to the survivors, is a blessing.

The academic year is hurrying to its end. Manfred Schöne stages three experimental plays at the school, and for his final class takes his students to the ultimate revelation—the Sistine Chapel ceiling and the wall of the Last Judgment.

In the seminar, Andrzej tears the students' poems apart limb from limb. My heart bleeds, but those who survive—Ellen, surely, and Joe, surprisingly, and tough-minded, classically trained Janet—will profit from his calculated severity. The others, who will likely never be poets, have pretty well known what to expect, and they meet the criticism, to my relief, with mature responses. Joe, for reasons I do not know, has quietly fallen out with his Tennessee sweetheart. I hope his final exams will not suffer as a result.

The pain in my ears continues.

Johnny Hallagan has a sudden heart attack and might have died, but Fr. Costello gets him to the hospital, with a police car clearing the last lap of the way, in a matter of minutes.

Between classes I ask Tim casually, on the stairway, if he will go home when the year is over, or stay in Italy.

"I'll go home. That's all set now. I can't stay here without a better job, which I haven't been able to find. And I should go back to Chicago because my mother needs me."

There isn't time to say more.

On a golden afternoon in the city, I realize that a year isn't going to be long enough to see, let alone savor, even those Roman sights to which the Blue Guide, with its rigid standards of excellence, grants a star.

Johnny Hallagan's quiet acceptance of his pain impresses the doctors and the nuns at Salvator Mundi. He sends instructions with me about wrapping up his history classes, which several of us are covering. He looks much older. The recovery is slower than any of us suspected it would be.

Tim has turned twenty. He worries about going home and wants, at last, to talk about his father.

"I don't want to see him. I don't want to hear him talk. He doesn't talk. He bellows. He's out drinking all night and then bullies us at home. He finds out what you like most, or are particularly good at, and he ridicules that. He never listens. He contradicts everything my mother says and makes fun of her—he really does—in public. My mother is grateful that they don't have to be seen together often. He's usually with the other yahoos he works with."

"Isn't that concentrating on his faults?" I ask. "He has good qualities—you said so yourself. You said he was fearless in speaking up for workers' rights."

"Yes, he loves to live dangerously. He's right most of the time, maybe all of the time, in what he says at those meetings. But he's really more interested in showing off in front of his friends than in seeing that justice is done."

"Are you being fair?"

"I think so. He called me into the kitchen before I left home, and slapped me in front of his friends. He said I shouldn't get any fancy ideas just because I talked to a congressman and was learning Italian and going to Italy to study. He told me to remember where the money was coming from. He was drunk."

"Did he make it up to you?"

"He took me to Comiskey Park when I had to prepare for exams.

I knew what he meant and what he wanted, but I couldn't respond. I couldn't accept it as an apology. He never said he was sorry."

"So you came to Italy and then supported yourself through a second year?"

"Yes. He hates me for it. He's taking it out on my brother, next in line. I guess Kenny got to be a pretty good wrestler, but my dad wrestled him to the floor, just to show him, and broke his arm. My mother wrote to tell me. Broke his arm! Deliberately, I'm sure."

"You can't be sure of that, not while you're still over here. Isn't he affectionate with any of his children?"

"We're all afraid of him, especially the three boys. The two girls he hardly notices, and they keep out of his way. If I ever thought he laid a hand on my mother—"

"He's worked hard all his life. He hasn't had many advantages, and he's put all of you through Catholic schools at considerable expense to give you what he never had."

"It's a matter of pride to him, that's all. He likes to brag about it to the guys at work who haven't been able to do it. Claiming he's kept all the kids unsoiled and virgin pure. You can imagine the blasphemies and the embarrassing remarks he makes."

"You realize he needs affection? Did you ever tell him you love him?"

"How can I tell him that, when it's not true. I hate him."

"You've got to make the effort. He fathered you. You are his flesh and blood. He does love you, even if he can't show it. He needs your love, probably more than the others because you're the firstborn. His acts of cruelty are a pathetic way of asking for love. Can't you be generous and find a way to give it to him? Hating him hurts you more than it hurts him."

I ought not to say such things, when Tim doesn't need advice but only someone to unburden himself to. And as I defend the man, feebly, I envy him the son he has and I haven't, intensely sorry for both of them, afraid of my own feelings, which are compounded of pity and rage.

"Get rid of all the feeling now," I say. "Then maybe you'll have no resentment when you see him again."

12

I T IS MAY, our last month together. I hurry to finish Lucretius in Latin and Thucydides in Greek, convinced by them both that humans are driven by fears and desires they must learn to control.

I am able to tell Ellen that she has real talent and, if she is prepared for a lot of heartbreak, she might think about submitting one of her stories for publication.

She is radiantly happy and says, "You know, Father, I don't have to write about 'Tom' any more. I think I've worked my way through that."

I'm not as happy for her as I should be. After all, if she could transmute her feelings about Tim into small works of imaginative craftsmanship, I ought somehow to be able to sort out my emotions and surmount them.

I visit Johnny Hallagan in the hospital, but can't tire him with my confused feelings about wanting to have a son of my own. The room is dark. A bespectacled German nun has set on the window sill, in a hospital vessel filled with water, a spray of glistening leaves and yellow berries. She warns me very strictly about the limits of my time in the room. Johnny has at least been able to give his attention to a book by Johannes Metz, who thinks we in religious life ought to show not just the world at large but our own church how to live the Gospels.

"Now that I can't be sure that the last day for me isn't all that far away," Johnny says from his bed, "I want to do right what I'm going to do with the rest of my life." His smile does strange things to his face. He offers me the book. "Remember when we talked about the vows? Tough old Metz says that the vows are protests."

I have visited Johnny almost daily, but something doesn't seem right between us this time. "Well at least Metz is in tune with the times," I say, resisting. "And he's not so old as all that, you know. He's about your age."

"I think he'll help you to sort out what we talked about. He says that when we vow to be poor we protest against all the having and possessing in the world. We reject materialism and join in solidarity with the other poor, the ones who haven't been given the option of choosing their poverty."

"And I suppose when we vow to be chaste and childless, we protest against those who regard wife and children as possessions and tyrannize them." My voice is as heavy as the remarks are rueful, and he looks at me with some apprehension.

"Well, we embrace a kind of loneliness. We choose it, and so cast our lot in with those who never chose it and feel trapped in solitary lives."

"It's too trendy for me, Johnny."

"It's a different rationale, seeing the vows as statements taken against society's injustices."

"I'd still rather see them as ways of perfecting myself."

"You might find Metz more congenial if you taught what I teach."

"And read Dickens."

"And read Dickens and were reminded of all the people in the world who are oppressed, in prison, or in need."

He has said "awl the people." I'm impatient with him. "I think I know pretty well what Metz is after. I can predict him on the third vow. We promise of our own free will to obey so we can stand in solidarity with all those who are forced to obey because it's their condition in life. So, even if we can do nothing about the death camps in Russia personally, we take a stand in favor of the Solzhenitsyns and against the gulags."

"We take a lifelong stand against them."

I'm still impatient, and he's disappointed in me.

"I don't want to tire you out, Johnny. Is there anything you need?"

"No, thanks. But *you* need something I wish I could give you."

"I'm OK."

"You're not at peace. Something's got hold of you and you're fighting it."

"So, what should I do?"

"If it's God, submit to it."

"What if I don't want to, or can't?"

"I've been humbled into submission here, Luke. I'm helpless as a baby, and there's nothing I can do about it. It's easier for me to say such things. It will take courage for you to submit."

"You're right, as always. Well, I'll do what I can, Johnny."

I give him my blessing and leave. His eyes are pleading with me. I do not take the copy of Metz that he offers me.

The German nun is suddenly there, brusque and unemotional. Behind the spectacles she has the sort of face Marcel Proust once spoke of, one in which you see no commiseration and no tenderness at the sight of human suffering. Only practical charity, ready to help, ready even to hurt, if charity demands it. "The impassive, unsympathetic, sublime face of true goodness." That is what Proust called it.

She tells me that I ought not to come back. I am not good for the young Pater, who is very weak. I should pray for him.

"Art thou slow to pray?" she asks, in her German-flavored archaic English.

It was what the Sibyl asked Aeneas. I look back into Johnny's room. My glance falls on the window sill.

13

I N THE EPIC COURSE, we've finished Homer and are now reading Virgil in translation. We've read about Aeneas escaping from the fall of Troy and his tragic love for Dido, who shelters him in Carthage, and the Golden Bough, which he plucks in order to see his father, and the wars he has to fight when he arrives at the place that will one day be Rome. We come at last to the last book of the *Aeneid,* book 12. By now it's clear to the class that Virgil isn't going to end his long poem as they had expected, with the founding of Rome and a glorification of its long future as a republic and an empire, ordained by heaven, civilizing the rest of the world. That is almost surely what Augustus, when he asked for an epic of his own, wanted as an ending. But the poem doesn't seem to be heading in that direction. It seems instead to be gathering together, in patterns of images, the thoughts and feelings I have faced in my own experience this year. That comes out strongly in the last lecture I give in Rome.

"As we come to the end of this long epic, I'd like to make a comparison between Virgil's compositional methods and those used in later centuries by composers writing large-scale pieces of music, where themes recur, often across considerable stretches of time, in new keys, in new combinations, with new instrumentation and new harmonies. When the themes reappear, each carries some of the emotional weight it has had in its previous statements, with additional connotations from the new context. Eventually the themes start pointing forward, toward the end of the piece. In a grand design by Beethoven in a symphony, or by Wagner in an opera, or by Virgil here, the recurrent themes are tensed toward some final statement to which they will contribute.

"The passage where we begin today illustrates this. It gathers up many of the themes and images we have met before and tenses them toward the last page of the epic.

"What happens today? Aeneas is struck by an arrow. He is brought back to camp wounded, supported by his son Ascanius, who is still too young to fight. Bleeding, stumbling, leaning on his great spear, Aeneas calls for someone to cut his wound open and extract the arrow and send him back to battle. But the efforts of Iapyx, the doctor who attends him, are of no avail. The arrow is lodged too deep in the flesh, and all the time the battle is going badly. The cries of young men dying echo around the tent.

"Then suddenly the pain stops, the blood ceases to flow from the wound, and the doctor finds that the arrow of its own accord follows his hand as he draws it from the flesh. He cries out that more than medical skill has wrought this wonder. He is right. Those present do not know it, but Aeneas's mother, the goddess Venus, unable to bear her son's pain, has with maternal tenderness plucked a healing herb and, bathed in a mist, carried it to the Trojan camp and plunged it into the water the doctor was using. Then Aeneas rises to fight his final battle.

"This passage is, to use a musical term, a recapitulation. It picks up several motifs from earlier places in the poem, restates them for us, and redirects them toward the unexpected last page.

"Iapyx, the doctor in this passage, is identified as the son of Iasus. Now a few weeks back, we met another son of Iasus. Do you remember? At the end of book 5. Aeneas is at last within easy sailing distance of his promised land, Italy, and yet his goddess mother knows that the gods who pursue him have blown him off his course before, and may again. She asks Neptune to give the Trojan fleet safe passage, and Neptune agrees, provided one life be given for many. The life he takes is that of Aeneas's faithful helmsman, Palinurus. The sea is quiet, and high in the stern, the helmsman is visited by the god of sleep, who comes though the mist. The helmsman hesitates for a moment and drops to his death in the sea, taking the rudder with him while the ship sails on. Father Aeneas reaches his destination.

"Motifs from that passage recur in this later one. In both passages Venus intervenes to save her son. The god of sleep in book 5, like Venus here in book 12, comes veiled in mist. The helmsman in book 5, like the healing herb in this passage, is plunged into the water. The rudderless ship in book 5, like the arrow here in book 12, moves of its own accord, furthering the passage of Aeneas on his mission.

"And the helmsman there, like the doctor here, is—it's a small point we might have missed—a 'son of Iasus.' They may be brothers.

They both help Aeneas on his way. They are both in some way heal-
ers, which is what the root 'ia'—as in 'psychiatry'—means.

"Virgil gives us, across hundreds of lines, those little motivic links.
Across hundreds of lines, yes, but I think that he hoped they would
keep working in our minds as we read, for it is at this point in the last
book—when a healing son of Iasus exclaims that a miracle has been
wrought—that Aeneas straps on his armor, embraces his own son
Ascanius, kisses him through the visor of his helmet, and speaks one
of the great passages in the poem. It is, in fact, the only time in all the
poem that Virgil gives us Aeneas's actual words to his son:

> Learn from me, my boy, what it is to be a man and to suffer.
> Learn from others what it is to be happy.

We *have* to think of Hector at this moment. Hector's son in the *Iliad*
was only an infant, shrinking in fear from his father's helmet. Hector
had to take his helmet off to kiss him. But Aeneas's son is already
learning about human suffering, about the *lacrimae rerum*. His
father, with his helmet already clapped on his head, kisses him through
the visor, reminding him of the war he did not want to fight.

"The lines addressed to the little son would be memorable even in
a context less well prepared, even without the echo of Homer. And if
we are sensitive to the way Virgil operates, we reflect that all the surrogate sons we have met in the long poem die. They die almost in
pairs. Palinurus the helmsman and Misenus the trumpeter. Lausus the
enemy's son and Pallas the ally's son. Nisus and Euryalus the older
and the younger male lovers. All of these have already fallen. And at
the very moment that Aeneas is healed of his wound, Virgil tells us,
the cries of other young men falling in battle echo around the tent.
Then we remember that the man who asked for the *Aeneid*, the most
powerful man in the world when Virgil was writing, Caesar Augustus,
also lost his adoptive son, Marcellus.

"There's a pattern that links all of these surrogate sons. Each is
given in death, like a recurrent leitmotif, a flower image. When, in the
world of the dead, Aeneas's father showed him the long Roman future
and saw Marcellus still to be born and destined to die young, he called
for lilies and bright flowers to scatter in the boy's honor. And, at pivotal passages throughout the poem, Palinurus is lulled to sleep on the
stern by a dewy branch the god of sleep has brought from Lethe,
Nisus and Euryalus die like poppies weighted down by the rain, and
the hues on Lausus's dying face are like those on the culled flower to

which the dead Pallas is compared. Most important of all, it is while he is preparing the funeral of his trumpeter Misenus that Aeneas sights the flowering growth that is central to all of these—the Golden Bough. The bough even hesitates before it comes in Aeneas's hands, as the helmsman hesitates before he drops into the sea, and the arrow refuses at first to move in the doctor's healing hand. All of that, I submit, is the work of an artist who works with small motifs in a design as vast as life itself.

"Well, you've now read through to the end of the *Aeneid* and you know what happens. You've noticed how, near the end, the motifs reappear. Venus once again appears out of maternal concern and plucks Aeneas's spear from a tree sacred to those who died at sea. You've noticed that, on the last page, as Aeneas poises that spear to slay his prostrate enemy, we have again that tantalizing word—and in Latin it's always in the same participial form—*cunctantem*, 'hesitating.' Aeneas hesitates before he kills because his enemy has pleaded for mercy in the name of his father, and Aeneas's father had told him 'Spare the suppliant . . . . Make utter war on the intransigent, but spare the suppliant.' He hesitates. Then the glitter of gold catches his eye. The armor on his enemy, blazoned with golden images of killing, tells him to kill. And he kills. That's how the *Aeneid* ends."

No one in the class is taking any of this down. It's much too complicated, too late in the term to be of any use as an essay topic, and, they sense, too personal to me to be asked as an examination question.

But finally a hand goes up. It is, of all people, Joe, the quiet one.

"Father, that's what I don't understand. Why, at the end, does Aeneas kill his enemy, when his enemy has asked for mercy? Aeneas is supposed to be a man of *pietas*."

"Well, it is a shocking and abrupt conclusion, Joe. But it is carefully prepared, built up like some vast symphonic movement out of many patterns. And it is an ambivalent statement for Augustus to ponder. How was Augustus, the *pater patriae*, 'the father of his country,' to read the ending of the epic that was supposed to be his own story? What was he to think of the hero that was surely intended as a figure for himself? How was he to react when, at the end of the epic he had requested of his poet, he is shown still to be no better than he was when he made his bid for power—a man who had killed off his enemies? I think that his poet left Augustus with that ending—or rather, with an epic without an ending—because his mission in life had not yet ended. He still had much to learn, and he seemed morally ill-equipped to learn it. The Golden Bough was right to hesitate.

"This is our last class, and I won't put a last interpretation on the *Aeneid* for you. I've already done too much, perhaps, pointing you in one direction. Ponder it for yourselves. It's about you as much as it is about the father of Rome. The way you read those recurrent motifs in that final recapitulation is the way you'll read the *Aeneid* and possibly the choices in your own lives as well.

"I'll look forward to reading your essays. Good luck on the examination."

14

THE PAIN IN THE EARS has lessened, but for weeks I have known that some of my hearing is leaving me.

During the days between the end of classes and the beginning of examinations, while the students are busy with their books, I take a final trip, buying a second-class train ticket at the window without benefit of rail pass, to Venice.

Even after previous visits to the city on the Adriatic, the feeling of stepping, suitcase in hand, from the railroad station landing into a boat—the low-cost vaporetto—as your means of transportation is unique and exhilarating. The city is rainwashed. Along the Grand Canal the rotting, sagging *palazzi* glisten in bright morning sunshine. The tower and façade of San Giorgio on its island are astonishingly clear across the water, a fairy-tale vision. The two squares that flank the campanile at San Marco are alive with every variety of the human species. Flags swirl gustily from their flagpoles—the tricolor, the banner of St. Mark, the papal insignia. One band is playing Neapolitan songs, another the overture to *Tannhäuser*. It is clear that recent rains have flooded parts of the city. The Doge's Palace, that supreme architectural emblem of the once Most Serene Republic, seems about to lift into the air like some rose-Gothic spaceship.

I find a room in a hostel for Catholic travelers and have a plate of scampi at a trattoria behind San Marco, chatting with two couples from Pforzheim who find Venice disappointingly *schmutzig*. I encourage them to see it with the soul. Somehow that sounds more convincing in German, and they actually agree to try.

I take the vaporetto to the Lido, alone in the crowd on the deck, facing back toward Venice. The city retreats across the water, its domes and bell towers set pink against distant white Alps.

The water at the Lido is cool this early in the year, but swimmable, and clear as crystal. The beach, still uncrowded, is hospitably warm.

The sand is fine. I lie on my back and watch small clouds drift into the sun. The salt stings my chest pleasantly. My ears throb.

Returned to the mainland, I explore the city on foot. Lights are going on inside the *palazzi*. They are more mysterious than the lights going on in any buildings anywhere else in the world. It is easy to conjure up tales of intrigue. In Venice nothing seems innocent. Cries of gondoliers echo around corners where the waves lap against chipped façades and stone lions crouch behind crumbling flowerpots.

I get pleasurably lost in the darkening maze of squares and bridges. I find the plaque on the Ca' Vendramin, which commemorates Wagner's death there, and I find the Teatro Fenice, where Verdi's *Rigoletto* and *Traviata* had their premieres.

That night this most beautiful opera house in Italy, its green-rococo interior delicately lit, presents a Verdi opera set in Venice, *I Due Foscari,* an early piece, based on Byron. The Doge of Venice—that terrifying figure, the Verdi father—is forced by his Council of Ten to banish his own son.

"I shall die in exile," says the son, handing the parchment back to his father. "Will we ever meet again?"

"In heaven, perhaps. On earth, no."

The exiled son says farewell to his own two boys.

"*Miei figli!*"

Inevitably, to a long-spanned Italian melody, an ensemble builds up, and everyone on stage voices his or her sentiments. The young girl next to me says under her breath, "Oh, how beautiful!" and the husband or lover who has been kissing her cheek more or less discreetly through the performance says, "How beautiful to die!"

The exiled son does die, and so, in the end, does the old father, his heart broken.

"My son, my son . . ."

At that point, the sounds start to blur in my ears.

The pain in my ears eases as I walk back through the city along its canals. San Marco and the Palazzo Dogale are alive with light and with music that scatters on the night winds.

I sight Manfred Schöne in the crowd. He scowls with moody recognition, makes a quick decision, which registers strongly on his face, and invites me to have coffee with him.

We retreat to a cafe on the square, to a table inside, as the night air is growing cold. It is the sort of place I've seen until now only from the outside—prohibitively expensive. Red plush seats, flowers, and glass-enclosed frescoes. The sounds of the square are both clearer and more muted when experienced through the place's elegant curtains. It is almost dark inside, and by now almost desperately quiet. There is no clatter of dishes, and the white-coated waiters whisper. Schöne always comes here, or so he says.

"The illusion is best when one artificial façade is seen from behind another."

"I've never seen Venice like this before. From the inside looking out."

"This isn't the real inside. The real inside is complete loneliness."

"Come on! The real Venice, I've heard you say in your classes, is an object lesson in intelligent town planning, laid out by intelligent men for the maximum benefit of people of all stations."

"That is true."

"It's a triumph of ingenuity, you said, the engineering of it as impressive as the art that fills it."

"That is true. I won't even separate the planning, the engineering, the architecture, and the art. They are all manifestations of the same spirit, which is intelligent and forward looking."

"And artificial?"

"What the tourist sees is artificial. The façade is artificial. We've made Venice a kind of toy. For the old Venetians it was a bold experiment that worked. The people who lived here when it was a republic had the answers to urban problems we have no answers for today. It was the most humane and livable city Europe had known for hundreds of years."

"And the inside is complete loneliness?"

"Not the inside of Venice. The inside of our illusions about Venice. This place," he stares around the cafe, "gets us part of the way inside the illusions. It stinks of illusion."

"I smell mostly aromatic coffee."

He is never amused at my attempts at humor. "You were at the opera tonight, as usual?"

"Yes," I answer. "Were you?"

"Yes. I've never seen *Foscari* before. It touched me, but I left after the second act."

He gives me a pleading look. He is tormented. He is probably en route, during the break, to Vienna to see his two boys. He didn't want to acknowledge me in the crowd. Now it is clear he has taken a risk of some sort with me and needs to talk. I ought to ask him a question. Instead he asks me.

"What is troubling you so much?"

I am startled by his saying to me what I might have said to him, and startled too by his sudden, overwhelming concern. He is open and vulnerable. His eyes look straight into mine, and say, "Tell me. I can bear your pain. That's why I'm here." The question comes so suddenly I don't try to deny the charge, or make excuses, or cover up.

"I think I'm losing my hearing."

"That is nothing. We all grow older and lose the quickness of our senses. What else is wrong?"

"I really am hearing less. My ears are in pain. You know what a loss this will be to me, if it grows worse. Music is a part of my life."

"See another doctor. If there is nothing to be done, you can learn to live with the ears you have. Pain is only a reminder of how finite you are. You can find room for it, if you have to. Even music you can do without, if you have to. It isn't as important as what you derive from it, and you can find that in other places, that nourishment for the spirit. Tell me, really, what is it that troubles you? I see it is something more."

This from a man as tormented as any I've known, a man I should try to help, an artist in constant pain. Idolized by his students but always unfulfilled. More intelligent and perceptive about the things that matter to him than anyone he knows, and so always lonely.

"Whatever it is that speaks to me in music *is* starting to speak to me in other ways. And I don't want to hear what it is saying."

"What is it saying?"

"I've got to give up everything I love. Let go of everything else and surrender instead to it, whatever it is. What I don't surrender willingly, it will take."

"That's the voice of your God. The voice of your God, I tell you. Your God, not mine. You made the commitment. Now he's holding you to the bargain."

I don't want to hear this. I change the subject. "What God is yours?"

"I haven't got a God. I envy you the one you're in love with."

I say nothing.

"You are in love with him, you know. It shows in many ways. But I don't think you're past the first stage of this yet."

I don't know what to say. He tries to help me.

"I envy you. You're a very contemporary man. You read and write a lot, you come and go as you please, you influence other people to think the way you do, and the enemies you make you scarcely know about."

"I know who they are, at least the ones at the school. There's no point in paying much attention to them. They're just small-minded. They're not real enemies. The real enemy, Manfred, is the God you say I love. He keeps trying to possess me."

"Why shouldn't he? If I believed in him I couldn't object to his possessiveness. You of all people have no case against him. You believe he made you, sustains you, surrounds you. And when you took the collar, you gave yourself to him."

"All right, Manfred. I'll tell you what keeps troubling me. What really troubles me. I want a son . . ."

His eyes narrow in pain.

". . . I want the son now I might have begot twenty years ago."

"Then you want sorrow such as you have never known. We help each other in this world because ultimately we are alone in it. We have friends. We observe charity and kindness to ease the pain of loneliness. Ultimately we are all separated from each other. But no people are more isolated than those in the same family. A father, sooner or later, is a stranger to his son. A man is a stranger to his wife, after they have children. Children are strangers to their father—especially, let me tell you, when they approach the age of twenty. And it hurts. Once a father and his son are strangers to each other, they easily become enemies."

I start to say something, and he anticipates me.

"You are going to say it isn't true. But you have never had a son, so how can you tell? You never married, so you can't know how your wife can use your children against you. You did have a father. How did you feel toward him?

"I'd like to make up to him now what I didn't do for him when he was alive."

"Did you ever tell him you loved him?"

"Not really. I wish I had."

"Did you love him?"

"I think I did."

"How can you tell? We hurt those closest to us. You've lost a little happiness by never marrying, but believe me, you've also spared yourself a lot more pain."

"How often do you see your sons, Manfred?"

"Three or four times a year. I take them away on trips."

"Away from their mother?"

"Yes. We are not legally separated, but we have an arrangement. We don't see each other except to be pleasant for a few minutes."

"How old are the boys?"

"Eleven and nineteen."

"And you love them, don't you? You see yourself in them?"

"I could when they were younger. Now the older boy is growing away fast. He won't interest himself in anything of interest to me. He sulks. I don't mind. He has to grow up, and part of growing up is growing away. It's the younger boy who hurts me. He believes everything his mother says about me. He's very self-possessed and distant. He's polite the way a magistrate might be. There's no real respect in him. Even when he looks at me he isn't looking."

"And so you can't feel that your sons are a part of you that will live on?"

"They will survive me—to be as different as they can be. That of course is their right and their choice. You're deluding yourself if you think fathers perpetuate themselves in their sons. Fathers cannot make their sons become what they themselves hoped to be. They're cruel if they try to force that, and they're set for a lot of pain if they expect it. But sons—a son can be crueler than any father."

"Even if I have no son, Manfred, and you have two, I can't believe what you say."

"It is true for me. It is my experience."

"I am sorry, Manfred."

"Thank you." He means it.

"Now I will tell you, Father, what you already know but need to be told. You *are* a father in the most important way. Your God is a father who has a son. He has a son, eventually, in the flesh—an incredible, beautiful mythology—but first and foremost he has a son in the spirit. First and foremost the son is a thought, an idea, a *logos*. The father is creative in him. That is true paternity. Not the son in the flesh, but the son in the spirit."

He leans closer to me.

"You, you are full of ideas. You have a head full of thoughts, most of which I find sentimental and absurd, but they are thoughts and ideas you are passing on to young people who accept them and want to live them. You are helping them to understand other languages and other cultures, to write poems and listen to music and read with some comprehension. You are encouraging them to believe in what you believe in, to love what you love. That is real fatherhood."

"You're doing the same, Manfred. Who is the most influential teacher in the school? There isn't one of us hasn't learned from you."

"That is why my own sons are such a disappointment to me. Do you see? What one can do with a student at the most receptive age, one cannot do with a son. A son turns away from you at the very time when you need him. You help him and love him for eighteen, nineteen years, then he rejects you and all you say and all you are. It defeats me. It almost makes me despair. But you, you are like your hero Hans Sachs. You are childless, and yet you have children. Your classes are full of Walthers and Evas. You help them interpret their dreams, to read and write and sing and listen. You show them how to observe the rules and respect traditions and make their youthful inspirations work for them. And when the time comes to let them go, like Hans Sachs, you let them go."

"I have to let them go. They have their own lives to lead. But this year I've found an ideal figure, an ideal son. A young Walther, perhaps. I can talk to him as I talk to you. He's full of promise, and I help him on his way. And I wish he were more a part of me than just someone I instructed and then let go."

"This year he's that boy from Chicago."

"This year he's that boy from Chicago. This year the problem has hit me hard."

He smiles ruggedly. "You know the old tag. *Aut liberi aut libri.* Either children or books. A wise man knows he can't devote himself to both. Your Hans Sachs gives up a wife and daughter in Eva. And a son in Walther. And they bless him for it in the end. He goes back to his books and his trade, and the love of others is his reward, their gratitude is his crown of laurel. You're moved by all that, aren't you?"

"I am, always." I am also eager to change the subject. "Do *you* like *Die Meistersinger?*

"I detest Wagner. A terrible man who wrote evil works."

"You mean, he wrote works that were put to evil purposes."

"There was something there already that encouraged that. A lot of him went into his music, including the hate. Wagner isn't for my generation. My boys have Jewish blood. Maybe they can grow up to forgive him. I can't. I'm a Gentile, and I still can't forgive him. I've seen too much."

"I respect that judgment. All the same, you'll agree that it isn't the insufficiencies of his character or his personality that matter with Wagner, or any other artist. It's the art itself. You'll agree to that, won't you?"

"Yes, I will."

"We're all flawed, after all. If Beethoven was syphilitic and Borromini suicidal, does it make any real difference to their art? It's their inner lives, not their propensities or physical afflictions, that are important to us. It's the inner life, tormented by and rising to meet the challenge of artistic creation, that produces great art."

"I think the case is very complicated with Wagner, but yes, what you say is true enough. A great artist doesn't seek his own ends and preach his own truths. He listens to himself, to an inner voice, if you like, and that voice is something more than himself, and he allows that to speak through him."

"He really is the instrument of a higher power?"

"Yes."

"Well, I think Wagner is such an instrument." I warm to the changed subject. "The archetypal quality of his work is almost a proof of it. The new interpretations—Donington's, using Carl Jung and depth psychology—show, at least to me, that Wagner intuitively reached levels of feeling that are common to all of us, but which we do not always acknowledge. Some of what he found within himself is terrible and repellent, some of it loving and healing. But I find I respond to it all. All of it is in me, at least potentially, and to experience it is healing. Or, to use his own term, redeeming."

He contemplates me with some alarm, but lets me go on.

"Wagner didn't really know he was doing all that, penetrating to the level of our suppressed feelings and giving them expression. At least, he didn't explain what he was doing that way, not in any of those volumes on volumes he wrote. He tried instead to justify what he was doing in terms of Greek drama or contemporary German philosophy. But he got the right word for the effect of it—redeeming."

"So, in *Tristan* and *Parsifal* you face what is buried deep within you?"

"Yes. I face it."

"And you find yourself, at the end of the opera, redeemed?"

"Yes. At peace with myself."

"And what you will do for this terrible man who may have intuitively struck on some 'collective unconscious' you will not do for the God who, you say, loves you and whom you love?"

He has cornered me as surely as any Greek in a Platonic dialogue.

"Father, I'm no Jungian, but I'll tell you something that that old Klingsor from Zurich, Carl Jung, once said. A truly religious person knows that God tries in the most inconceivable ways to enter a man's heart. God can set a man to battle with himself, divide him in two, as Faust is divided when he says, 'Two souls, alas, dwell in my breast apart.' God can tear a man apart, as your Tannhäuser is torn, between the sensual and the spiritual. You Christians are supposed to feed and clothe and shelter the poorest on earth. You are supposed to love your enemies. Well, your Mr. Jung says, what if the poorest on earth, the one most in need, the enemy himself, is within you? Can you be kind to yourself, feed and clothe and shelter yourself, heal your own hurt?"

"When did I ever see myself poor and in need, and not respond?" I almost quote the words of the last judgment, and I am afraid of what he is going to say.

"When did you ever see yourself poor and in need? When you found someone you could talk to like you are talking to me, and you realized he was young enough to be your son, and then you wished he *was* your son. You couldn't forgive yourself for wishing it, and yet you couldn't forgive yourself for promising away a son when you took your vows a long time ago. Now your God is trying to heal you. He's saying, 'You trusted me then. Can't you trust me now?' I think you should listen to him."

I pause for a long time. Outside the window the lights of Venice are going out.

"You don't believe in him," I say wonderingly, "but you're like his messenger to me."

"So are all the things you love, all messengers. God speaks in them all—Homer and Virgil, Verdi and Wagner. You know what Wagner does in his operas? Divides himself up into Amfortas and Kundry, Parsifal and Klingsor, and then starts draining off the evil and bringing together the good and healing his own hurt. His operas are gigantic dramatizations of his own perennial problems with himself. I don't like that. We all can love Verdi because he sings about all of us. Wagner sings only about the torment going on inside himself. I admit it's fascinating. He was a great genius, and a real man of the theater. But no one can love his work unless he is ready, as you are, to submit to it on his terms. If you do, you suffer along with all the Amfortases and Kundrys and, as those big calculated dramas move to their stupendous climaxes, you are redeemed with them. Well, Father, your God can do

what Wagner does, if you'll surrender to him, and you don't need ears
for His kind of music."

There is a long pause.

"So what do I do? I forgive myself—"

"For making a religious commitment, and then trying to take some
of it back."

"And then?"

"You let happen what will happen. Good or bad, whatever it is,
accept it. That is the quiet way he wants you now to renew the
promises you made enthusiastically when you were young. Then, it
seemed anything was possible, and it probably was. If you wanted
something strong enough, you could get it then by sheer force of will.
And you probably did. Now you learn, and Wagner tells you in Hans
Sachs and the other characters, that there are some really beautiful
things you cannot have. Cannot ever have. I hope that what you're
feeling now is the worst of what you will feel about failed realizations.
I've seen many more ruins on my personal landscape. We've all got to
renounce those unrealizable dreams and hopes. Renunciation—that's
the great Wagnerian theme, isn't it? Accept the inevitable and embrace
it. Choose it. It is good. It is *God*, coming into your life. Accept it, and
you will grow, *O Sachs, mein Freund*."

"Maybe I don't understand what I have done with my life, but I
believe what you say. And I am very grateful, Manfred."

"No one understands his own life. We are mysteries to ourselves.
Do as he keeps asking, your God, and you'll probably suffer more, but
you'll grow. Not to grow is to die. You remember Sant' Ivo? You were
there when I gave the talk to my class. The tiny little place has to rise
up to support a circular dome, to set it floating. It's a star and it has
to transform itself somehow to support a circle. It struggles upward
to a higher, simpler state. It succeeds by transforming itself. Your God
is within you, speaking to you, but he's also outside and above you,
floating like a dome. He's both immanent and transcendent—isn't
that what the theologians say? Deep within you he urges you to transform yourself and struggle upwards to him high above you."

"Do *you* believe he is within each one of us?"

"What I believe is of no consequence here."

"Tell me."

"I believe that the world is a violent place, that we have only slightly
tamed our violence, that we are all hurrying toward meaningless
deaths which, to some extent, we can foresee. That is to say, I proba-

bly believe in nothing. I find those who do believe, and who build their beliefs into beautiful structures, the ones I admire most. I envy you your optimistic beliefs, and that is why I wanted to help you believe in them when I saw you were troubled."

The white-coated waiters have long since turned out the lights in the cafe, and are standing politely at the glass door for us to see that it is past closing time. We ask their pardon and hurry out to the square. It is cold and almost empty, and never has it looked so vast to me.

"Thank you, Manfred. You have helped me, perhaps more than I know."

"Thank you, Father. You will help me, too, if you really believe what you say you believe. We nonbelievers depend on you who believe."

"Depend on me, Manfred."

As he takes my right hand in his, he places his left on my shoulder.

I move on the vaporetto down the darkened Grand Canal. The moon rises over the rooftops. The water laps quietly and glimmers with reflected light. A gleam, not quite a gleam, of gold. Schöne seems a kind of hero to me.

That night I have a dream that is Venetian in its half-lit baroquery.

I have an arrow in my side, and I plead with someone to extract it. The walls of Sant' Ivo rise gradually to transform themselves into a forest of cypresses and old ash trees.

A knightly figure is walking on the Rhine. He lifts his flashing helmet from his head. He is too young to die. He hesitates, as if any minute he will sink into the waves. A trumpet sounds a single note, coming nearer. Ellen, with her glasses all clouded over, cries out to me. "Art thou slow to pray? Art thou slow?"

"Let me see my father," the knightly figure says. "Show me the way to him."

I try to cry out, "Here I am." But there is a wall built of images between me and the vision, and the vision fades. Johnny Hallagan is bending over me. His face shines like a saint's. Parts of him are broken off, and the edges glimmer like stars. He touches my ears, and says:

"God is within you and without. Submit. Surrender. Let go."

The throbbing in my side ceases. I sleep peacefully the rest of the night.

In the morning, though I have time to stay in Venice one more day, I take the early train back to Rome. Italy's rocks seem harsher, its lakes more opaque, its sunlight and shadow more pronounced, than before. I try to conjure up the memory of the silver trumpet that sang of the Holy Grail. I remember the notes, but the sound of it has gone out of my ears.

In Rome, it has been raining heavily, and there is a rainbow along the Tiber.

At the villa Fr. Costello sees me coming along the palm-lined way and comes out on the porch to meet me.

"Johnny is dead."

I drop my suitcase. His strong hand grips my shoulder.

"He died last night. A massive attack. We'll have a funeral Mass here before we send him back to Philadelphia."

My ears blank out completely for a minute.

15

JOHNNY LIES UNHELMETED at his wake. I try to think of something joyously childlike, maybe something from *Four Saints*, to recite at his Mass. But the words that hammered away at me when I first came to the villa have left me now.

Ellen suggests this from Rilke, and it is Rilke I read at the Mass. The monk to his God:

> Put out my eyes. I can see you.
> Close up my ears. I can hear you.
> And without feet I can go to you.
> Without a mouth I can call on you.
> Break off my arms. I will fasten on you
> with my heart as with a hand.
> Stop my heart, and my brain will beat.
> Thrust a brand into my brain
> and I will carry you on the surface of my blood.

So we send the body of John Robert Hallagan home.

The final examinations are written quietly, under less tension than any in my experience.

It is Andrzej who says to me the most consoling thing about Johnny's death: "This is a death clear in meaning. So many of the hundreds of deaths I saw during and after the war seemed to have no meaning. They still have no meaning for me. This death has."

For once he has nothing more to say.

The next Sunday is Pentecost Sunday—the day on which, though he left us, he sent his Spirit, to see us through time until time would end. The bright day is appropriately windy, and the ash trees and cypresses toss their branches beneath the chapel windows.

After Mass, Ellen, apprehensive about her impending transatlantic flight, asks me to hear her confession, and then we walk slowly from the chapel along the sunny porch of the villa to my office. Andrzej has pretty well relinquished the office to me these days so I can, as he puts it, "play Hans Sachs for the final act."

Ellen explains, "I'm always afraid of taking long trips."

"And this one closes a chapter. Can you believe the year is already over?"

"No. I wish it would start again. Whatever am I going to do back home? " She sits down tentatively. "How are the ears, Father?"

"Oh, they're not the obedient servants they once were. I don't suppose they'll ever let me hear music as well as I used to. But I'm learning to live with them. I liked your poem."

"Fr. Zielinski was hard on it."

"He was cruel only to be kind. There was too much Rilke in it to please him. He has a quick eye for faults. But I, with my failing senses, liked it. How did it go, now . . . ?"

Ellen, shy in many ways, is not shy about her writing. She speaks the poem without embarrassment.

> God, I was made as salt upon your tongue
>   And pain within your heart.
> As word I seared your brain, as song unsung
>   I wrenched your womb apart.
>
> Now I am made the sunlight on your face,
>   The rain upon your cheek.
> You breathe my breezes, wander through my space
>   And listen when I speak.
>
> Then take me, God, as everlasting day,
>   As elemental night,
> As gentle wind and rain, as world of play
>   And garden of delight.

"He must love you for saying that."

"He or She."

I laugh. "Of course. Well, we know so little about God. Maybe the only thing we really know is that God knows and loves. I hope, Ellen, that your love affair with God is rich and full, lasts all your life, and expands your mind and heart."

"Thank you, Father."

It sounds as if she is about to cry. But she is not. She takes her glasses off, and she is clear-eyed.

"You know, Father, I asked about your ears because, well, it may be the Roman sunlight, but more and more I find I don't really need these as I used to."

"Italy is a land of miracles!" I exclaim. "Ellen, I'm overjoyed! We'll see if your eyesight is stronger under gentler light back in Minnesota."

"I'll write and tell you. Father, you're busy and I won't take up more of your time. I wanted to leave you this."

She takes a loose page from her notebook.

"Don't read it now. It's more about the senses, and it's my own version of the *Book of Hours* again, so I'm talking to God, of course. But you know Rilke's God was no ordinary God. Anyway, I want you to have it."

She stands up quickly and, as she lays the page on my desk, the glasses go back on, and she is shy again.

"Thank you, Ellen. I'll look forward to reading it. We won't say good-bye now, will we? There's still tomorrow."

She smiles and nods. Then she is gone. The poem, simpler than anything in her stories, reads:

> I touched unspoken music,
> Heard unremembered light,
> Reflected time unknown, before
> You called me from the night.
>
> I know, because you touched me
> With fragrant murmurings.
> My darkness lights remembering
> The silence in me sings.

Janet stops by the office briefly. She is really looking for Andrzej.

"Fr. Zielinski was one of the best teachers I've ever had anywhere. When I came here I'd never met a Catholic priest before. He changed my whole image of what you people are like. He's helped me a lot since the last class, you know. We've gone over a lot of my work, and he's told me bluntly what is good in it and what has got to go."

"I'm glad to hear it, Janet. He's some sort of genius, of course. It was a pleasure for me to be teaching in tandem with him."

"Well, Father, no disrespect, but I really think he beat you in every one of your encounters."

"You think so?"

"Yes. He went right to the point every time. You always took one step back for every two forward. You were bland, much too concerned with images and so on. But you were a good foil for him. I guess that was your strategy, wasn't it?"

"It's time to take that one step back . . . You certainly did well on your Greek exam."

"Yes, I felt good about it. But in the first semester I thought a lot of Plato's ideas were scary, though you tried hard to explain them away. And in the second semester I couldn't work up much interest in Thucydides at all, except for the topographies of those battles. I'm going to see Pylos and Sphacteria one of these years. But I may have had my last course in Greek. I want to do other things."

"With your languages you might consider going on in comparative literature."

"Yes, the poetry seminar is the sort of thing I wouldn't mind teaching some day. But we ought to have read more poems by women."

"Emily Brontë and Emily Dickinson?"

"Well, perhaps, but even more the women who are still writing. I think you'll see in the future that literature by women will begin to take over the curriculum. I don't see much of a future for your Greek philosophers and your medieval saints. You're going back to Canada, aren't you? Have you read Margaret Laurence and Margaret Atwood? Mavis Gallant? Anne Hébert?"

"Not much. *Mea culpa*. But only Ms. Hébert would have made it on our course. You'll remember that, after Robert Frost, we read only foreign languages. And your four Canadian ladies are all of them better at prose than verse."

"Well, I'm going to do my graduate work on Willa Cather."

"Oh, fine! Now *there*'s someone I've read quite a bit of—*The Song of the Lark*."

"Not one of her best."

"Oh, but the passage where the country doctor tells the girl who wants to be a singer that there are only a few really splendid things in life, and they're so easy to miss, and she should reach for them while she can . . ."

"I don't remember that. But I remember how she eventually makes it big in the opera world. Well, Father, good-bye." She extends a hand.

"Good-bye, Janet, and good luck."

Tim has immersed himself in his books through the examination period, and perhaps for other reasons has kept his distance from me since the day he told me about his father. On the night before the student flight back to Chicago, when I am well into marking the papers on Homer and Virgil, he comes to my office door. He is tentative, almost distant.

"I wanted to say thanks for a good year, Father."

"Want to sit down?"

He does.

"It *was* a good year, Father. I think when Fr. Hallagan died a lot of us became aware, suddenly, about the sacredness of life and death. And you . . . you taught me to think and feel in new ways. I learned a lot, and I think I've grown."

"Thanks, Tim. I too was helped by Fr. Hallagan this year. And I'm grateful for the times you and I have had together, especially, I think, for the time we went to the Virgil places. I've learned from you."

"From me?"

"Well, there's no one we can't learn from." He thinks for a minute that I am just being pleasant. "But you, Tim, you are a chosen vessel. I've often thought to myself, 'Tim is more like me now than I was myself at his age.' Except that you are so much more than I am, more generous and more concerned about the problems of the world and about helping people. I've often thought that you loved God more, far more, than I do."

"A chosen vessel. You mean to say, like St. Paul—"

"Like St. Paul told Timothy, yes. You should be a priest. You have all the signs."

"I was afraid you'd say that, and I didn't want to hear it. Now, on the last day—"

"On the last day, I've said it. Well, I intend it as a compliment, and it's true. You do have all the signs of being a good priest. It wouldn't be right for me to say good-bye and never tell you that."

"Something's been telling me that for months now. But I didn't want to listen. I think I want to marry and have children."

"Well, Tim, you'd be just as good a man, and probably do just as much good, too, if you married and had children. You're full of love, and you would be a good husband and a dutiful father."

"A father or a Father."

"Mister Brannigan or Father Brannigan. Either one. They're two kinds of love and two kinds of fathering, but many of the same good qualities are needed for either."

"What are those?"

"What St. Paul told Timothy—justice, faith, charity, and peace with those who call on the Lord from a pure heart. Being gentle towards all, ready to teach, ready for every good work."

He puts his head in his hands and says nothing for a while. I break the silence.

"All right, that's enough about that. It was meant to be a compliment, not a complication."

A long pause. I say, "What would you want me to do—think it and never say it? It's said."

"Well," he comes back, his dark eyes misting up, "it certainly caps a year of learning and searching."

I try to change the subject. "So—what did you learn this year that is most valuable?"

He thinks for a minute.

"You make something beautiful when you love it. Or maybe just that there's more to life than any surface meaning indicates. Everything you taught us pointed to other meanings. Nothing is quite as it seems, because God is everywhere."

"You knew that when you came in here the first time."

"I know it better now . . . OK, Father, tell me what *you* learned this year?"

It is the pedagogical trick I used on him when he first came to see me, and it breaks the emotion of the moment.

"Well, I've seen more operas than in all the previous years put together, and I'm more convinced than ever that God speaks to us through great works of art. Through classics and music especially, in my case."

He waits expectantly for me to say more. "So you don't think, with Virgil and Verdi, that the world is a chaotic place after all? It's not violent and full of destructive forces?"

"It appears to be that way. But you just said, Tim, nothing is quite as it seems."

"Because God is everywhere."

"Yes, feeling with us and helping us. Maybe you should help me with these Virgil papers."

He laughs. "Are you serious?"

"You didn't take this course, but you've had a firsthand encounter with Virgil. Besides, you'd come fresh to these papers and be more objective than I can be. Everyone in the class is saying that a hero is someone who leads us into a new area of awareness. I've read it so many times now I'm not sure I believe it any more."

"What are they saying about the Golden Bough?"

"You have to find it if you want to know the secret of life and death."

"And if you want to talk to your father." He casts the flashing eyes downward. There is a moment's silence.

"You'll talk to him, Tim, and you'll say the right thing. I'm sure of it."

"I hope you're right. I'll let you get back to the papers."

We stand up. "So this is good-bye?"

"Looks like it," he says.

"Chicago for you, Toronto for me."

"I'll remember you as part of Rome."

"Tim, I think you'll always be part of me."

We shake hands. He leaves quickly, already a part of the past. The sound of his footsteps echoes down the corridor.

We cannot hold or grasp. Only cling to God, the eternal present, who tries in every way to enter the human heart.

In the morning the three big chartered buses drive up again between the lazy palms and umbrella pines. Pino and his fellow workers pack the baggage below. The buses fill up quickly, and those of us not flying back to Chicago try to say good-bye to each passenger as he or she boards. It happens with a suddenness that leaves many students unprepared. There are embraces and tears. The good-byes to those well and those casually known are about equal in duration. Joe, the quiet one, suddenly has more to say than I can take in. I can't remember saying the final good-bye to Ellen, but I vividly recall a girl I hardly knew saying, "I don't like this, Father. I'm afraid to leave you and all my friends."

"Oh, you'll make many more friends. But I hope you'll remember me."

There is an unearthly quiet in the villa when just a few of us are left in it. Maria Parenti says you never remember what the last thing is that people say at such good-byes. She settles down to a stack of registrar's papers, lowering the heavy glasses from her forehead to her Roman nose.

"I suppose you'll be leaving us soon as well, Father Mozart."

"Mozart? I'm generally known around here as the Wagner man."

"Oh, no. Mozart. I've heard you talking to your Theophilus. Isn't that Mozart? Johann Chrysostom Wolfgang Amadeus Gottlieb Theophilus?"

"Theophilus," I say, "is anyone loved by God."

But it's Mozart the radio plays as I pack away the books in my office, soon to shelter another occupant who will have to come to terms with Andrzej. It's the *Sinfonia Concertante* the radio plays, in that key of beginnings, E-flat. Andrzej would of course know the Köchel number. The violin and viola question and answer one another as Andrzej and I did in class. Andrzej is the viola—deeper, wiser than the violin, and almost surely the part Mozart wrote for himself.

It's Wagner I play when I make my way down one last time to the piano. This time Manfred Schöne doesn't come in to tell me what *Tannhäuser* means. He has already left in his car for Vienna. The E-flat measures swell under my fingers, proclaiming how the pope's staff, which he thought could never bear leaves again, has burst into flower at the death of the young minstrel. Manfred said it touched him when he was young.

No one has touched Johnny's room yet. His books still line the desk. His coffee mug, pillow, slippers, and robe are all in place. His old football helmet still hangs by its strap on the closet door. Down past the corridor window is the sacristy. I vest for Mass and say it alone. It is a Requiem Mass, so I can choose the Gospel. How could I not choose the passage about Jesus putting a little child in the midst of his disciples, saying, "I bless you, Father, for hiding these things from the learned and clever and revealing them to little children"? I speak the words of consecration, and lift the host and the chalice on high, asking God to receive into his sight the clear-seeing childlike man he sent this year from Philadelphia to Rome.

I take the vestments off and open my Book of Hours. Amid the official prayers and psalms, another Rilke poem is there:

God speaks to everyone only once. Before he creates him.
Then he walks silently with him out of the night.
And the words he says before life begins,
those cloud-swept words, are these:

"Sent forth with the gifts of consciousness,
go to the farthest limit of your longing.
Give me substance.

Grow like a flame behind the things you experience,
so that the shadow that they cast
may cover me always, far and wide.

Let everything happen to you—beauty and terror.
Only go. You must. No experience is the ultimate one.
And let not yourself be separated from me.
Near is the land, that they call life.
You will recognize it by its seriousness.

Give me your hand."

16

T HAT WAS THE END of the year in Rome, Theophilus. Now you know that it wasn't a year in which I solved all, or perhaps any, of my problems. But I saw into some of them, and was granted several graces. No one is saved by one grace or one flash of light. But grace leads to grace, and light to light. It was a year of epiphanies.

How many doors and how many floors and how many windows are there in it . . .

I haven't seen many of the people from the year in Rome in the years since.

I rejoined my religious community in Toronto and resumed my life with people I knew better and had known longer than those I knew in Rome. Most of the staff and students from Villa Soratte I've lost contact with completely.

Andrzej I have seen from time to time. He comes through Toronto. He has published more poems in the years since we shared the office and has become a kind of celebrity. Pope John Paul II gave him a special commission in Poland. His clear-sighted pessimism enabled him to speak to officials there, stubbornly and with no respect for persons, long before the Communist government went under. Since we taught together, a battle of the books has raged on university campuses, and the classic authors he and I favored have come under fire. Predictably, he regards the new orthodoxies, political correctness and the rest, as self-serving nonsense. Perhaps we were ahead of the times teaching Sappho and Li Po along with all those "dead white European males." I hope that Andrzej has forgiven me for saying, one time when we met recently, that he was a forerunner of deconstructionism. He wasn't pleased at that. At least he pretended he wasn't.

Fr. Costello stayed on for several years at the villa and was then for a long time in charge of campus ministry at a midwestern college. He has deplored, as have we all, the instances of clerical abuse of children that have come to light in the years since; he has helped to bring the guilty to punishment and to put new rules in place to prevent such tragic happenings in the future. He has also pleaded the cause of nuclear disarmament and has helped bring ecological thinking to the fore. If we do not destroy ourselves and our earth, future generations who never knew him will owe their existence partly to his efforts. He will have brought children into the world in the most humane sense, and will have earned many times over the name we at the school respectfully gave him—Father.

The thick-necked Hector and the lovely Andromache married, after he spent a year in Wisconsin and she in Israel. They settled down near Racine. They called their baby boy Homer. I hope that the homely name has not been a hindrance to the boy. I saw him on a visit to Wisconsin shortly after he was born. He was a merry-hearted little prince, caressed and kissed by his father.

Janet is teaching in California, married and divorced, with a string of books to her credit. She is very au courant on campus. She is also adept at skewering those meretricious plays that have proliferated about brainless nuns and malicious priests. She is convinced that Catholic education can and should be a model for the larger varieties, and she has the statistics to prove it.

Ellen married a naval officer and had three babies. She is, in her pictures, no longer plain. She is busy and fulfilled, and has seen a lot of the world—but, in time, through glasses again. Her stories have appeared in print where they count the most, in New York. She still writes to me.

Joe, the quiet one, was drowned in a boating accident in Indiana.

Manfred Schöne was killed, with his two boys, in a car crash in Austria.

Tim failed to make friends with his father, found making movies involved him with people he couldn't respect, entered a seminary, left, fell in love two or three times, reentered, completed his theology, was ordained a priest, and serves in a parish on Chicago's South Side. I never hear from him. Perhaps his church has not become the better church we had hoped for in our year together, but I am sure he still believes in it and believes too that, despite all contrary appearances, the world makes sense.

When I returned to Venice, the Lido was no longer swimmable. The opera house has since burned to the ground. Arson was suspected. Rebuilding has been slow.

I've been back to Dresden, to see again the charred buildings on the Elbe. The Semper Opera House has risen at last from the ashes, its wall of bright new stones interlaid with tragic stone remnants forever blackened by the firestorm. When I was there, Mozart's E-flat *Magic Flute* blessed the stage with its fire-and-water symbols of rebirth, while, outside, floodlights seemed to summon the vanished baroque splendors back to life. The city is German again and, though there are many problems, this time I felt as welcome there as ever I did in Mannheim.

Hans died with his children around him, and Anna ran the *Gasthof* until her two daughters and their husbands took over. They tell me that my shoes are still welcome in the warmth of the kitchen. The smiling husbands, like younger Germans everywhere, seem to know nothing about Hans Sachs.

Toronto has since seen the local première of *Die Meistersinger* and some of the other Wagner operas, and at its overcrowded, underfunded university some students still want to know about the languages and literatures of Greece and Rome, about poetry and music, about Catholicism, about the long traditions of all of these, about the Golden Bough and the Holy Grail and the inscrutable love of God— and those are what I, despite my insufficiencies, busied myself with until I reached these emeritus days.

The year in Rome was one year in forty years' teaching. I recall it more vividly, Theophilus, as it recedes in memory. I am at peace with it. But sometimes I wish I had asked Manfred Schöne, while I still had the chance, about those lines at the end of *Faust*, where the questing hero finds his eternal present:

> Everything in the past is only an image.
> Everything insufficient finds fulfillment here.

Perhaps someday in that "here" I'll be able to ask Manfred about the past, and he will explain it to me. Meanwhile, from the recurrent images in my memory I must make sense of my small life, of the choices I have made, of the graces I have been given, of the world in which I was given them, and of the One who sent them.